GLOBALIZATION
AND POSTCOLONIALISM

GLOBALIZATION
Series Editors
Manfred B. Steger
*Royal Melbourne Institute of Technology
and University of Hawai'i, Mānoa*
and
Terrell Carver
University of Bristol

"Globalization" has become *the* buzzword of our time. But what does it mean? Rather than forcing a complicated social phenomenon into a single analytical framework, this series seeks to present globalization as a multidimensional process constituted by complex, often contradictory interactions of global, regional, and local aspects of social life. Since conventional disciplinary borders and lines of demarcation are losing their old rationales in a globalizing world, authors in this series apply an interdisciplinary framework to the study of globalization. In short, the main purpose and objective of this series is to support subject-specific inquiries into the dynamics and effects of contemporary globalization and its varying impacts across, between, and within societies.

 Supported by the Globalization Research Center at the University of Hawai'i, Mānoa

GLOBALIZATION AND POSTCOLONIALISM

HEGEMONY AND RESISTANCE IN THE TWENTY-FIRST CENTURY

SANKARAN KRISHNA

ROWMAN & LITTLEFIELD PUBLISHERS, INC.
Lanham • Boulder • New York • Toronto • Plymouth, UK

ROWMAN & LITTLEFIELD PUBLISHERS, INC.

Published in the United States of America
by Rowman & Littlefield Publishers, Inc.
A wholly owned subsidary of The Rowman & Littlefield Publishing Group, Inc.
4501 Forbes Boulevard, Suite 200, Lanham, Maryland 20706
www.rowmanlittlefield.com

Estover Road
Plymouth PL6 7PY
United Kingdom

Copyright © 2009 Rowman & Littlefield

British Library Cataloguing in Publication Information Available

Library of Congress Cataloging-in-Publication Data:

Globalization and postcolonialism : hegemony and resistance in the twenty-first
century / Sankaran Krishna.
     p. cm.
  Includes bibliographical references and index.
  ISBN-13: 978-0-7425-5467-2 (cloth : alk. paper)
  ISBN-10: 0-7425-5467-8 (cloth : alk. paper)
  ISBN-13: 978-0-7425-5468-9 (pbk. : alk. paper)
  ISBN-10: 0-7425-5468-6 (pbk. : alk. paper)
  eISBN-13: 978-0-7425-5764-2
  eISBN-10: 0-7425-5764-2
  1. Postcolonialism. 2. Colonies—History. 3. Colonization—History.
4. Globalization. 5. Hegemony. I. Krishna, Sankaran.
  JV152.G56 2009
  327.101—dc22   2008032485

Printed in the United States of America

♾ ™ The paper used in this publication meets the minimum requirements of
American National Standard for Information Sciences—Permanence of Paper
for Printed Library Materials, ANSI/NISO Z39.48-1992.

For Jorge Luis Andrade Fernandes (1968–2004)

CONTENTS

ACKNOWLEDGMENTS

There are at least two reasons to delight in composing the acknowledgments page of a book: it means you are almost done, and it is always a pleasure to record the support of friends. I owe a big thank you to all my colleagues at the department of political science at the University of Hawai'i, especially Jon Goldberg-Hiller, Mike Shapiro, Kathy Ferguson, Noenoe Silva, Nevzat Soguk, Neal Milner, Bianca Isaki, Samson Opondo, and Rohan Kalyan. Patrick Johnston was coolly efficient as he made the tables, hunted down references, prepared the index, proofed the manuscript, and offered sensible advice on content and style. Itty Abraham and Srirupa Roy have long shared my obsession with India, postcoloniality, the 1950s, and sundry other matters, and they remain my co-tenants in that strange niche between political science, critical theory, and South Asian studies that we have carved for ourselves. I thank Manfred Steger for inviting me to contribute this volume to the globalization series and for his confidence that I was the right person for the topic. I have tested Susan McEachern's patience greatly and her cheerful support and encouragement has been invaluable. I should also thank an anonymous reviewer for a robust critique even if I have not allayed all the concerns raised therein. Every time I telephoned home, that is to say every other week, my dad would inquire about the progress of the book. The pressure to give him some upbeat news was relentless and undoubtedly did a great deal to ensure its completion. I hope he will find it was worth the wait.

This book is dedicated to my dear friend and colleague, Jorge Fernandes. Jorge did his Ph.D. in our department and wrote a brilliant dissertation that has since been published as a book (*Challenging Euro-America's*

Politics of Identity: The Return of the Native, Routledge, 2008). He left the islands in the fall of 2004 to accept a position at Bowling Green State University in Ohio. A few months later he died in a car accident. Jorge enriched our lives immensely. He was a voracious reader with an incredible ability to discern nuance and was always a supportive and constructive critic of our work. His quiet and completely unselfish presence made a huge difference to so many of us, and I miss him terribly. There were many times during the writing of this book when I felt the task was beyond me. At such moments of despair, I would recall Jorge and the gentle and funny ways in which he would help shore up your spirits and get you back on track. Even as I dedicate this book to his memory, I realize that yet again I owe Jorge more than he does me.

INTRODUCTION

GLOBALIZATION AND POSTCOLONIALISM: HEGEMONY AND RESISTANCE IN THE TWENTY-FIRST CENTURY

SUMMARY OF THE ARGUMENT

In 1492 Christopher Columbus embarked on an intrepid voyage to find the fabled riches of the Indies. The India of his fervid imagination was a space of immense wealth and exotic goods. His voyage was underwritten by royal patronage of Queen Isabella and King Ferdinand of Spain, and its success was seen as greatly enhancing the prestige of the kingdom. Yet, barely five centuries later, India, or the Indies, was synonymous with poverty, squalor, backwardness, superstition, and overpopulation. Far from being a desired space, it was the quintessential third-world country, exporting nothing but communicable diseases, as a former U.S. ambassador to New Delhi, Daniel Moynihan, once acidly remarked.[1] How did this space get transformed in the imagination of the world from one of unsurpassed wealth to degrading squalor in a matter of just a few centuries—the blink of an eye in historical time? In many senses, the story of the decline of India in the European imagination is also the story of relations between the West and the non-Western world. This book is about two competing stories that seek to explain or make sense of this historical development—the narratives of modernization and underdevelopment. It argues that neoliberal globalization is the latest intellectual heir of the first story, namely, modernization, and postcolonialism is the child of the second story, that of underdevelopment and of resistance to the story of modernization.

Even a casual observer of the academic and intellectual world of today will be struck by the ubiquity of two words: globalization and postcolonialism. This book will investigate the intimate relationship between the historical and contemporary socioeconomic processes that these two terms attempt to capture. In a nutshell, the book argues that although globalization is a movement that is suffusing the entire world with a form of production based on free-market capitalism and an attendant ideology of individualist consumerism, postcolonialism articulates a politics of resistance to the inequalities, exploitation of humans and the environment, and the diminution of political and ethical choices that come in the wake of globalization. If neoliberal globalization is the attempt at naturalizing and depoliticizing the logic of the market, or the logic of the economy, postcolonialism is the effort to politicize and denaturalize that logic and demonstrate the choices and agency inherent in our own lives. In brief, this book will argue that if globalization is the reigning or hegemonic ideology in the world today, postcolonialism, at its best, constitutes one of its main adversaries or forms of resistance to its sway.

Although there are important differences in the way various authors use the terms *globalization* and *postcolonialism*, a preliminary and provisional definition of these terms is appropriate here. *Globalization* can be seen as the accelerated spread of a free-market–based, capitalist style of production over an increasing swath of nations on this planet, especially over the past three decades. The entry of previously closed or inward-looking economies like China and India (together constituting almost 40 percent of the world's total population of 6 billion), as well as that of the communist bloc of countries in Eastern Europe, into the world market means that capitalism and the ideology of free markets reign over a greater part of the world than ever before. There has been a tremendous increase in the volume of international trade, especially in the scale and mobility of investment capital over the past two decades. This expansion in trade and mobility of capital is further underlain by phenomenal increases in the speed of communications and transportation that have literally shrunk the world. This is sometimes referred to as *time–space compression* and is one of the most important characteristics of globalization.[2]

The impact of such time–space compression exceeds just the economic realm: there are profound changes in the way people in different parts of the world view themselves, their futures, and the ways in which they are, in turn, impacted by developments in distant places as a result of such a compression. Thus, the collapse of the Thai currency (the baht), which triggered the Asian economic crisis of the late 1990s, was transmitted with breathtaking speed—within hours—through the economies of faraway nations like Russia, Mexico, and Brazil, as world financial markets are now integrated to an unprecedented degree. Similarly, there were long lines of shoppers waiting for the release of the last book in the Harry Potter saga in downtown Chennai in India, at the same time as similar lines were forming in New York and London. Young men and women in South Korea are undergoing cosmetic surgery in huge numbers to shape their faces and bodies to conform to an image of beauty derived from international soap operas and television shows and to enhance their desirability as employees in the eyes of multinational firms. These changes have had important consequences for social, cultural, and psychological aspects of human life in ways that we are still trying to fully fathom.

In this book the more capacious term *globalization* is used to refer to the combined economic *and* sociopolitical cultural changes of the contemporary epoch, while the term *neoliberal globalization*, or occasionally, *globalism*, is used when the focus is mainly on the economic—trade, investment capital, and policy-making aspects of these changes.[3] This is done, however, while recognizing that distinctions between the economic and the noneconomic domains are themselves a matter of politics, and that much that is important and crucial for our well-being as humans and a planet depends on where and how this distinction is made. Globalization, especially in its neoliberal form, presents itself as the rational commonsense and as the triumph of the economy over politics, with the latter invariably seen as something that interferes with or corrupts the functioning of the "natural" and rational logic of the economy. It is important to signal at the very outset that this view is an interpretive standpoint that has to be contested rather than accepted as a given.

Postcolonialism can be provisionally defined as the perspective or worldview of those who believe that it is possible to understand today's world only by foregrounding the history of colonialism—defined in a very preliminary way as the domination of certain societies and peoples by others—over the past five centuries. It commences by noting that capitalist development and colonial conquest or domination were coeval historical processes that were and are intimately related. Postcolonialism contests the claim that free-market ideology is a natural commonsense and that it produces prosperity or improved lives for all. It points out that both historically and now unregulated capitalist growth have always been highly unequal, producing prosperity for the few and immiserization for the many, both within particular nations and across the world. A postcolonial perspective argues that the claims of neoliberal globalization's proponents that the logic of markets should dictate policy and the economy is something above politics are themselves quintessentially political claims and should be contested. Political compulsion of weaker nations and peoples, and military coercion over them, has always underlain so-called free trade, and this is true today as well.

An important aspect of postcolonialism is its sensitivity to issues of cultural domination: economically developed and dominant nations invariably set the standards and constitute the model against which others are evaluated or evaluate themselves. This domination of the West over the world in the realms of knowledge production and culture, or Eurocentrism, is an enduring legacy of colonialism, and postcolonialism argues that reversing economic domination is inextricably linked to cultural decolonization. It should be apparent at this point that dominant narratives that equate modernization with civilization, development, and progress can also become instruments of oppression in the hands of once-colonized elites and nation-states in the third world. The latter can justify their political rule and claims of cultural superiority over their own countrymen in the name of their privileged access to the narratives of modernization. Postcolonialism, in its widest sense then, can be seen as a discursive or theoretical standpoint that opposes Eurocentrism in all its forms, not just when deployed by a geographically demarcated West upon a non-West.

In this book, the term postcolonialism is used to refer to this wide perspective on global history, that the developments of the past five centuries are inexplicable outside the history of colonialism, conquest, and control. Postcolonial theory, on the other hand, will be used to refer to a more bounded set of authors and writings, dating back to the late 1970s, which share the postcolonial perspective in many ways, but also depart from it in others. Postcolonial nations refers to the Afro-Asian and Latin American countries commonly grouped into the third world in recent decades.

PLAN OF THE BOOK

The first chapter looks at two perspectives, that of modernization and postcolonialism, and essentially argues that they can each be signposted under the iconic figures of Adam Smith and Karl Marx. The chapter will detail the bifurcation of human life on our planet from a situation of diversity and relative equality across the continents, to one of stark inequality between first and third worlds. It demonstrates the internal coherence of, and the fractures within, these alternative stories. The chapter is sensitive to the fact that while at a planetary level one can discern a clear polarization between an affluent first and an impoverished third world, and that there are salient differences within these worlds as well. Thus, for instance, the Native Americans who were indigenous to America and the African slaves who were transported to the first world were possibly worse off than many in the third world, while the elite classes of many such third-world societies, especially those engaged in colonial trade and the rising professions, had lifestyles that were closer to the first world in economic and social terms. That is, a global polarization between first- and third-world countries is underlain by a more complex and nuanced polarization between richer and poorer classes, regions, ethnicities, and races within each of these zones.

If the first chapter lays the historical (colonialism) and ideational (Smith and Marx) bases for the modernization and postcolonial perspectives, the second chapter focuses on developments in the twentieth century. It shows how the rise of American hegemony, the decades of development, decolonization and debt, and the rising neoliberalism of the last quarter of that century have set the grounds for current debates over globalization. It ends by suggesting this debate is between those who seek to privilege the logic of the economy over that of politics and morality against those who would privilege the latter over the former. A postcolonial perspective is an invaluable ally in the struggle against the hegemony of the idea of the market as the sole and best arbiter of decisions about the allocation of resources, the means to alleviate poverty, and the collective well-being of the planet as a whole.

The third chapter details the emergence and shifting meanings of the term postcolonial over the past few decades. It begins by looking at certain important works that have emerged from a postcolonial perspective, and then takes a detailed look at four exemplars of postcolonial theory. In the latter section, we look in some detail at the works of Edward Said, the Subaltern Studies Collective, Homi Bhabha, and Gayatri Spivak.

Chapter 4 examines some of the more influential critiques of postcolonial theory that have emerged in recent years, both from a leftist perspective and from other standpoints. Chapter 5 looks at a prominent site of encounter between globalization and postcolonialism: the issue of Islamic terrorism. It argues that the issue of "terrorism" perfectly illustrates the utility of a postcolonial perspective and its distinctive take on globalization in advancing our understanding of the historical and contemporary issues that underlie the so-called war on terror.

The conclusion returns to the issue of the competing logics of the economy and polity that we inaugurated in the first chapter. It looks at the sites of resistance to neoliberal globalization all across today's world and argues that a central thread running through these movements is the desire to recover human agency over our own future. Rather than accepting the neoliberal argument that the economy is a natural force, these movements reassert the political: the capacity of humans to collectively alter their present as well as their future through thought and action. In the assertion of the primacy of the political over the economic, such movements have found much of value in postcolonialism and in postcolonial theory. It argues that in its main variants, postcolonialism articulates a humanist commitment to a politics of change, even as it refuses the seductions of essentialist identity, or a vacuous celebration of contingency and indeterminacy.

CHAPTER 1

INTELLECTUAL AND HISTORICAL BACKGROUND: THE STORY OF UNEQUAL DEVELOPMENT FROM 1500 TO 1900

SMITH/MARX; MODERNIZATION/UNDERDEVELOPMENT; GLOBALIZATION/POSTCOLONIALISM

Although the specific terms postcolonialism and globalization have become popular only in the past two decades or so, they emerge from a far longer intellectual history on the growth and decline of various regions and nations in the world economy and the intertwined histories of capitalism and colonialism. The pages that follow sketch out one version of this history as a backdrop for the emergence of these terms, as well as define certain key concepts and terms that recur throughout this book.

When one looks at the world today, an inescapable fact is the vastly unequal distribution of assets, wealth, affluence, and life prospects. We live in a world where a relatively small number of people, about one-sixth the world's total population of approximately 6 billion people, have a preponderant share of the planet's wealth and resources, while a significant majority of the remaining 5 billion lead lives marked by insecurity, poverty, and misery. The relatively affluent 1 billion are largely concentrated in an area of the world often termed the "West" or the first world (which includes Western Europe, North America, Australia, New Zealand, and Japan), while the rest are distributed across the continents of Africa, Asia, Latin America, the Pacific islands, and parts of Eastern Europe and the Middle East, which together are often termed the third world.[1] Of course it should be noted that seeing the world as divided into first and third worlds can be misleading in the sense that there are many pockets of affluence in the third world, just as there are pockets of severe poverty and deprivation in the first world. Throughout this book, there sensitivity will be shown to the differences between classes, races, genders, and regions, within first and third worlds, even as it is argued that such a planetary distinction between the two worlds still holds much empirical truth and analytical utility.

As much as half of the world's population, 3 billion people, subsists on less than two dollars a day, while the world's three richest individuals' assets exceed that of the total GDP of the 48 poorest countries of the world. In 1997 the combined income of the richest 20 percent of the world's population, concentrated in the first world, was seventy-four times as much as that of the poorest 20 percent who live mostly in the third world.[2] The differences between the first and third worlds in life expectancy, literacy, per capita income, energy consumption, infant mortality rates, daily caloric intake, access to health care, and other indicators reveal the polarized world we live in today. As noted above, within the West there are areas of striking poverty and insecurity, and in the rest of the world there exist areas marked by affluence and prosperity—but this global picture of a widening inequality between first and third worlds is accurate.[3]

At an everyday level the different life prospects between first and third worlds is indicated by the large numbers of people in the latter desirous of emigrating—legally or illegally—to the former, and the marked absence of a movement of people in the opposite direction, except for tourism. The media are full of stories about the desperate efforts of would-be migrants from the third world to gain entry into the first world, be it in ramshackle boats over dangerous seas, on foot across deserts and past trigger-happy border security patrols, in container trucks, or as stowaways on international airlines. A common sight in many leading third-world cities is that of serpentine queues of men and women outside Western embassies and consulates, armed with certificates and papers, seeking work- or education-related visas for entry into the first world.

There is fairly substantial agreement that this polarization of the world into relatively concentrated areas of affluence and larger swathes of poverty is a relatively new phenomenon. It is, at best, about four or five centuries old, perhaps even less—the blink of an eyelid in comparison to the length of time that human civilizations have existed. Historical data, travelogues, memoirs of merchants, pilgrims, explorers, and other evidence show that different parts of the world were not so unequal until around 1500 A.D., and the distribution of affluence and poverty was nowhere near as polarized as it is today. According to one source, while the average per capita income of someone in Europe was about three times that of someone in the third world in 1500, that ratio had increased to five to one by 1850, to ten to one by 1960, and to fourteen to one by 1970.[4]

Over the decades, many trees have been felled as scholars from various disciplines explained the inequality of our world, and one can discern two dominant explanations in the literature on comparative economic development: the first, which is the dominant or the reigning paradigm, here labeled modernization, and the second, here termed the underdevelopment paradigm. To presage the argument, I hold that neoliberal globalization is the intellectual and political child of the modernization school, while postcolonialism traces its ancestry to the underdevelopment paradigm. Moreover, I suggest that while neoliberal globalization owes its ultimate inspiration to the Scottish economist Adam Smith, postcolonialism derives from the work of Karl Marx.

Modernization theory had its heyday in the decades immediately after World War II, experienced a brief decline in its popularity in the late 1960s and 1970s, and has made a comeback today, albeit in somewhat modified form. It explains the world since 1500 by focusing on a set of individual-level attributes seen as desirable and conducive to economic growth, political democracy, and a scientific approach to natural and social life.[5] For a variety of reasons, often left unexplained by modernization theorists, these desirable attributes happened to be more prevalent among individuals in the societies of Western Europe and relatively lacking among those in the rest of the world during the seventeenth and eighteenth centuries. A brief list of such attributes conducive to development according to the modernization school would be: (a) understanding the world in scientific rather than spiritual or religious terms, and seeing it as amenable to human action and change, rather than as incomprehensible; (b) the capacity to defer consumption or enjoyment and use one's savings for investment in productive activities that would multiply the initial capital; (c) the tendency to evaluate oneself and others through achievement or accomplishment in the material world rather than what has been inherited or by other criteria of social status such as family, ancestry, caste, or color; (d) acting in rational, self-interested ways to better one's own life and to get the most out of interactions with others and with nature; and (e) being free of medieval prejudices against profit, interest, usury, commerce, or speculative investments.

Since the source of dynamism is traced to the individual, the role of the state or of politics more generally should be limited to providing security for the individual and to underwrite the sanctity of the contract for trade and commerce. In fact, in the modernization school of thought, the individual is the center of social analysis and is in many ways the sole reality, with society, state, and other forms of collective being seen as abstractions that are less than real, that is, metaphysical. This premise, that the only "real" entity in social analysis is the individual, is often referred to as *methodological individualism* and is a key tenet of the modernization approach. To this view, the state should, by and large, stay out of direct production or interference in the workings of the economy. It should moreover not engage in wasteful expenditures that weaken the nation's currency by increasing deficits or debts (something that complements the emphasis on individual thrift and self-discipline) and should ensure that its laws and taxes do not contravene the essentially competitive and individualistic character of society, as that is the source of its dynamism and progress. Similarly, the state's provision of a safety net for its less fortunate citizens should guard against what is called the moral hazard, that is, it should never be so comprehensive that it negatively impacts their work ethic, competitiveness, and entrepreneurial drive. In other words, for genuine success to occur in a society, the possibility of failure has to be real.

Some modernization theorists offer historical explanations as to why desirable individual- and state-level attributes came to be concentrated in Western Europe in the early modern period. They emphasize the European Renaissance in the late medieval period and the efflorescence of interest in science, mathematics, astronomy, and the democratic polities of the ancient Greek city-states, which fueled both the scientific breakthroughs and the Enlightenment. They also place a great deal of emphasis on the Protestant Reformation and its multiple impacts—its focus on this-worldly life, its ascetic character in contrast to the pomp and splendor of Catholicism, its more tolerant and permissive attitude to the needs of commerce on matters like interest, and its emphasis on secular and civic associations rather than the clergy or religious order. In addition they point to the rising prosperity and power of a mercantile class of burghers, who thrived in the cities and towns in important crossroads as long-distance trade within Europe, with the New World, and with Asia increased rapidly after 1492. The political and economic rise of this class of merchants, or burghers, often at the expense of the feudal aristocracy, gave a great fillip to individual rights, freedom of religion and the press, and the rise of civic and secular institutions. The rise of this class and its emerging bourgeois ideology of individual liberty weakened the hold of a stifling and hierarchical feudal society with its equally conservative church and clergy. It was the interaction of these multiple and complex events over centuries—the Renaissance, the Reformation, the rise of the burghers, and other societal changes in Europe as a whole—that constituted the background against which the modern individual emerged first in the West.

Although attention to history is occasionally part of modernization theory, its primary mode of explanation, however, is more narrowly empirical or behavioral. That is, it looks at the Western developed world of today, sees what the dominant characteristics of individuals, states, and society are, and freezes them as always characteristic of such societies, as both lacking in other societies and worthy of emulation by them if they wish to progress. This viewing of world history and development through a particular narrative or story about the West and defining the past, present, and future of the whole world through that perspective may be defined as *Eurocentrism*. In this sense, modernization theory is essentially Eurocentric. Most importantly, modernization theory sees development as primarily a result of individual attitudes occurring within reasonably self-contained societies or regions: it is the attributes of people *within* these societies or regions that are crucial. Modernization theorists operate out of an unconsciously national cartography—they see the world as populated by distinct spatial containers (be they nations or kingdoms) of societal, state, and individual attributes that can then be assessed as modern or traditional. In other words, the methodological individualism of this approach is complemented by a methodological nationalism at the planetary level.

Economic growth and development are seen as the work of risk-taking, rational, and enterprising individuals. By definition, politics, society, and the state become at best facilitators for the actions of such individuals, and at worst interferences in the efficient and optimal allocation of resources by them. From this perspective, one can readily see why modernization theory dovetails neatly with a laissez-faire, or free market, view of the economy. Within a particular region or nation, the job of the state is limited to underwriting the legal sanctity of contracts and providing security to its citizens and their property. Thereafter, individuals, operating in a freely competitive system and equipped with modern rational value systems, can be trusted to produce the best results for society as a whole. Each of them will specialize in the production of whatever his or her unique genius best enables that person to produce. Such self-interested, rational, utility-maximizing individuals will interact in a market and exchange his or her own products with that of others at prices or terms determined by the logic of supply and demand. Skillful, well-made, and scarce products that satisfy needs or wants will command premium prices, while shoddily made, plentiful, and inessential goods will not sell. Investment and talent will flow into areas that seem likely to return a profit and steer clear of dead ends. Specialization makes each of these individuals more knowledgeable about his or her own niche of the market than anyone else, and certainly the state. Specialization impels individuals to make an infinite series of improvements and innovations under the gun of competition, and this is the fount of technological progress. The operation of this logic, when unimpeded by monopolies, price fixing, state interference, unequal access to information, and other distortions, will not only awaken each individual to give his or her best, but will redound to the benefit of society as a whole. The innate competitiveness of the process, and its relentless culling out of all those who are inefficient, ensures that it works in an ever-increasing upward spiral in terms of productivity and growth.

The first and most influential exponent of this logic of the economy was Adam Smith, a Scottish philosopher who wrote in the mid-eighteenth century. Smith placed much emphasis on specialization or the division of labor, alongside the "invisible hand of the market," to ensure the optimal allocation of resources and the societal benefit that ensues.[6] Individual producers, acting in their own self-interest, and interacting in an overall context of equal information, will rationally and inevitably act in ways that collectively produce a situation that is best for all, even if that was not necessarily their intention. This same logic is extended out of the local or national to that of the global or the international. Given that different parts of the world (like individuals with differing aptitudes working in various trades) are endowed with different kinds of material resources, geographic and climatic characteristics, and other factors, each part of the world is uniquely equipped to produce certain commodities or goods more efficiently than others. As with individuals, a global free market or unrestricted international trade among various countries with differing specializations will redound to the collective benefit of all the world's peoples.[7] The logic is compelling, commonsensical, and parsimonious, and it remains powerful and hegemonic to this day.

An exemplary work from within modernization theory is Walt Rostow's *The Stages of Economic Growth: A Non-Communist Manifesto*, first published in 1960 and an oft-cited work on development.[8] Rostow posited that every nation in this world can be placed in one of five stages of economic growth, and the whole point of development was to transition through these stages to reach the desired end point, namely, a modern society marked by high consumption, very evocative of the United States circa 1960. The first stage was the "traditional society," with "pre-Newtonian science and technology," and a ceiling on the productivity of its inhabitants. They were predominantly agrarian and their populations were largely static and at the mercy of nature. Rostow has characterized their value systems as "long-run fatalism," and their political structures were incapable of dynamism. People in such societies lacked the qualities of the modern individual—rational, individualistic, risk taking, and capable of deferring pleasure and immediate consumption. The second stage, "the preconditions for take-off," is marked by the rise of these individualistic values and first occurs in England in the late seventeenth and early eighteenth centuries, and soon becomes true of Western Europe, sometimes in autochthonous fashion and more often by war or the import of such ideas from other societies. Rostow's description of the third stage, "the take-off," essentially recounts the process of the Industrial Revolution, with science and technology revolutionizing production in both industry and agriculture, mechanization, the destruction of the self-contained agrarian estates of the previous era, and mass production. What is crucial in his story is the presence of a critical mass of those with modern values in society, a political system open to their rise to influence, and a threshold level of rates of effective investment and savings that exceed 10 percent of the national income. The multiplier effects of such rates of investment and savings transform traditional society into a modern industrialized nation. All that is left (to stay with Rostow's airline metaphor) is to attain cruising altitude and maintain it. In Rostow's terms, the fourth stage is called "the drive to maturity," and the final stage is called "the age of high mass consumption."

To Rostow, different nations are like runners poised in distinct lanes on a race track. Britain, for example, leaves the starting block as early as the late eighteenth to early nineteenth centuries during its Industrial Revolution, followed by the United States and Germany (in the mid-nineteenth century), followed even later by France and Belgium (in the late nineteenth century), and Russia in the early twentieth century. The rest of the world is either suited up and waiting to step on to the race track, entering the stadium, or at varying distances from it. The essential point is that each country's development is seen as a discrete and largely self-contained project. Each country seems to step on to the race track in conditions deemed identical, whether it was in the late eighteenth century or the mid-twentieth century: time literally stands still for it. Rostow does not entertain the notion that earlier development of some countries may have irrevocably altered the prospects of later developers. It is in that sense a static and ahistorical model. To put it differently, he believes that when it comes to development you can step into the same river not merely twice but an endless number of times.

In its emphasis on modernization or development as a largely national, self-contained, ahistorical, and autochthonous process based on individual attributes and enterprise, Rostow's work is exemplary of the modernization school. Three points are crucial about the model in light of our earlier discussion about current global inequality. First, as the success or failure of a nation to take off is seen as largely a domestic matter, today's poorer nations have largely themselves to blame for not making the transition. Second, there is no secret to the growth and development of nations: you need to cultivate individuals with modern values, have a state structure that encourages free trade, and attain a certain threshold of investment and savings. And third, given that the ideal values for progress and development were initially Western, modernization and development are equated with Westernization. Indeed, according to this Eurocentric model, the future of the entire world should be the past and present of the West.

A very different story about the world over the past five centuries emerges when one turns to the underdevelopment approach.[9] First, at a fundamental level, this approach sees politics and economics as indivisible, as inextricably intertwined. It harkens back to the eighteenth and early nineteenth centuries when there was no distinct field of economics but rather that of political economy. This field, which included among its adherents Adam Smith and Karl Marx, emphasized that the realm of the economy cannot and should not be understood apart from the overall polity that it was embedded within, that economic choices always had political implications, and vice versa. From an underdevelopment perspective, laissez-faire or free trade is better understood as a particular political choice made by the state and leading sectors of the market as the most appropriate policy at that time. There is nothing timelessly true or rational about laissez-faire, and efforts to make it appear natural or commonsensical are themselves political claims that should be contested. In contrast to the modernization school of thought, which emphasizes the negative impacts of politics on the freedom of trade and the rational choices made by investors and consumers, the underdevelopment approach sees politics as the domain of ethics, as the place from which one resists the often impoverishing and unequal effects of economic development based on private enterprise.

From the underdevelopment perspective, it is instructive that often the world's leading economic power in a particular epoch is invariably supportive of laissez-faire globally (as was Britain in the nineteenth century or the United States for close to three decades after the end of World War II). With their competitive edge over others, it is in their self-interest to have a relatively unrestricted world economy in which their products can outsell everyone else and their investments go unimpeded all over the world. Unsurprisingly, the leading world economy becomes a major proponent of the universal "logic" of free trade and presents it as natural and commonsensical. In contrast, the second-rung nations and others further behind invariably find laissez-faire a recipe for losing their economic sovereignty and their own industries being swamped out of existence by the cheap imports from the leading power. Such nations (for example, the United States or Germany vis-à-vis Britain in the nineteenth century, Japan vis-à-vis the West in the late nineteenth century, or third-world nations relative to the developed nations in the twentieth century) are less inclined to see laissez-faire as either natural or commonsensical, and view it as good for the leading power but disastrous for themselves if applied indiscriminately.

Indeed, one could make a persuasive case that tensions on the issue of free trade and the desire of a growing second-rung economy to protect its infant industries from the world's premier industrial power were in substance partly why the thirteen colonies in northern America seceded from Great Britain to form the United States. One of the founding fathers of the new country, Alexander Hamilton, wrote his *Report on Manufactures* in 1791, which remains an eloquent critique of laissez-faire from the perspective of a society trying to ascend the industrialization ladder by initially protecting its fledgling manufacturing base from premature exposure to imports from the advanced nation.[10] Similarly, Friedrich List, the German nationalist and philosopher, wrote his *The National System of Political Economy* in 1841 in which he argued the case for protectionism from free trade as a necessary step in the evolution of self-reliant and mature economies.[11] The Meiji regime in Japan argued an essentially similar case for that country beginning in the late 1860s—in fact, they explicitly based their argument for economic nationalism on the writings of Alexander Hamilton and Friedrich List, among others.

The underdevelopment approach begins its explanation for the global inequality of our times by posing the following questions: Is it a coincidence that the rising prosperity and affluence of a handful of nations in the West occurred during the same centuries as the conquest of the New World and the colonization of Asia and Africa? Is there any relationship between, on the one hand, the discovery and plunder of gold and silver from the New World, the profits from the slave trade, and monopoly trade with Asia by the trading companies of Europe, and, on the other hand, the rising powers of the bourgeois class, and the occurrence of the Industrial Revolution first in the societies of Western Europe? Can one better understand the economic success and political stability of a particular region or nation in terms of the innate attributes of its citizens, or is it more useful to focus on the ways in which that particular nation or region has interacted with the rest of the world economy in preceding decades and centuries?

These questions are rhetorical in the sense that the underdevelopment approach considers the answers to be obvious. To this view, it is *not* a coincidence that the growing inequality of the world in recent centuries was coeval with conquest and colonialism; and development *should* always be understood as taking place in an interconnected world economy rather than within nation-states. This approach argues that development and underdevelopment are simultaneous and interrelated global processes best understood at the level of an integrated world economy. The word *underdevelopment* is crucial in this regard. It suggests that the third world was not *un*developed during the centuries in which countries like Britain, the United States, or Germany achieved their take-offs, but was actively *under*developed during that time. An undeveloped society—akin to what Rostow describes as a traditional or "pre-Newtonian" society—is one that is premodern and has minimal trade and other relations with the rest of the world, whereas an underdeveloped society is one that was part of the world economic system of trade and exchange but in a subservient position and exploited in ways that primarily benefited the Western colonial powers. Although a certain degree of economic growth and prosperity did occur as part of underdevelopment, it was confined to narrow enclaves and benefited only the elite classes, while leaving the rest of society worse off.

Thus, Latin America had its mineral wealth (gold and silver) forcibly extracted and siphoned off overseas beginning in the early sixteenth century, while much of its indigenous population was wiped out by genocide and its political regimes destroyed. The arrival of settlers from Spain and Portugal, along with the emergence of the idea of private property in land (in contrast to previously existing communal forms of access to lands for all sections of the people), converted the Latin American countryside into giant landed estates, or *latifundias*, producing cash crops and livestock for export to Europe rather than for the needs of domestic society. The *latifundias* used highly coercive forms of labor organization, including slavery, which precluded the rise of democratic or individualistic values. Instead, it froze social relations along deeply hierarchical and racist lines. On the industrial front, imposed free trade made Latin America an importer of manufactured goods paid for by its mineral and agricultural exports. Given the narrow and elitist character of the domestic market and the imposition of free trade, the Latin American colonies imported their manufactured goods from Europe rather than manufacturing them locally. This form of extraverted growth represented the underdevelopment of Latin America. To this day, the countries of Latin America remain among the most unequal societies in the world, with incredible concentrations of wealth among a few, usually of Iberian ancestry, and generalized poverty and squalor for the rest.

Underdevelopment was much more than the transfer of wealth or profits overseas. It profoundly changed the socioeconomic, political, and cultural structures of these countries. This process is briefly illustrated through the exemplary instance of India. The British East India Company established its first trading depot in western India in 1600 at a time when the ruling Mughal dynasty was at the apex of its power, wealth, and control in that country. From then until about the mid-eighteenth century, it had a monopoly on British trade with India, and the profits from this trade steadily made it an important player in British politics and power. From around the early decades of the eighteenth century, the Mughal dynasty in India went into a slow decline. As its power receded and various regional satraps began to assert their autonomy, the East India Company became embroiled in contests between rival kingdoms and heirs to power. It became a political and military player in India and by the mid-1700s had acquired the rights to collect land revenue in the province of Bengal. Having organized a powerful militia to protect its factories and warehouses in India, increasingly armed with the latest weapons invented in Europe, and informed by European developments in the organization of armies, the

East India Company began to dictate terms to the regional kingdoms and principalities, and its conquests brought it to power over an ever-widening territory in India.

The decades after the initial acquisition of political power in Bengal (i.e., from the 1750s onward) saw the further political fragmentation of India alongside the growing political and economic rise of the East India Company. This period, coinciding with the first Industrial Revolution in Britain, marked the decisive colonization and underdevelopment of India. From here on, the Indian economy was steadily extraverted—that is, designed to meet the economic needs of Britain rather than her own domestic population. India was forced to specialize in the export of minerals, raw materials, and agricultural commodities, often at unremunerative prices, and to import industrial or manufactured goods from Britain. In a matter of a few decades, around the turn of the eighteenth century, India's once flourishing textile and handicrafts industries were wiped out by the cheap machine-made imports from Britain. Almost overnight, India went from being one of the world's largest exporters of textiles and clothing to being a major exporter of raw cotton and an importer of finished goods. At the same time, British-imposed free-trade policies on India prevented the rise of any significant domestic manufacturing entities to absorb the millions displaced from work by the deindustrialization of the textile and artisanal crafts. In Britain the serfs thrown off the land during the enclosure movement and the agricultural revolution that followed it were gradually (if violently) redeployed in the growing industrial sector, a process now termed urbanization. In contrast, in India, displaced workers, artisans, and craftsmen moved in the opposite direction—from towns and cities to villages, swelling the numbers trying to eke out a living from agriculture—a process that one might term forced ruralization. In the villages, the institution of private property in land replaced previously existing communal rights of access to land, making it alienable. This, alongside ever-increasing demands by the colonial state for land revenue, led to the immiserization of landless peasants, small farmers, and other rural classes. The nineteenth century saw the creation of one of the most manifest signs of underdevelopment in India—a mass of rural, impoverished landless and small peasants eking a precarious living, alongside a narrow class of absentee landlords who were supporters of colonial rule, and an alien colonial elite living in high style.[12]

The human costs of such colonization were truly staggering. In a recent work Mike Davis meticulously delineates the interaction of the collapse of community in rural areas due to the introduction of the ideas of private property in land; the climatic variations due to El Niño currents, especially on monsoon rains; the imposition of ideas of free-trade, market economics; and hostility to state intervention, even during a climatic disaster, on societies like India, China, northern Africa, and Brazil during the Victorian age, in the second half of the nineteenth century. By his estimates, anywhere between 31 million and 61 million farmers, landless laborers, and their families, perished during this time in these countries due to famines attributed to the vagaries of nature.[13] Davis argues convincingly that these were preventable deaths occurring as they did during years when colonial governments continued to export food (alleged grain surpluses) from neighboring regions rather than use them to avert starvation. Davis deliberately uses the word "Holocaust" to describe this human-engineered catastrophe rather than the more commonly used terms natural disaster, act of nature, or famine. He connects the emergence of modern economic ideas to this disaster, in other words, he emphasizes the dialectical nature of development and underdevelopment, when he notes:

> We are not dealing, in other words, with "lands of famine" becalmed in stagnant backwaters of world history, but with the fate of tropical humanity at the precise moment (1870–1914) when its labor and products were being dynamically conscripted into a London-centered world economy. Millions died, not outside the "modern world system" but in the very process of being forcibly incorporated into its economic and political structures. They died in the golden age of Liberal Capitalism; indeed, many were murdered . . . by the theological application of the sacred principles of Smith, Bentham and Mill. . . . Although crop failures and water shortages were of epic proportions—often the worst in centuries—there were almost always grain surpluses elsewhere in the nation or empire that could have potentially rescued drought victims. Absolute scarcity, except perhaps in Ethiopia in 1889, was never the issue. Standing between life and death instead were new-fangled commodity markets and price speculation, on one side, and the will of the state . . . on the other.[14]

In colonial India, without factories to absorb the millions thrown off the land, unemployment and underemployment were rising. The lack of innovations or investment in agriculture alongside ever-increasing and efficient collection of land revenue by the colonial regime made for agrarian stagnation. The culmination of the Victorian-era holocausts examined by Davis came decades later in the Great Bengal famine of 1943 (just four years before Indian independence from Britain) in which a colossal 3 million Indians died, at a time when Britain continued to export food from her Indian colony to various parts of the world in the war against the Axis powers. Although the millions killed during the Holocaust in Germany and Poland, or the tremendous loss of life in the Soviet Union, or in Japan, during World War II have received a great deal of attention and caused much debate among historians, the deaths of 3 million people in India during that same period has often gone virtually unnoticed. Underdevelopment is thus an omnibus term that refers to agrarian stagnation, underemployment, deindustrialization, small enclaves of growth in sectors that are parasitic off the colonial regime, and extraversion of the entire economy to suit the needs of an alien government and people.[15] The consequent creation of mass poverty and lack of economic dynamism has political, social, cultural, and psychological ramifications that are powerful and enduring.

Variations of Indian underdevelopment during British colonialism characterized nearly all of Afro-Asia and Latin America, thereby creating the third world over the course of these centuries. In Latin America, formal independence from Spain and Portugal was achieved relatively early, in the nineteenth century, but the structural effects of colonial underdevelopment continued unabated. The political and economic elites were largely Iberian, and the pattern of economic development was oriented toward the interests of this narrow elite and of their European forebears. The domination of their economies after independence by European nations and the United States and their political subservience to the latter, exemplified by the Monroe Doctrine, indicated the continued colonial status of much of Latin America.

Unlike Rostow's supposition that all countries come to the development race track at varying points in time with roughly similar assets or endowments, the underdevelopment approach argues that neither the runners nor the track is the same over time. The early development of the frontrunners came at the expense of the latecomers and decisively handicapped the latter in their efforts to catch up with the former. The underdevelopment approach sees free trade or laissez-faire not as economic commonsense but rather as a political ideology imposed by leading powers on weaker nations and a critical instrument in their exploitation and colonization. The individual attributes prized by the modernization school—rationality, independence, competitive drive—are not intrinsic characteristics unique to the West or any specific set of peoples, but are themselves socially or historically produced in certain contexts and precluded in others. Just as underdevelopment was a product of the interaction between global politics and economics, development of the third world would also have to come from active state or political engagement with the economy, and not merely by relying on the benign dispositions of a so-called free market or the inculcation of modern values from the West.

The linkage between the underdevelopment of the third world and the rise of the first world was more complex than just direct plunder and a transfer of wealth from the former to the latter, although the latter should never be minimized.[16] Although both Marx and Smith agree that the role of monopoly profits from colonial trade and of plunder and pillage in the early rise of the West was critical, there is a crucial difference in emphasis between them. Consider the following quotes from their works about the role of such "primitive accumulation" prior to the onset of modernization and development in the West during the seventeenth and eighteenth centuries. Here is Marx on the subject:

> The colonies secured a market for the budding manufactures, and through the monopoly of the market, an increasing accumulation. The treasures captured outside Europe by undisguised looting, enslavement, and murder, floated back to the mother-country *and were turned into capital.* . . . As a matter of fact, the methods of primitive accumulation are anything but idyllic. . . . In actual history, it is notorious that conquest, enslavement, robbery, murder, briefly force, plays the great part. . . . In fact, the veiled slavery of the wage workers in Europe needed, for its pedestal, slavery pure and simple in the new world. . . . Capital comes [into the world] dripping from head to foot, from every pore, with blood and dirt.[17]

Adam Smith, writing nearly ninety years before Marx on the same issue:

> The discovery of America, and that of a passage to the East Indies by the Cape of Good Hope, are the two greatest and most important events recorded in the history of mankind. Their consequences have already been very great. . . . One of the principal effects of those discoveries has been to raise the mercantile system to a degree of splendour and glory which it could never otherwise have attained to. . . . The countries which possess the colonies of America, and which trade directly to the East Indies, enjoy, indeed, the whole shew and splendour of this great commerce. . . . Europe, however, has hitherto derived much less advantage from its commerce with the East Indies, than from that with America. . . . *By opening a new and inexhaustible market to all the commodities of Europe, it gave occasion to new*

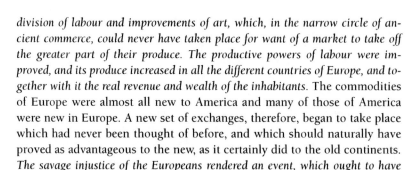

division of labour and improvements of art, which, in the narrow circle of an-
cient commerce, could never have taken place for want of a market to take off
the greater part of their produce. The productive powers of labour were im-
proved, and its produce increased in all the different countries of Europe, and to-
gether with it the real revenue and wealth of the inhabitants. The commodities
of Europe were almost all new to America and many of those of America
were new in Europe. A new set of exchanges, therefore, began to take place
which had never been thought of before, and which should naturally have
proved as advantageous to the new, as it certainly did to the old continents.
The savage injustice of the Europeans rendered an event, which ought to have
been beneficial to all, ruinous and destructive to several of those unfortunate
countries.[18]

Smith highlights the impact of production for larger markets, virgin territories with new resources, and the huge expansion of trade on European
social division of labor (specialization) and technological improvements
and innovations ("improvements of art"). He is clear that political factors
("the savage injustice of the Europeans") ensured that benefits of such expanded trade were confined to Europe and led to immiserization of the
Americas. Although this constitutes an important recognition of the centrality of colonial conquest and trade to the rise of the West, and moreover
something that twentieth-century modernization theorists (like Rostow
above) are loath to even admit into their analyses, the emphasis in Smith
is on the beneficial effects of trade that an expanded market brings in its
wake. To Smith, the essential engine of change that leads to the rising prosperity of the West was the expanded market and a larger range of goods,
resulting in specialization and technological innovations. It is in this sense
a trade-centric or "circulationist" logic of explanation for the rise of the
West.

This characteristic of the Smithian logic prevails in mainstream or liberal economics to the present and constitutes a core tenet of many variations of contemporary globalization, especially what has come to be called
neoliberal globalization. The expansion of international trade and exposure to competition through the dismantling of (political) protectionism
will awaken the always already present enterprise of individuals in a society, their innate tendency to "truck, barter and exchange one thing for another," in Smith's language,[19] and will culminate in development and prosperity for all. The focus on expanding trade often comes at the expense of
attention to issues such as class conflict, inequality, and regional variations
in the growth that is thus generated. The assumption that trade and expo-

sure to international competition will inevitably raise the GNP (which it undoubtedly does) and that this increased GNP will inevitably percolate down to all classes within society (an assumption repeatedly belied in the economic history of third-world nations) is central to proponents of globalization in its present avatar—and its genealogy to the Smithian logic should be obvious here.

However, Smith's emphasis on the liberatory aspects of expanded trade and markets cannot explain why, in that case, Spain and Portugal did not emerge as vanguards of industrial modernity in the West. They were, after all, first to conquer the New World and to find the new sea route around the Cape of Good Hope (South Africa) to eastern India. Instead, after a burst of conspicuous consumption by the state and elites (i.e., construction of magnificent capital cities, palaces, and cathedrals), Spain and Portugal subsided into second-rung European powers over the next few centuries. What accounts for the difference in the longer run fortunes of Spain and Portugal on the one hand and Britain or Holland on the other? The answer lies in the contrasting emphases in Smith's and Marx's accounts above.

Marx tellingly argues that the treasures looted from the New World and the profits of the monopoly trade with Asia floated back to Europe and "*were turned into capital.*" It is their conversion into a new socioeconomic and political entity, namely, "capital" that is critical here. Capital is not merely wealth or money, and it becomes capital only in the context of crucial changes in the class character of a society, of changes in the social, economic, and political context of its entry. For plundered wealth and profits from long-distance trade to serve as capital, social changes that have created a class of competing producers interested in reinvesting profits and expanding production, generalized commodity production, and monetized wages, laborers alienated from any rights to personal or communal lands and working for wages, and a state committed to the expansion of the economy through the reinvestment of surplus rather than spending it for its own glorification, are all indispensable components. Marx argues that primitive accumulation in this period (seventeenth to early eighteenth centuries) interacted with and energized a profound ongoing social and political revolution in northwest Europe, especially England, and together inaugurated a distinctively new, dynamic, and continuously innovating form of production, that of capitalism.

This period in the social history of Britain saw the consolidation of previously fragmented landholdings into giant estates (as a consequence of the "enclosure movement"), which produced wool and other commodities central to her growing foreign trade. The declining military power of feudal lords relative to a centralized state occurred alongside the rise of an independent class of tenant cultivators who were more attuned to production for exchange or the market. The alienation of the serfs from their traditional plots on the lords' estates, from access to communal lands (the Commons) due to the enclosure movement, as well as from the tools of their craft, created a relatively mobile labor force or working class. Whereas home-based artisans had previously been organized by guilds that jealously guarded their skills, controlled membership through a process of apprenticeship and in other ways ensured their economic status and survival, the power of the guilds was now broken as production was being centralized and as skilled artisans were being replaced by mechanization. The demise of home-based artisanal production systems and the creation of a mobile and uprooted labor force had profound implications for the division of labor within the household, for patriarchy, for gender relations, and the raising of children. This artisan class now had no means of survival except offering its labor power to the factory owners or capitalist farmers in return for cash wages. Production was relocated from highly dispersed households using the worker's own tools and materials to a centralized system with tools, materials, and workspace (the factory) all owned by the capitalist. The laborer was theoretically "free" to not work in the factories, but given the lack of access to land (personal or communal), the demise of feudal traditions of noblesse oblige, and the need to earn wages in order to buy all necessities of life for himself and his family, this freedom was more apparent than real. Other social changes such as the decline of wealthy churches (as their lands were alienated) and the repeal of laws that guaranteed a certain ceiling on the price of bread (for example, the abolition of the Corn Laws in Britain in 1846) or other staple foods further rendered the situation of the laboring classes more precarious. Quite simply, one had to work in order to live.

This system of organizing production through the provision of capital (the factory, tools, and materials) by the owner, and the "free" laborer working through the day in exchange for a fixed wage, in a competitive system, has historically proven to be an incredibly dynamic and efficient form of production. It vastly exceeds the productivity of labor and of profits produced by other, prior forms of organizing production, whether on feudal estates or slave-based plantations or home-based craftsmen. The monetization of economic exchange and the improved exaction of revenues by the state interacted to pressure tenant farmers to increase their yields and the productivity of their lands. Unlike prior social epochs, when such pressures would have been met by increasing the overt and "extra-economic" coercion of the serfs, in the prevailing political conditions (the weakness of the feudal nobility, the dispersal of the erstwhile serfs, a strong and centralized state, and the rising political power of the bourgeoisie), that was not as easy. The result was an agricultural and industrial revolution in England based on improved technology and the "superior" organization of free labor, where the pressures of the market and possible loss of livelihood served as the impetus to enhance labor productivity rather than explicit coercion (slavery or serfdom) as in preceding epochs.

Among other things, the exploitation of "free" labor by the pressure of the market and by the need to earn wages in order to ensure one's subsistence hid the political character of such exploitation. Although in feudalism or slave society the intertwined character of political and economic power of the lord or the slave owner was inescapable and stared the laborer in the face, under this new regime of production, the political and economic aspects seemed to diverge and embody separate realities. The emerging divide between the public/political and the private/economic, itself a constitutive moment in the emergence of modernity, concealed (or better still, naturalized) the exploitative character of capitalist production. Alongside the emergence of ideas of individual liberty, equality of all before the eyes of the law, secularism or separation between church and state, and other significant bourgeois freedoms, economic inequality was subtly taken out of the domain of the political or the contestable and placed within that of the natural. If you were poor, it was now up to you to show the dynamism, energy, drive, and discipline necessary to succeed. The political domain, or the state, was committed to no more than the minimalist liberal provision of equality before the law and the equality of opportunity for all. Beyond that, it was up to the individual to determine his or her economic fate in this world.

Although the English agricultural revolution and its role in creating conditions for the Industrial Revolution merit a fuller analysis than is possible here, for our purposes the crucial point is this: the influx of wealth from plunder in the New World and the profits from the triangular global trade under European dominance that linked Latin America, Africa, and Asia, for the first time in human history, were not frittered away in an orgy of conspicuous consumption by the state and elites or in military adventurism. Rather, the interaction of this wealth with the profound social changes in northwest Europe—that is, its conversion into capital—is crucial.

This uniquely new social structure for accumulation based on competition, private production, and the separation of the worker from the means of production, what we call capitalism, therefore emerged from the depths of the English countryside. It was the first system of organizing humans for production oriented not so much toward the fulfillment of necessities, or the ostentation of state or king, but of accumulation for accumulation's sake. The overwhelming purpose of capital is to multiply itself, to transmute itself into more of itself through reinvestment of profit, to intensify the returns.

Marx and Engels, writing in their *Communist Manifesto* in 1848, convey a graphic sense of the energy, enterprise, dynamism, and earth-shattering power of this new method of production led by the bourgeoisie:

> The bourgeoisie cannot exist without constantly revolutionizing the instruments of production, and thereby the relations of production, and with them the whole relations of society. Conservation of the old modes of production in unaltered form, was, on the contrary, the first condition of existence for all earlier industrial classes. Constant revolutionizing of production, uninterrupted disturbance of all social conditions, everlasting uncertainty and agitation distinguish the bourgeois epoch from all earlier ones. All fixed, fast frozen relations, with their train of ancient and venerable prejudices and opinions, are swept away, all new-formed ones become antiquated before they can ossify. All that is solid melts into air, all that is holy is profaned, and man is at last compelled to face with sober senses his real condition of life and his relations with his kind. . . . The need of a constantly expanding market for its products chases the bourgeoisie over the entire surface of the globe. It must nestle everywhere, settle everywhere, establish connections everywhere. The bourgeoisie, by the rapid improvement of all instruments of production, by the immensely facilitated means of communication, draws all, even the most barbarian, nations into civilization. The cheap prices of commodities are the heavy artillery with which it forces the barbarians' intensely obstinate hatred of foreigners to capitulate. It compels all nations, on pain of extinction, to adopt the bourgeois mode of production; it compels them to introduce what it calls civilization into their midst, i.e., to become bourgeois themselves. In one word, it creates a world after its own image. . . . The bourgeoisie, during its rule of scarce one hundred years, has created more massive and more colossal productive forces than have all preceding generations together. Subjection of nature's forces to man, machinery, application of chemistry to industry and agriculture, steam navigation, railways, electric telegraphs, clearing of whole continents for cultivation, canalization of rivers, whole populations conjured out of the ground—what earlier century had even a presentiment that such productive forces slumbered in the lap of social labor?[20]

With the advent of capitalism, and its distinctive social relations of production, the quantitative gap between the northwest of Europe and the rest of the world now widened into a qualitative difference between first and third worlds. Those parts able to resist the political, economic, and social domination of England and other early industrializers were able to join them as developed societies in due time, and those that could not were invariably colonized and underdeveloped as a result. Thus, the thirteen colonies that coalesced to form the United States asserted their political and economic sovereignty from England on the issue of imposed free trade and controlled their own destiny. Fragments of capitalist England established in distant parts of the world as settler colonies, aided by the genocide of the indigenous or aboriginal populations therein, as in Australia, New Zealand, and Canada, became part of the developed West. Similarly, societies like France, Germany, Holland, Scandinavia, and Japan, which were able to protect their economic sovereignty, did likewise at later times.[21] Russia retained its economic and political sovereignty from Western imperialism, but through a communist revolution in 1917–1918 that enabled it to resist colonialism and capitalism by withdrawing from the world economy. China was never fully colonized in the way that India was, but the unequal treaty port system and the depredations of various colonial powers through this mechanism ensured its underdevelopment, until 1949, when a peasant-based communist revolution took it out of the ambit of Western dominance and the world market.[22] By the late nineteenth century, Britain, France, Germany, the United States, and smaller powers like Italy, Belgium, and Japan established new colonies in various parts of the third world. At the start of the Great War (World War I) in 1914, the entire planet was divided into either colonizer or colony.

The advent of capitalism was thus both a result of an ongoing social revolution in the northwest of Europe and a cause of tumultuous and unprecedented changes there and in the rest of the world. Although it would be impossible to depict all of these changes, the period from the late seventeenth to the late nineteenth centuries can be seen as the inauguration of modernity on a planetary scale. The late nineteenth-century analytical division of political economy into the distinct domains of politics and economics was an important sign of the emerging modern. It hinged on a division between public and private and between political and civil society. It was a key step in the consolidation of a liberal imagination in which politics is deemed to be the domain of public affairs, matters of state and governance, maintenance of law and order, and increasingly, of parties and elections—while economics, or the production of wealth and its distribution, was now the realm of the private, the nonpolitical, and the individual. This distinction between public and private, and the consignment of economic matters to the domain of the private or civil society, is of enormous significance in the emergence of modernity. Inter alia, it depoliticizes issues of economic inequality because, in the liberal imagination, the state has to be merely neutral, and everyone should be equal in the (blindfolded) eyes of the law. Thereafter, each individual succeeds to the extent of his or her ability, hard work, and good fortune. Innate competitiveness is the engine of societal development and not to be dampened in any way. This "minimalist" definition of equality (limiting it to equality before law, rather than equality of assets, wealth, or material circumstances) is premised on the prior separation of politics and economics as distinct domains. It is this same separation that allows for the "logic of the economy" to be presented as something natural, scientific, and, if allowed to work on its own, redounding to the collective benefit of everyone. Thus, justifications of free trade or contemporary globalization on grounds that "the economy" should not be sullied by political interference arise from this prior separation of economics and politics—a separation that has been described as itself a profoundly political act and at the core of a liberal order. The excision of overt discussion of the politics of economic inequality, of the history of the unequal distribution of property and wealth between classes and nations, and the growing fascination with the quantitative idiom in contemporary neoclassical economics can be traced back to this original separation.[23]

The contrast between Smithian and Marxian theories of development and their roles as progenitors of globalization and postcolonialism can now be thrown into relief. The Smithian/modernization approach emphasizes free trade and commerce as the engine of national and international development, irrespective of historical, political, social, and other factors. Given its (essentialist)[24] belief that humans have an innate proclivity to truck, barter, and trade, that commerce awakens their innate creativity and competitiveness, it argues that liberalization of the economy will inevitably result in development for everyone. The consequent emphasis is on the free market and limiting intervention of states or political factors in the freedom of commerce. Indeed, this approach is actively suspicious and hostile to the domain of politics and urges the liberalization of domestic and international trade in order for everyone to develop. In its contemporary form, this understanding of the primacy of international trade in economic development can be called neoliberal globalization. The intellectual lineage from selective readings of Smith, through modernization theory, to contemporary proponents of neoliberal globalization should be apparent here.

In contrast, with its focus on interrelations between economic, social, and political domains, the Marxian/underdevelopment approach argues that trade and commerce do not always work like a deus ex machina to produce development everywhere. The history of capitalist development shows that political and economic domination of some countries or regions by others (colonialism), and some classes by others, ensures that the fruits of development are distributed highly unequally. It argues that historically development and underdevelopment are two sides of the same interrelated process, that the class structure of a society and the actions of the state are critically important in determining whether trade and commerce will have a positive impact on general well-being. Postcolonialism is the intellectual child of the Marxian/underdevelopment approach, and its contemporary concerns reflect a clear lineage to that tradition of inquiry. For postcolonial works, the simultaneous and related production of development and underdevelopment represent both the dynamism of capitalism and its greatest flaw.[25] From this perspective, capitalism and colonialism are understood as the seminal processes of the past few centuries. They underlie the global inequality that is seen today and are a quintessential part of modernity itself, not some aberration from an otherwise pacific and progressive story of development.

Capitalist colonialism has rendered our understanding of the world Eurocentric, and we are unable to think outside the categories and concepts that emerged in post-Columbian Europe. Answers to regional, national, and international inequalities are not to be found in the mantra of free trade or liberalization—if anything, history teaches us the opposite. It is only through the relentless focus on the world historical experience of capitalist colonialism and its contemporary manifestations everywhere that we can begin to understand and reverse its effects and embark on human development. Such human development must, of necessity, also be an act of profound decolonization that tries to reverse the political, social, economic, and cultural domination of the rest by the West. The underdevelopment approach emphasizes the role of the third world in the making of Europe. The latter would not be what it is without the material, social, intellectual, and cultural interactions with the colonial world over the past few centuries. Thus the West and the third world are seen as mutually constitutive entities that have emerged with their distinct characteristics due to their interaction. The idea that one of them (the West) is the source of modernity and that the other (the third world) has to learn how to modernize itself through imitation is fundamentally flawed for this reason. This emphasis on the interrelated historical contexts of colonialism and capitalism and their constitutive role in the emergence of modernity makes underdevelopment theory one of the important sources of postcolonial thought. In its wake, postcolonialism, unlike globalization, is motivated by a desire not for mimesis but rather for a form of human development that is decolonized and beyond Eurocentrism.

CHAPTER 2

INDEPENDENCE OR NEOCOLONIALISM? THIRD-WORLD DEVELOPMENT IN THE TWENTIETH CENTURY

INTRODUCTION

In the previous chapter, the historical and intellectual genealogy of modernization and postcolonialism as narratives was examined. Tracing these two narratives back to the iconic figures of Adam Smith and Karl Marx it was shown that although modernization accounts for the rise of the West in terms of its individualism, free markets, and its supposedly rational and scientific outlook, postcolonialism emphasizes colonial plunder, a complex structure of underdevelopment and external political control, in explaining the decline of the East. This chapter will examine the developments from the beginning of the twentieth century until the present in the relative fortunes of the first and third worlds. The figures of Smith and Marx remain as salient as ever in the competing explanations and economic strategies attempted by various nations in their efforts to reach the exalted club of developed nations.

Britain's domination of the world economy, her underwriting of a global system of lower tariffs, an international currency system premised on the gold standard, and expanding international trade ended by the first decade of the twentieth century.[1] It had already begun to fray some years before, with the United States and Germany having caught up, if not exceeding, British industry in terms of organizational innovations and productivity. The invention of the assembly line, the increase in efficiency and productivity under new economies of scale, the impact of Taylorism in further deskilling and routinization of labor, and the transition to a society based on mass production for mass consumption represented a revolution in capitalist production. These developments, usually coalesced under the title "Fordism" after its pioneer Henry Ford the U.S. automobile manufacturer, marked a radical shift within capitalist structures of production.[2]

The United States' replacing Britain as the world's leading economy and as upholder of a new liberal global trading regime by the mid-twentieth century was a tumultuous process. It witnessed two devastating world wars and a decade-long economic depression (1929–1939) that severely affected the entire world. Although there are many aspects to this period worthy of discussion, for a work focused on the relationship between globalization and postcolonialism, the following points are crucial. The first is the decolonization of former colonies in Asia and Africa. When the dust from World War II settled, it was clear that direct control over the third world through colonialism was no longer viable. The Afro-Asian continents were afire with national liberation movements for independence in the interwar period, and the colonial powers (mainly Britain, France, Holland, and Japan, but also Germany, Italy, Belgium, Spain, and Portugal) were militarily and/or economically devastated by recession and war. India gained independence from the British in 1947, followed soon after by Indonesia from the Dutch. Korea, Manchuria (eastern China), and Formosa (Taiwan) had come out from under Japan, which also lost its briefly won colonies in much of Southeast Asia and the Pacific. China overthrew the quasi-colonial domination of her economy and polity by the West and Japan through the communist revolution of 1949. The fifteen or so years after the Chinese communist revolution could well be called the era of decolonization, as one country after another in Asia and Africa liberated itself from colonial rule. As wars in Vietnam, Algeria, Angola, Mozambique, and Palestine and civil war in South Africa, Rhodesia (now Zimbabwe), and other places showed, the process was by no means pacific or without resistance by the colonial powers. Yet the tide had turned against overt political and economic domination of Afro-Asia by alien Western governments, and decolonization became a reality.

A second critical point of the aftermath of World War II was the emergence of the New World economy under U.S. hegemony. Pegged at $35 per ounce of gold in 1944 (at the historic Bretton Woods conference in New Hampshire), the U.S. dollar replaced the British pound as the currency of choice; it offered a stable and guaranteed medium of international exchange for a world still embroiled in war. The creation of the International Monetary Fund (IMF) and the International Bank for Reconstruction and Development (IBRD; better known as the World Bank) on this occasion were important steps in the consecration of a new and relatively open world economy under U.S. auspices. The IMF was established to lubricate international trade through the provision of hard-currency credit in a postwar context where most countries had no reserves of foreign exchange and could ill afford imports to rebuild their economies. The World Bank was set up with the initial purpose of providing loans and assistance to the devastated economies of Europe and Japan and reconstructing their infrastructure, and thereafter began lending to the developing world as well (its first third-world loan recipient being India in 1950). Soon after Bretton Woods, in 1948, the General Agreement on Trades and Tariffs (GATT) was established with the long-term goal of steadily whittling down barriers to international trade, such as protectionist tariffs and taxes.

Third, a significant difference between American underwriting of the new liberal order and its precursor (Britain in the late nineteenth century) is worth emphasizing. Bretton Woods occurred in the aftermath of the Great Depression of the 1930s and amid the ongoing devastation of World War II. The importance of maintaining international trade to avoid interconnected recessions across the capitalist world, as had happened in the late 1800s and recurred during the 1930s, was now self-evident. Similarly, the role of national governments in dampening the boom-and-bust cycles inherent in capitalism was recognized with unprecedented clarity. Already, during the depression, many Western countries had realized that governments had a crucial role to play: when demand fell and recession was around the corner, instead of tightening the belt as conventional economics of the previous era had recommended, now it was seen as the role of the government to stimulate the economy through expanded investments, generating employment, and using deficit financing if needed to "prime the pump." Such Keynesian policies (named after the British economist John Maynard Keynes) represented a departure from conventional liberal economic thinking that saw little or no direct role for the state (i.e., politics) in the efficient functioning of economies, was actively hostile to the idea of inflationary state spending to stimulate the economy, and recommended tightening the belt rather than expansion of credit in times of recession. Keynesian thinking was evident in Franklin Roosevelt's New Deal in the 1930s United States and in the efforts of England and other European countries to get over their recessions as well. The Bretton Woods institutions revealed the imprimatur of Keynesian thinking at the level of global economic institutions. The long-term health of the world economy was to be restored by providing cheap credit through the World Bank and international liquidity for trade through the IMF, thereby creating demand and employment across all the Western economies. Among other things, the creation of these institutions and their loan and credit programs, which were tied to purchases from the United States, allowed the latter to gradually taper off its full-employment levels and soft land its economy in the aftermath of the frenzied, all-out production of the war years.

Fourth, Bretton Woods and the establishment of the New World Order after World War II occurred in the shadow of communism and working-class and peasant militancy throughout the world. It is easy now to forget that in most Western European countries during World War II communists played a prominent part in underground resistance to the Axis powers. After the war, they emerged with a credibility that few centrist or confessional political parties (many of whom, in Italy, France, and Germany, for example, had collaborated with the fascist movements of the interwar period) had. In the first elections after the war in a number of Western European countries, communist and socialist parties proved to be formidable contenders and gained a sizable share of the popular vote.[3] Even before the war, the depression of the 1930s had provided a tremendous fillip to socialist and communist ideology in nearly all Western countries, including the United States. The depression in the Western world contrasted with the rapid strides in industrialization, with full employment being made under central planning in the Soviet Union. During the war, the Soviet Union played a huge role in the defeat of Nazi Germany, and its de facto occupation of the eastern half of the European landmass at the end of the war brought communism to the very edge of Western Europe. The global presence of a viable alternative to the capitalist way of life was inescapable.

In the third world, the socialist or communist alternative was even more visible and militant. The success of a peasant-based revolution in China meant in effect that the communist bloc had just been enlarged by as much as one-sixth of the world's population. The consolidation of communism (a version of) in North Korea in the early 1950s after the inconclusive Korean War and the rise of peasant-based communist insurgencies in a wide variety of theaters constituted a world in which capitalist development, far from being the sole choice, seemed locked in a battle for its very existence on a global scale. Communist insurgencies and anticapitalist leftist movements spread across parts of India (in Telengana, Bengal, Kerala, and the northeast generally); Southeast Asia (including Laos, Cambodia, Vietnam, Burma, Malaya, parts of Thailand, Indonesia, and the Philippines); and all across both Africa and Latin America. In many countries (as witnessed in Indonesia in 1965, or India during the Naxal uprising of the late 1960s and early 1970s, or Malaysia in the mid-1960s), third-world nationalist governments resorted to incredible levels of repression in order to combat these insurgencies, often with the help of Western governments and aid. The success of the Cuban revolution in 1959 and the emergence of Che Guevara as an iconic symbol of peasant-based anticapitalist ideology in Latin America in the 1960s were further indications of the battle for the soul of third-world nationalism. In Africa, communists were prominent in the struggle against French colonialism in Algeria and Morocco, in the forefront against apartheid in South Africa, against settler colonialism in Rhodesia, as well as against Lusophone colonialism in Mozambique, Angola, and other theaters. Communists and socialist parties and cells were also part of the nationalist and anticolonial movements in the Middle East, especially in Iran, Iraq, and Syria. As discussed in the next chapter, particularly in the work of Robert Young, the possibility of a socialist revolution sweeping across the third world was a palpable reality in the 1950s and 1960s, and this hope underlay much of what would come to be described as postcolonialism.

Keynesianism, the proximal presence of communist societies in Eastern Europe, the decade-long recession of the 1930s, the electoral clout of working-class parties in Western societies, and the popularity of a people-based anticapitalist alternative in many third-world countries all tempered the free-market ideology of the United States and the institutions established in 1944. One summarization of the Keynesian underpinnings of Western economies in the period 1945–1975 lists: "a state-managed *modus vivendi* between labour and capital; limited capital flows; managed trade; dependence of corporations on retained earnings for investment; strong regulation of banks and the financial sector; fine-tuning of the economy through monetary and fiscal mechanisms; and fixed exchange rates."[4]

The presence of the communist alternative and the threat it represented to market societies also explained the inordinate amount of financial assistance, covert military operations, intelligence-based destabilization, and political-ideological support provided by the United States through its foreign policy of containment in various parts of the world.[5] In Western Europe, Japan, and all across the third world, the United States stood as the bulwark of capitalism and anticommunism (which, despite U.S. rhetoric, was never the same thing as democracy). Just as British underwriting of so-called free trade relied upon gunboat diplomacy, U.S. underwriting of the postwar order relied upon a foreign policy that combined carrot and stick to keep the world safe for, in theory, democracy and freedom, but in reality capitalist trade and investment.[6] As discussed in later chapters, this history of U.S. involvement worldwide on the side of capitalism and private investment and against what was perceived as communism (but was often an effort by the recently decolonized to assert national sovereignty and ownership over their own assets) would constitute an important reason for the great degree of divergence between U.S. self-perceptions and the way in which it is viewed in the third world.

These factors constituted the background against which the newly independent countries of Afro-Asia and the formally free but U.S.-dependent Latin American countries embarked on their development in the postwar period. In the mid-twentieth century, at a theoretical level, these countries were faced with two starkly contrasting developmental models. The first was that outlined by the modernization school of thought, which was capitalist, based on private enterprise, relatively open to Western investment and imports under a free-trade model, and one that saw expansion of international trade and investment as the engine of economic growth. It saw the direct involvement of the state sector—in economic planning and in production—as, at best, a temporary phase, and one that should be rapidly left behind after a certain measure of consolidation. The second was a Soviet-inspired, centrally planned, and state-led developmental alternative, with an emphasis on import substitution, protectionist tariffs, and national self-sufficiency, especially in the domain of manufactured goods. This model was pessimistic on the importance of export growth, international competition, and foreign direct investment in the developmental process.

In reality, third-world countries followed many divergent models of economic growth, and the above contrast between the free-market model and the state-centric inward looking models is more useful as an ideal type. Many third-world countries went for a "mixed" economy: with private, capitalistic, industrial, and agrarian sectors, alongside a measure of state planning and direct participation in the economy, especially in key infrastructural industries.[7] Such departures from strict adherence to free-market strategies and keeping the state out of the economy was understood, in the context of global Keynesianism, as inevitable and perhaps necessary for balanced growth, even by the United States.[8]

The Cold War was also a quintessentially ideological battle for the minds and beliefs of those in the developing third world, and the United States and Soviet Union spent an enormous amount of resources to win them over. Given their long period of colonial domination, much of it with a selective imposition of ideas of free trade, many newly independent countries were lukewarm to the modernization school, especially given its undiluted Eurocentrism. But their need for capital, technological know-how, the inertia of preexisting patterns of colonial trade and investments, and cultural domination of third-world countries during the era of colonialism made them dependent on the West. Modernization theories were underwritten by the richest nation in the world, disseminated through textbooks and educational strategies, magazines and movies, lectures by visiting academics and intellectuals, and scholarships for third-world students to first-world universities. Such ideological emphasis on private enterprise, openness to foreign direct investments, and protection of the assets of Western multinationals was backed by military force whenever necessary. Thus, when the democratically elected Iranian Prime Minister Mohammed Mossadegh sought to nationalize the oil industry (which was dominated by a British multinational) in the early 1950s, he was overthrown in a coup engineered by the Central Intelligence Agency (CIA) in collaboration with the British. He was replaced by Shah Mohammad Reza Pahlavi, who went on to establish one of the most ruthless and repressive dictatorships of the twentieth century. The shah was a faithful ally of the United States for close to three decades thereafter, until his ouster in the Islamic revolution of 1979. The case of Iran was emblematic of U.S. foreign policy during these decades, consistently preferring authoritarian third-world regimes to democratic economic nationalists and justifying this preference on grounds of the containment of communism.

The two superpowers divided the world anew into strategic blocs of countries allied to one or the other. The United States sought to contain the Soviet Union through a series of treaties signed with countries bordering it, while the Soviet Union offered assistance (both overt and covert) to regimes sympathetic to its foreign policy goals and committed to at least the idea of state-led, if not communist, development.

For many leading third-world countries (such as Egypt, India, Indonesia, Ghana, Nigeria, Kenya, and others), economic and ideological competition between the two superpowers offered both opportunity and danger. On the one hand, they jealously guarded their hard-won sovereignty and were loath to ally too closely with either bloc. Such independence from either bloc (or nonalignment as it came to be called) allowed them the opportunity to get the best of their relations with either superpower, to further their own plans for self-reliant economic development, and to make an important ideological or symbolic statement regarding their sovereignty and status in world affairs. On the other hand, as a long list of countries literally going from Angola and Afghanistan to Vietnam and Zaire shows, the military and ideological standoff between the United States and the Soviet Union was often played out in third-world countries as proxy wars, at a severe cost to the latter.

At an aggregate level the success of the Bretton Woods institutions, as far as the Western world is concerned, was reflected in the unprecedented growth rates and expansion in trade that occurred in the three decades after the end of World War II. Overall annual growth rates of GNP in the developed Western world had been about 2.5 percent per annum in the period 1873–1913, and this fell to an average of 1.9 percent per annum in the 1913–1950 period. But after the war, it increased to a resounding 4.9 percent per annum for the 1950–1973 period for the Organization for Economic Cooperation and Development (OECD) nations. As discussed below, such growth in the developed world was matched by unsurpassed GDP growth rates as well as per capita growth rates across the developing world. Such generalized growth at the height of Fordism led Arthur Lewis, the Nobel laureate economist, to describe it as "the greatest boom" and many others to describe the period as the "American century." During this same period (1950–1973) exports of the OECD countries to one another increased at a rate of 8.6 percent per year, indicating the stunning expansion in trade under U.S. leadership of the world economy.[9]

Although the immediate aftermath of independence in most third-world countries was marked by heady optimism and the belief that self-government would soon result in generalized development for all, the reality has proven to be different. With the exception of a handful of Newly Industrializing Countries (NICs) (South Korea, Taiwan, Hong Kong, and Singapore), and in more recent years China, which have seen rates in excess of 6 percent per annum in per capita economic growth rates, most countries in the third world have grown at a much lower rate of between 2 and 3 percent per annum in per capita terms. Thus for the period 1950–1980, Lloyd Reynolds's sample of a large number of third-world countries distributed across the continents of Africa, Asia, and Latin America finds that the median GDP growth rate was a relatively healthy 4.9 percent per annum. However, medical breakthroughs, such as the advent of antibiotics in the 1930s, the worldwide distribution of preventative medicines and vaccines (through organizations such as the World Health Organization), improved neonatal care, and the political fact of self-government, resulted in improved life expectancy, reduced infant mortality rates, and generally lowered mortality rates in most third-world countries. This led to a veritable demographic explosion across Asia and Africa in the twentieth century. The total world population, which was less than a billion in 1800 and had barely increased to a little over a billion in 1850 and about 1.6 billion in 1900, now increased exponentially to 2.5 billion in 1950, 4 billion by 1980, and over 6 billion people in 2008. Since population growth rates have been low (well below 1 percent in the postwar period) among the developed nations, the vast bulk of this population increase has occurred in the third world. The median aggregate GDP growth rate of 4.9 percent per annum (1950–1980) for the third world averaged out to a median per capita growth rate of just 2.3 percent per annum. At this rate, it would take an unconscionably long time for a structural transformation of the third world into a developed area. Moreover, the gap between the first and third worlds was widening even faster as a result of this disparity in per capita growth rates.[10]

Table 2.1 summarizes Michael Todaro's findings regarding the growth in GNP per capita in the period 1966–1985 for various parts of the world. The average annual GNP per capita increase was of the order of 2.7 percent for developing countries as a whole, but within this, Africa saw only a 1.1 percent increase in GNP per capita. Moreover, the thirty-one low-income African countries actually experienced a decline in their per capita GNP of the order of 0.3 percent per annum. The picture of a diverging world is substantiated by the enormous discrepancies between the first and third worlds in terms of per capita GNP, life expectancy, infant mortality rates, literacy levels, and the physical quality of life index.

Contrasting with sub-Saharan Africa has been the sustained and substantial increases in GDP per capita of a handful of East Asian economies. South Korea (6.6 percent), Hong Kong (6.1 percent), Singapore (7.6 percent), and to a lesser extent Malaysia (4.4 percent), Thailand (4.0 percent), and Indonesia (4.8 percent) have all grown at rates that have transformed

Table 2.1. Growth in GNP Per Capita in the Period 1966–1985

	Avg. ann. GDP growth rate per capita 1966–1985 (%)	Per capita GNP 1985 ($)	Life expect-ancy at birth (Years)	Infant mortality per 1,000 live births	Literacy (%)	PQLI 1985[a]
Developed countries	2.7	10,169	74	15	99	96
Developing countries	1.7	720	61	72	61	66
Africa	1.1	683	52	111	45	49
Africa—low income[b]	–0.3	231	48	126	41	43

Source: Adapted from Michael Todaro, Economic Development in the Third World, 4th ed. (New York: Longman, 1989), 48–49.
[a]The Physical Quality of Life Index (PQLI) is "a composite index based on life expectancy at age one, infant mortality, and literacy." See Todaro, 60, 108–13.
[b]There were thirty-one of fifty-three African countries in this category, all of which were located in sub-Saharan Africa. Low-income countries had per capita GDPs under $470.

their economies, while Taiwan's GDP grew at 9.1 percent per annum in the period 1966–1982.[11]

The contrasting emphases of the modernization/globalization school of thought and the underdevelopment/postcolonialism model are reflected in the debate that ensued over NIC success. Initially, the success of Korea, Taiwan, Hong Kong, and Singapore, the East Asian Tigers, was thought to be proof of the veracity of the free enterprise, market-model and was touted as such by the World Bank in its analyses of East Asia. However, later research by scholars committed to a political-economy approach has produced a more nuanced understanding. For example, the works of Robert Wade, Alice Amsden, and others have shown that the Korean state has played a prominent role in the developmental surge of that country.[12] Through selective credit policies and controlling access to hard currency, it subsidized sectors seen as competitive in global markets. It was not open to foreign direct investment across the board, but judiciously combined protectionism in certain sectors and liberalization in others according to well-articulated strategies. It was draconian in terms of labor laws and re-pressed workers unions during the critical growth decades. Central ministries coordinated research and development of private firms in ways that minimized duplication and destructive competition between them.

Perhaps most importantly, the economic success of countries like Korea and Taiwan rose less from their export orientation or openness to the world economy (although this was undoubtedly a factor in making their firms globally competitive) and more toward the fact that they had enacted thoroughgoing land reforms in the 1950s that greatly diminished landless-ness and rural poverty, eliminated landlordism, and expanded the domestic market beyond urban enclaves. Land reforms also thwarted any rise in peasant militancy and communist ideology. The state invested heavily in areas of general concern to the population, such as primary education, health care, rural infrastructure, and women's development. It was a combination of all these factors (and other exogenous and fortuitous ones such as U.S. aid, since countries like Korea and Taiwan were front-line states in the struggle against global communism; their role as economic subcontractors for the United States in the Vietnam War; and by riding the coattails of a resurgent Japanese economy in the postwar period) that caused their success, and not a laissez-faire economic policy. The impressive growth rates of Korea and Taiwan have resulted in general prosperity rather than enclave growth, and this mainly on account of the prior history of land reforms and rural investments.[13] This is today seen in their low

Gini indices of inequality, in comparison with most other third-world countries.

Once again, one can discern the argument between those who would emphasize Smithian trade-centric explanations ("NIC success arose because of participation in international trade—their export orientation and liberalizing foreign investment—and keeping state interference in the economy to a minimum") versus political economists ("NIC success was more on account of judicious state planning and policies, land reforms, and investment in social capital which meant their external orientation generated widespread domestic prosperity"). The phenomenal growth rates (both gross and in per capita terms) achieved by Japan after the end of World War II, and China from the 1980s onward, did not occur exclusively on account of free-market principles and liberalization across the board either. On the contrary, in Japan, the period of U.S. occupation after the war enacted a thoroughgoing land reform, and thereafter, state ministries and bureaucracies played a key role in the developmental surge in that country.[14] Sectors (such as rice farming) remain highly protected to this day in Japan. In China, private ownership of industrial enterprises, competition, and export orientation have all been state-directed policies under the control of a single-party dictatorship that remains communist in name but not in ideology. The Chinese revolution leveled rural inequalities to a substantial degree, invested heavily in the formation of social capital, namely, primary education, health care through "barefoot doctors," women's education, and welfare, and limited population growth. To this day, China refuses to consider full convertibility of its currency or liberalization of its capital market accounts. In a similar vein, the success of India in the information technology sector in very recent years was in substantial part a product of prior decades of state-sponsored educational institutions in technology; selective subsidies, incentives, land, tax breaks, and import licenses offered to software startup firms; and a decades-long protectionist legacy that led to firms such as International Business Machines (IBM) actually leaving India in the 1970s, forcing the domestic computer industry to become self-reliant.[15] Clearly, it is not so much the liberalization of trade and investment by itself, but rather the wider sociopolitical economy in which such liberalization occurs and the critical role of the state in the timing and nature of such liberalization that are critical to success. This is analogous to the crucial point made in the previous chapter: it was not just the plunder and pillage of the New World that fueled the industrialization and modernization of European countries. It was rather the state and societal contexts into which such wealth entered that is important. Thus, the plundered wealth was frittered away in Spain and Portugal, while it fed the Industrial Revolution in England and Holland.

In other words, the debate between the modernization/globalization/ Smith model and the underdevelopment/postcolonialism/Marx model continues to the most recent events in the global economy such as explaining NIC success or the rising growth rates in China and India.

UNEQUAL GROWTH, DEBT CRISES, AND THE CONSOLIDATION OF NEOLIBERALISM

The picture of comparative GDP per capita growth rates in the postwar world outlined in Table 2.1 changed significantly in more recent decades. As Table 2.2, adapted from the work of Richard Cooper, indicates, there was a slowdown in growth rates across the developed world, but the areas hardest hit by the reversal in growth in per capita GDP were Africa, Latin America, the former Soviet Union, and Eastern Europe. In sharp contrast to Lewis's "golden era" of growth for the postwar decades, the contemporary era has seen a marked slowing down everywhere except Asia.[16]

By the early 1970s, the "American century" was already showing signs of strains, and the social structure of accumulation that had underwritten the postwar boom across the world was coming unraveled. First, profit margins all across the developed world were steadily narrowing as competition between the United States and the now-robust economies of Western Europe and Japan intensified. The rising share of the NICs in the export of manufactured goods represented a new development, as they successfully altered their economies from production of raw materials and agricultural

Table 2.2. Annual Increase in Per Capita GDP (%)

Region	1950–1960	1960–1970	1970–1980	1980–1990	1990–2001
USA, Canada, Australia	1.7	2.9	2.1	2.2	2
Western Europe	4.2	4	2.5	1.9	1.7
Eastern Europe	3.8	3.4	3	−0.6	0.7
Former USSR	3.3	3.5	1.5	0.7	−3.5
Latin America	2.2	2.4	3	−0.7	1.3
Asia	3.8	4.1	2.9	3.2	3.1
Africa	1.9	2.5	1.2	−0.7	0.2

Source: Richard N. Cooper, "A Half Century of Development," Paper No. 04-03, Weatherhead Center for International Affairs, Harvard University, Cambridge, MA, May 2004. www.cid.harvard.edu/cidwp/pdf/118.pdf (accessed 22 May 2008).

goods to more value-added manufactured goods higher up the commodity chain. Initially targeting specific labor-intensive sectors opened up to them by the ongoing rounds of negotiations under GATT, the NICs displaced U.S. workers in fields such as textiles, shoes, steel, shipbuilding, electrical and electronic appliances, small cars, and a number of other sectors. The response of Western capital to such diminishing profit margins within the industrialized world was predictable: on the one hand, it sought to rene-gotiate the social pact with labor that had characterized the three-decade-long period of growth and expansion, and, on the other, it increasingly be-gan to relocate production and services outside the high-wage domestic economy and in the rising economies of the third world.

The late 1970s saw the first sustained assaults on the Keynesian welfare state and the power of organized labor (under Margaret Thatcher in Britain), and this was consolidated in the 1980s (especially during the presidency of Ronald Reagan in the United States and Helmut Kohl's chan-cellorship in Germany). In Britain, the nationalized firms and sectors were privatized, and the power of unions and the working class was decisively decimated by the Thatcher regime in a series of highly publicized con-frontations. Millions of state employees were fired as a result of privatiza-tion. Meanwhile, London and the southern counties prospered greatly un-der the liberalized economy and especially the liberalization of capital markets and the financial sector, and the financial district surged in wealth. The midlands and northern counties (once the industrial and mining heartland of Britain) fell into a steep decline, which is still ongoing. In-equality within the country increased greatly. In the United States, similar changes were occurring, with the shift of the economic center of gravity away from the industrial Northeast and around the Great Lakes to the Southwest and Western states. In the decade of the 1980s, under Reagan and George H. W. Bush, the average family income of the top 10 percent of society increased by 16 percent, and the family income of the top 1 percent of society increased by a staggering 50 percent. At the other end, the bot-tom 10 percent of U.S. families lost 15 percent of their incomes (moving from an annual income of $4,113 to $3,504 over the decade). Such rising inequality was characteristic not merely of England and the United States, but rather "virtually all countries have seen inequalities increase over the past twenty years because of neoliberal policies."[17]

The power of capital to renegotiate terms with labor, strengthened by the neoliberal ideology of conservative governments across Western coun-tries, was greatly augmented by changes in communication, information, and transportation technologies that now enabled production to be globally parceled out. The NICs, economies such as Mexico, Brazil, Thailand, Indonesia, Malaysia, China, and various export-processing zones all across the world, became favored sites for the relocation of U.S. industrial production. The wage differential between the United States and these new sites of production far outweighed any increase in costs due to transportation. Such nonunionized labor in societies with large "surplus" populations (itself a legacy of prior centuries of underdevelopment, as seen above), with lax environmental regulations, and with governments competing to attract foreign investments (by providing tax holidays, cheap access to land, power, credit, and the like) constituted the basis of a renewed cycle of accumulation, one that would soon gain the name globalization.

The most striking aspects of the period after the end of the "American century" (usually dated to 1973, which was the year of the first oil price hike by the Organization of Petroleum Exporting Countries [OPEC] and two years after the United States detached the dollar from gold and the world economy went from fixed to floating exchange rates) are (a) the worsening of an already bad situation in much of sub-Saharan Africa, (b) the rising per capita GDP growth rates in China and India, which has arguably made a dent in the extent of world poverty in recent years, (c) the negative growth rates and the deterioration across most indicators in the former Soviet Union and the ex-communist countries in the period from about 1989 until very recently, (d) the debt crisis that swept across Latin America and other parts of the third world in the 1980s, and which continues to be a major factor in their development today, (e) the East Asian meltdown of the late 1990s, its rapid export to the former Soviet Union and Latin America, and the role of the IMF and liberalization of capital markets in this crisis, and (f) rising inequalities both internationally and within the countries of the world in the era of globalization.

The key to the above developments has been a profound change in the temper of global economic ideology. If the post–World War II period marked the heyday of development economics[18] and Keynesianism within nations and multilateral institutions such as the IMF and World Bank, the period since 1980 has seen the resurgence of market ideology and ostensible hostility to statist or political interference in the functioning of the economic domain. Ironically, this period has actually seen a tremendous increase in the degree of political interference by institutions such as the IMF and its Structural Adjustment Program on the economies of third-world countries, done in the name of defending free-trade principles!

The power of institutions such as the IMF and World Bank to dictate policies to third-world governments arose in large part due to the debt crises that swept these nations in the 1980s. The genesis of such third-world debt goes back to developments in the 1970s. Following the first and second oil price hikes of 1973 and 1979, respectively, huge dollar deposits (often termed petrodollars), totaling as much as $350 billion by 1979, lay in Western banks, desperately looking for profitable investment avenues. These were augmented by what are commonly called Eurodollars: internationally held U.S. dollars in offshore bank accounts outside the purview of the U.S. government. As the premier economic power of the postwar era and as the general provider of liquidity for international trade, the United States had exported millions of dollars overseas in preceding decades. These included the dollar exports needed to finance the almost continuous balance of payments deficits run by the U.S. economy once the Western European countries, Japan, and the NICs had effectively eliminated its edge in manufacturing. Further, the export of dollars was compounded by the costs of the foreign policy of containment, the war in Vietnam being the most prominent instance. By 1979, such Eurodollars were estimated to have reached $425 billion, and like petrodollars, desperately seeking investment outlets. These were the source of the incredibly aggressive and profligate lending engaged in by private banks to third-world nations through the later half of the 1970s and the early 1980s.[19]

The loans were contracted by various third-world nations—predominantly in Latin America—on variable interest rates and based on highly optimistic forecasts regarding their earnings from exports to the first world in the near future. Many third-world countries borrowed heavily at this time, not merely because there were so many lenders eager to lend, but also because their oil import bills had suddenly quadrupled. However, the late 1970s saw the terms of trade between third-world exports (still largely dominated by minerals, agricultural goods, and other raw materials for the non-NICs) and first-world exports (manufactured goods) deteriorate sharply to the detriment of the former. Oil-exporting third-world countries, such as Venezuela and Mexico, borrowed heavily on the assumption that the prices would remain high into the future. Such forecasts and calculations went seriously awry by the early 1980s when the U.S. Federal Reserve, in a bid to contain inflation in the United States and to stave off a potential collapse in the value of the dollar, sharply raised interest rates. The tightening of money supply and the increased costs of borrowing for investment quickly plunged the United States, and soon the rest of the

Western world, into a sharp recession in the early 1980s. This supply-side retreat from Keynesianism was accompanied by a larger attack on labor unions and the idea of welfare in general in the United States and in Britain, as outlined above. The rise in interest rates made third-world debts (contracted at variable rates) balloon suddenly, while the Western recession made their chances of exporting their way out of debt virtually impossible and sent the prices of primary commodities plummeting further. As the reality of one major third-world borrower after another being unable to service its debt (let alone repay the principal) came home, private banks that had engaged in the indiscriminate lending were faced with imminent collapse, leading to possible catastrophe for the world financial system as a whole.

It was in this context that the IMF in its role as a "lender of the last resort" stepped in. To put it simply, the IMF provided credit to these indebted third-world countries to enable them to service their loans from Western private banks and to continue to maintain levels of investment (in the hope that their exports would soon pick up to a West that was still mired in recession). In exchange for a bailout in a moment of crisis, these third-world countries would, in effect, be forced to put their financial houses in order. They would agree to a Structural Adjustment Program that was constructed on putative principles of sound finance, balanced budgets, and liberalization of international trade, but which represented in reality a retreat from Keynesianism and a return to previously regnant ideas of belt-tightening and contraction as a response to an economic crisis. The reasons for the debt crisis had to do with a number of factors: the floating billions of "hot money" (in the form of Euro- and petrodollars) seeking investment outlets anywhere and everywhere; the dilution of capital controls and international banking regulations in the aftermath of the fixed-rate regime of the Bretton Woods systems; a U.S. corporate and banking sector, and stock market, obsessed with showing quarterly profits and dividends rather than slower but sound investments; deregulation of the domestic U.S. banking and savings and loans sector; the growing presence of bureaucrats in the finance ministries of third-world countries who were amenable to the neoliberal logic being pushed by the World Bank, the IMF, and the U.S. Treasury Department; the collapse of nonoil primary commodity prices in the 1980s; the sharp rise in oil import bills of most third-world countries; and a host of other factors. But these were largely ignored, and blame for the debt crisis was exclusively laid on undisciplined borrowing by corrupt third-world nations. (A similar selective reading would also prevail during analysis of the East Asian meltdown during the late 1990s, as we will soon see.)

In exchange for the bailout, these nations were instructed by the IMF (a) to eliminate "subsidies" and "wasteful" budgetary expenses on public transportation, provision of food staples especially to the urban poor, and other such instances of "profligate" spending; (b) to devalue their currencies in order to enhance their export potential, while also directing investments into sectors that favored exports; (c) to liberalize trade by removing restrictions and tariffs; (d) to privatize or sell off nationally owned public sector enterprises; (e) to be more hospitable to foreign direct investment from Western firms and multinationals; (f) to modify labor regimes to keep wages low; and (g) to strive for a balanced budget and the elimination of deficits. This package of reforms came to be called the Structural Adjustment Program of the IMF in the 1980s, and it constituted a key step in the emergence of neoliberal globalization in the 1980s.

The contrasting views of the modernization/globalization model and the underdevelopment/postcolonialism model once again stand out in analyses of the debt crises of the late 1980s. To the former, the debt crises were a result of profligate borrowing, lack of economic discipline, incomplete liberalization, state subsidies, and irrational behavior on the part of third-world countries, while the latter emphasizes the unequal power structure of international institutions and third-world governments and the continued salience of political and economic neocolonialism.

Exemplifying the underdevelopment/postcolonial approach, Cheryl Payer likens the international financial system of the early 1980s and the debt crisis that ensued to a Ponzi scheme.[20] In such a scheme each person is promised double his or her original investment so long as he or she brings a certain number of new investors into the scheme. Thus, if I were to enter with an initial investment of $100, I would immediately get $200 so long as I was able to convince another five investors to enter the scheme by paying $100 each. They would be inclined to do so, because they too would see their investments double immediately so long as they each brought in another five investors to enter the scheme. In its simplest version, a Ponzi scheme pays off the investors in round (n-1) by using the money gained from investors in the nth round. Theoretically, the game can go on forever even in a finite population because the same investor can play it any number of times. In reality, as the number of players needed ratchets up exponentially, most Ponzi schemes end with the last (and largest) round of investors being gypped out of their money and the organizers of the scheme disappearing with a nice bundle. The crux of such games lies in the confidence that players have in them—they continue so long as it is still available—hence they are called "con games."

Payer argues that private banks that had lent to the third-world countries could recoup their loans only by convincing a new round of lenders about the essential soundness of the loans to these nations. They were like investors in round (n-1) trying to convince a new round of investors to buy in, in order to recover their own investments. Since the name of the game is confidence, that is where the IMF comes in according to Payer. The Structural Adjustment Programs were like a certification process forced upon third-world countries by the IMF in order to shore up global confidence in them. The latter's pronouncement regarding the sincerity of the efforts of debtor nations to put their economic houses in order sent a signal to a new round of lenders, whose loans (along with those of the IMF) enabled these countries to service their debts, that is, for the prior round of lenders to recoup their investments.

To Payer, the IMF was not so much interested in the welfare of debtor nations as it was in averting the collapse of the global financial system on account of a mass default, salvaging investments of Western private banks, and using the situation as an opportunity to coerce third-world nations into the emerging neoliberal consensus about free trade as the engine of economic growth. The debtor nations were over a barrel and in no position to resist the IMF. Standing up to the latter would ensure that no lender, institutional or private, would step into the breach, ensuring the default of their loans and the collapse of their economies. In other words, for Payer if earlier centuries of so-called free trade were imposed on third-world countries via gunboat diplomacy, today it is done through ostensibly neutral international financial institutions like the IMF and the World Bank.

The 1990s saw the extension of the Structural Adjustment Programs under the IMF and World Bank auspices to the countries of the erstwhile second world (the former Soviet Union and its Eastern European allies) as they disbanded communist regimes and began to adapt to market economics. The "shock therapy" of their conversion from state-run communist societies to free-market economies has entailed a huge social cost, revealed in the plunging GDP per capita levels and indicators such as infant mortality rates, life expectancy levels, and daily caloric intake. The Structural Adjustment Programs imposed by the IMF demanded immediate and drastic cuts in welfare expenses and subsidies in societies that had had them for decades; the privatization by sale of state-run industries and organizations (often to carpet baggers from Western nations); dismantling barriers to trade and financial flows; and other reforms in line with the World Bank–IMF package. The resultant immiserization of the former Soviet bloc and the no-holds-barred gangster-style capitalism that has come in its wake reveal a great underestimation of the difficulties of the transition from state-run socialism to free-market capitalism, and one that seemed unconcerned about the social impact of free-market dogmas.

As with many economic issues, the impact of Structural Adjustment Programs on growth and inequality is mired in controversy. Such programs aim at macroeconomic policies of governments, and one can argue that a drop in GDP growth rates in the aftermath of such a program might have been the result of many intervening variables, including the defective or incomplete implementation of the Structural Adjustment Program itself. Critics, such as Cheryl Payer, Susan George, Joseph Stiglitz, and Walden Bello, have argued that an unelected international institution should not play a role that directly contravenes the national sovereignty of debtor nations, and that the policy prescriptions of the IMF have dovetailed altogether too neatly with the interests of private Western banks, the U.S. Treasury Department, and Western corporations and investors desirous of access to third-world countries and ex-socialist nations on favorable terms. They point out that IMF bailouts are equivalent to a worldwide taxpaying public bearing the costs of mistakes made by private lenders, and meanwhile there is no denying that austerity programs of the IMF disproportionately impact the poorest sections of third-world societies. Thus Cooper's data in Table 2.2 reveal that there was an annual *decrease* in per capita GDP of the order of 0.7 percent between 1980 and 1990 in both Africa and Latin America. The shock therapy administered under the neoliberal prescription coincided with an annual *decline* in GDP per capita of the order of 3.5 percent per annum in the period 1990–2001 in the former Soviet Union, one of the sharpest reversals in growth in the twentieth century. Africa's GDP per capita growth rates in the period 1990–2001 is barely discernible at 0.2 percent.

What cannot be denied is the worldwide retreat of Keynesian principles since the late 1970s and the rise of what even analysts sympathetic to the idea of liberalized world trade as an engine of economic growth, such as Joseph Stiglitz, have called "market fundamentalism." They use this term to indicate the unthinking application of ideas of free trade, irrespective of time, space, or economic sector. The architects of the rise of such market fundamentalism in recent decades in the Western world were conservative leaders such as Reagan, Thatcher, and Kohl, while the role of the IMF and the World Bank was in exporting the "neoliberal consensus" across much of the developing and ex-socialist world, as outlined above. The spread of such a form of market fundamentalism is an inescapable reality of globalization at the present time.

One of the most dramatic instances of the application of such market fundamentalism and of the information and communications revolution at the heart of globalization to exponentially magnify its disastrous impact occurred during the Asian financial crisis. The crisis began in July 1997 with the decision of the Thai government to depart from the regime of pegged exchange rates and float its currency, the baht. The government was responding to the tremendous pressure on the baht as a result of an unsustainable policy that it had adopted in preceding years, in large part on the advice of the IMF and the World Bank. This policy was in effect a combination of fixed exchange rates (important for foreign investors concerned about currency risk), liberalized capital accounts (that is, unrestricted movement of investment capital into and out of the country), and high domestic interest rates relative to Western markets in order to attract capital and investments. For the preceding decade at least, the market fundamentalists of the IMF and the treasury branch of the U.S. government had been rigorously evangelizing for liberalization of capital market accounts, especially in the capital hungry Rising Asian Tigers, such as Thailand. The hypermobile capital of Western investment banks like Goldman Sachs and Merrill Lynch, pension funds, mutual funds, hedge funds, and private investors roamed all over the world at the touch of a computer keyboard, seeking rapid profits from small divergences in currency values, interest rates, stock prices, and the like on a global level.[21] Such funds invested heavily in emerging market economies such as Thailand, as they generally had higher rates of return than those prevalent within the developed world. Intent as they were in short-term profits rather than investing in projects with long gestation periods, such money moved into stocks, on arbitraging differences in interest rates and currency values, and in real estate speculation.[22] The fixed rate of the baht meant that it appreciated in tandem with the rising dollar in the mid-1990s, which adversely affected Thai exports. As the trade deficit ballooned and exports stagnated, the contradictory mix of policies signaled a highly overvalued baht. The problems were now compounded with hedge funds and individual investors such as George Soros betting on the imminent devaluation of the baht by converting billions of them into dollars before the fall.

With the announcement of the floating of the baht, the Thai government was in effect signaling that it could no longer sustain the contradictory set of macroeconomic policies that had made it such an attractive emerging market for Western speculative capital in the first place. Other investors and banks joined Soros and the hedge funds in offloading the currency as fast as possible, leading to the virtual elimination of the country's foreign exchange reserves as the Thai government paid up. The Thai stock market plunged as investment capital left the country as fast as it had come in, and soon all across Asia markets went into a free fall. As investors competed with one another to get out of the plummeting Asian market before it hit the ground, the crisis was rapidly exported to Russia and Latin America, especially Brazil and Mexico, where there too the countries had liberalized their capital market accounts, dismantled capital controls, removed standstill provisions or trip wires that would have kicked in to slow down the sale of stocks or currency, and eliminated taxes or penalties on short-term investors. The crisis resulted in a sharp downturn in growth rates across East and Southeast Asia as investment capital suddenly dried up on projects midway through their construction. It led to the collapse of many banks, financial houses, and small and medium-sized industries; sent unemployment levels spiraling upward; reduced the savings and assets of millions of people in countries like Thailand, Indonesia, South Korea, and Malaysia to worthless paper; and led to the overnight collapse of a real estate boom that had gone on for years prior.

Debate about the causes and means to get out of the Asian financial crisis had an eerie resemblance to earlier debates about the third-world debt crises of the 1980s (as described above). Leftist analysts such as Walden Bello, Susan George, and Cheryl Payer, and pro-capitalist supporters of liberalized international trade, such as Joseph Stiglitz and Jagdish Bhagwati, for example, targeted their ire on the indiscriminate liberalization of capital market accounts (under the tutelage of the IMF) and on the rapacious movements of speculative capital across the world by money managers and funds based in the West. Stiglitz, a proponent of liberalized trade as an engine for economic growth, lit into the IMF for its insistence on capital market liberalization in the third world and the convergence of its views with the interests of the U.S. Treasury Department and private banks and investment houses. He decried the poor quality of its research and expertise on the economies of countries it professed to advise and argued that the IMF operated out of a dogmatic attachment to theories of free trade and liberalization without taking into account country- or sector-specific details and variations. He further pointed out that the "solutions" recommended by the IMF for the Asian countries to come out of their crisis, which essentially prescribed more of the medicine that had already nearly killed them, had actually prolonged the crisis. Malaysia, which went against the IMF's explicit recommendations and instead raised barriers to the exit of mobile financial capital, refused to devalue its fixed currency, embarked on a program of expansionary state financing and investment, and imposed fines and penalties on rapid speculative financial movements and came out of the crisis in much better shape than those (such as Indonesia, Thailand, Brazil, or Russia) that towed the line of IMF orthodoxy. India and China, neither of which had liberalized their capital markets, had been relatively immune to the Asian financial crisis.

On the other hand, then U.S. Treasury Undersecretary Lawrence Summers and Michael Camdessus and Anne Krueger of the IMF, influential columnists like Thomas Friedman of the *New York Times*, the *Wall Street Journal*, and news magazines like the *Economist* rehashed familiar charges that these third-world countries had weak or corrupt financial institutions; that their banks and industrialists had made poor decisions and borrowed indiscriminately; that the Asian financial crisis was a reflection of "crony capitalism" and nepotism that disregarded sound economic principles in borrowing. They made little or no mention of the movement of giant, unregulated waves of capital across the world, based on practically no research at all, into the fundamentals of the economies they entered or exited, creating and bursting "bubbles" with serious consequences for those caught in its wake.[23] Nor did they own up to the role of the IMF in creating the conditions for the financial crises (through its insistence on liberalization of capital market accounts of borrowers) and in prolonging it (by insisting on belt-tightening and its opposition to capital controls).

When it comes to allegations of Asian crony capitalism, one wonders why the rich history and contemporary reality of robber barons, the buying of political influence through electoral donations, union-busting through goon squads, outright racism, misogyny and anti-Semitism, the revolving door between the Pentagon and the arms industry, Enron, the savings and loans scandals of the 1980s and 1990s, the ongoing crisis over hyped-up adjustable-rate subprime home mortgages sold by companies like Countrywide Finance, and many other unsavory aspects of U.S. capitalism have never led to the charge that it too is a form of crony capitalism. This does not even touch upon issues such as the influence of well-financed Political Action Committees in securing legislation in the interests of capital in the U.S. Congress, and various state legislatures, or the fact that no one but the well heeled or corporate sponsored can even think of running for public office in the United States today. The selective memory of critics such as Krueger, Camdessus, Summers, and Friedman was breathtaking. Asian Tigers like Korea, Taiwan, and Singapore, and emerging markets such as Malaysia and Indonesia had been touted for over two decades as shining exemplars of what openness to the world economy could produce. Their export orientation, along with rising growth rates and prosperity, was lauded as proof of the success of the neoliberal model and prescribed for all other countries, especially relatively inward-looking economies like India. East Asian success had even led to pseudo-scientific theories about Confucian or Asian values, family ties, and ethnic styles of management as worthy of emulation by the West. There was certainly no talk of crony capitalism then as these countries were held up as ideal models for everyone else, including the West, to follow. Overnight many of these same economies were now described as preternaturally corrupt and in dire need of reform.

The silence about the lemming-like behavior of financial money market managers in the West, unable to see beyond their own short-term profits, only furthered the impression that the IMF was busy blaming the victim instead of owning up to its own share of the blame for the crisis. In a typical instance of selective memory, in his best-selling book *The Lexus and the Olive Tree*, Thomas Friedman celebrates the financial money market managers and hedge fund investors as the contemporary equivalent of the "invisible hand of the market"; they are the savvy, rational investors who decide which countries have their fundamentals right and which ones do not and invest accordingly.[24] One gets a very different picture about the detached rationality of these same financial analysts when one reads Jeffrey Winters's paper. Here is his description of their actions during the Asian meltdown in 1998:

> Suddenly, you receive disturbing news that Thailand is in serious trouble, and you must decide immediately what to do with your Malaysian investments. It is in this moment that the escape psychology and syndrome begins. First, you immediately wonder if the disturbing new information leaking out about Thailand applies to Malaysia as well. You think it does not, but you are not sure. Second, you must instantly begin to think strategically about how other EMFMs (Emerging Market Fund Managers [SK]) and independent investors are going to react. And third, you are fully aware, as are all the other managers, that the first ones to sell as a market turns negative

will be hurt the least, and the ones in the middle and at the end will lose the most value for their portfolio—and likely to be fired from their position as an EMFM as well. In a situation of low systemic transparency, the sensible reaction will be to sell and escape. Notice that even if you used your good connections in the Malaysian government and business community to receive highly reliable information that the country is healthy and not suffering from the same problems as Thailand, you will still sell and escape. Why? Because you cannot ignore the likely behavior of all the other investors. And since they do not have access to the reliable information that you have, there is a high probability that their uncertainty will lead them to choose escape. If you hesitate while they rush to sell their shares, the market will drop rapidly, and the value of your portfolio will start to evaporate before your eyes.[25]

It is important also to realize that in many ways crony capitalism is a redundant term, as there is no other kind in existence. It is a truism that emerging markets lack strong and well-established state and financial institutions, transparency, layers of impartial and incorruptible bureaucratic insulation between state elites and economic institutions, clear guidelines regarding banking regulations, areas earmarked for investment and the movement of capital, and other aspects that are taken for granted in the West. Yet, *it is precisely such characteristics that make them "emerging markets" in the first place and offer the opportunities for super-profits to Western hedge fund managers, investment banks, and individual investors.* Whereas returns on investment are of the order of a few percentage points in Western developed markets, they can run as high as 40 and 50 percent per annum for brief spells in emerging markets because, not despite, of the lack of institutionalization.

In her searing analysis of Indonesia in the 1980s and 1990s under the Suharto regime, Anna Tsing shows the nexus between Western investment capital, corrupt state officials beginning with the executive and his family and ending with village-level mayors, and functionaries, produced a "miracle economy" with high rates of growth and huge returns on investment, alongside growing poverty, landlessness, and environmental collapse. The result was the "privatization" of national wealth and territory, the wholesale destruction of forests in Kalimantan in a breathtakingly short period of time, the destruction of the rights of indigenous peoples and poor farmers to access to what had been hitherto communal lands and forests, and the incredibly swift extinction of thousands of species of flora and fauna. Tsing's analysis emphasizes that it was precisely the weak institutions, poorly developed financial rules and regulations, unclear property regimes (especially for the poor and the indigenous), and related characteristics that underwrote Indonesia's miracle economy and its high returns in the first place. She notes in a succinct and brilliant fashion:

> Imagine for a moment a contradiction between capital and governance. Governance requires rationalization, clarity and order. Capital, in contrast, thrives where opportunities are just emerging. The exceptional profits that allow a firm or corporate sector to get ahead are made where bureaucratic visibility is not yet firmly in place. In the deregulation zones where government is at the end of its tether, capital can operate with the hyperefficiency of theft. Capital cooperates in the spreading of governance measures that facilitate and legitimate this theft; some visibilities and rationalizations develop rapidly, while other economic standards are fluid and even purposely muddy. In the midst of contrasts between clarity and haze, discipline and free-for-all are uncannily bundled together.[26]

In sum, a contradictory set of policies (mandated by the IMF) led to the liberalization of capital accounts and removal of exchange controls in emerging markets, while requiring them to exercise tight fiscal and monetary discipline, leading to high interest rates domestically, alongside fixed exchange rates to maintain the value of their currency. This created the conditions for short-term speculative capital to enter in the form of billions of dollars seeking quick and extraordinary profits on overvalued currencies, disproportionately high interest rates, short selling on overheated stock markets, and real estate speculation. These are not aberrations in the ongoing globalization of the world but are a core component of the way in which capital revalorizes itself and the ways in which emerging markets are constructed to produce precisely such ends. However, when the bubble burst on account of the contradictions, such capital moved out of these countries just as rapidly, leaving them high and dry. Both the debt crisis of the 1980s and the Asian financial crisis of the late 1990s were results of a supply-driven excess of investment capital seeking profitable outlets in emerging markets that were hyped beyond all reason. It was precisely the lack of institutional controls and the contradictory policies that often made profit rates in such markets significantly higher than in the more established bourses and economies of the Western world. When these debt-ridden and devastated economies turned to the IMF for relief in a crisis, this was an opportunity to bring them more firmly into the ambit of neoliberal globalization.

In assessing explanations for the debt crisis or the Asian financial meltdown of the late 1990s, the difference between the modernization/

globalization model and the underdevelopment/postcolonialism model should be readily apparent. Although the former tends to blame the victims for not being adequately modern (i.e., they are corrupt, nepotistic, lack institutions, and cannot defer gratification), the latter emphasizes the historical fact of Western developed capitalist nations using the international system and its institutions to their own advantage and at the expense of the developing countries.

Today, a widely prevalent definition of a poor person is someone who is living on less than one dollar per day (U.S. dollars valued in terms of purchasing power parity [PPP]). When one looks at the world in terms of the percentage of poor people, as shown in Table 2.3, and the trends over the past three decades of globalization, one is immediately struck by the regional disparities.[27]

The sharpest reduction in the percentage and numbers of poor people has occurred in China (which dominates the "East Asia and Pacific" region in Table 2.3). In South Asia (dominated by India), while there has been an impressive reduction in the percentage of poor people, in terms of absolute numbers there are more of them than in 1981. In Latin America, since the percentage of poor people has stayed roughly the same over the past two decades, the absolute numbers have been increasing. The sharpest increases in the numbers of poor in the past quarter century have occurred in sub-Saharan Africa and in the former Soviet bloc countries. In sub-Saharan Africa, there was an increase of 100 million poor people between 1990 and 2001, while in the former East bloc countries, the numbers increased from 23 million to 93 million over the same period.

Table 2.3. Decline in Income Poverty, 1981–2001 (%)

Region	1981	1984	1987	1990	1993	1996	1999	2001
East Asia and Pacific	56.7	38.8	28.0	29.5	24.9	15.9	15.3	14.3
Europe and Central Asia	0.8	0.6	0.4	0.5	3.7	4.4	6.3	3.5
Latin America and Caribbean	10.1	12.2	11.3	11.6	11.8	9.4	10.5	9.9
Middle East and North Africa	5.1	3.8	3.2	2.3	1.6	2.0	2.7	2.4
South Asia	51.5	46.8	45.0	41.3	40.1	36.7	32.8	31.9
Sub-Saharan Africa	41.6	46.3	46.9	44.5	44.1	46.1	45.7	46.4
World	40.4	33.0	28.5	27.9	26.3	22.3	21.5	20.7

Source: World Bank report cited in "Human Development Report 2005: "International Cooperation at a Crossroads: Aid, Trade, and Security in an Unequal World," United Nations Development Program (2005), 34.

A crucial statistic from Table 2.3 is that the percentage of the poor in terms of overall population declined more sharply in the period 1981 to 1996, and since then the rate of decline has slowed considerably. Although this is to some extent an inevitable statistical effect, critics of neoliberal globalization point out that such figures encourage one to be cautious about linking globalization to reduced poverty. They do this for a number of reasons, the most important of which are the following:

1. To the extent that substantial percentage reductions in poverty often occurred in the 1980s, prior to the full impact of neoliberal global-ization on India and China, it indicates that market liberalization by itself may not be the main reason for the drop.[28]
2. The strong performance of China in this regard should give pause as the country has followed a mixture of policies that departs quite dra-matically from the neoliberal consensus and whose trade liberaliza-tion came after radical equalization of many aspects of Chinese so-ciety during decades of communist rule.
3. Indian growth (which in per capita terms has approached 4 percent over the past decade) has to be qualified by data that indicate re-gional, class, and urban-rural inequalities rising sharply and rising growth rates having little impact on unemployment in the country.
4. The areas that have borne the greatest brunt of neoliberal globaliza-tion, in terms of Structural Adjustment Programs, such as Latin America, sub-Saharan Africa, and the former East Bloc, are also the regions with the poorest performance in terms of poverty reduction.

Although the debate over poverty and neoliberal globalization in recent times is ongoing, the data are more unequivocal when it comes to global inequality in the longer term. Here, the picture of rising inequality and a growing divergence between first and third worlds over the past two cen-turies is inescapable. Table 2.4 summarizes two crucial sets of figures: first, GDP per capita growth rates for various parts of the world going back to 1820, and second, the x-fold increase (that is, the number of times in-crease) in per capita GDP rates for various parts of the world going back to that year.

Although the developed world as a whole has seen a nineteenfold in-crease in its GDP per capita over the past two centuries and Japan has wit-nessed a staggering increase of almost thirty-one-fold, the story for Africa and India is abysmal, with the rest of Asia, Latin America, and the Eastern

Table 2.4. GDP Per Capita Growth Rates and x-fold Increase Since 1820

Region	X-fold increase 1820–2001	Annual average compound growth rates of GDP per capita growth (%)				
		1820–1913	1913–1950	1950–1973	1973–1980	1980–2001
Developed World	19.0	1.3	1.2	3.3	1.9	1.9
Eastern Europe	8.8	1.0	0.6	3.8	2.1	0.2
Former USSR	6.7	0.8	1.8	3.3	0.8	−1.6
Latin America	8.4	0.8	1.4	2.6	2.7	0.3
Asia	6.9	0.4	0.1	3.6	2.8	2.3
China	6.0	−0.1	−0.6	2.9	3.5	5.9
India	3.7	0.3	−0.2	1.4	1.4	3.6
Africa	3.5	0.4	0.9	2.0	1.2	−0.1

Source: "Growth and Development Trends, 1960–2005," from *World Economic and Social Survey, 2006: Diverging Growth and Development,* United Nations (2006).

Europe (including the former Soviet Union) doing only marginally better. Clearly, the idea of development as something that structurally transforms a society and makes for a generalized society of self-sufficiency or affluence has passed by much of the world.

This picture of a diverging world economy is further confirmed by Table 2.5, which shows the ratio of GDP per capita in the different parts of the world relative to the developed world. With the sole exception of Japan, the rest of the countries in the world have regressed relative to the developed world over the past two centuries; in fact, in most instances,

Table 2.5. A Bifurcated World with Growing Inequality, 1820–2001

Region	Ratio of GDP per Capita Relative to the Developed World					
	1820	1913	1950	1973	1980	2001
Developed world						
Eastern Europe	0.57	0.42	0.34	0.37	0.38	0.26
Former USSR	0.57	0.37	0.45	0.45	0.42	0.20
Latin America	0.58	0.37	0.40	0.34	0.35	0.25
Asia	0.48	0.22	0.15	0.15	0.16	0.18
China	0.50	0.14	0.07	0.06	0.07	0.16
India	0.44	0.17	0.17	0.06	0.06	0.09
Japan	0.56	0.35	0.35	0.85	0.88	0.91
Africa	0.35	0.16	0.16	0.11	0.10	0.07

Source: "Growth and Development Trends, 1960–2005," from *World Economic and Social Survey, 2006: Diverging Growth and Development,* United Nations (2006).

they have gone from being about half as well-off as the developed world to being a quarter, or a fifth, as well-off. Although the average Japanese had 56 cents to every dollar owned by a resident of the Western developed world in 1820, today he has about 91 cents to that dollar. In contrast, whereas in 1820, the average African had about 35 cents to each dollar of a first-world resident, today he has as little as 7 cents to that dollar. The Indian has regressed from having 44 cents to every dollar of a first worlder in 1820 to having just 9 cents in comparison. The Latin American, who used to have 56 cents to every dollar of the Westerner, today has 25 cents, and similar figures obtain for East Europeans and Russians.

The gap between the first world and the rest has widened since 1820 and has further intensified over the past three decades; this is one of the inescapable realities of the contemporary world. Since the early nineteenth century marked the industrialization of the Western world and is often coterminous with the beginning of the modern era, what Tables 2.4 and 2.5 collectively signify is that this era has seen the inexorable polarization of the world.

Against this background, one may see the period since the end of World War II as marked by the continuous tussle between those wedded to the idea of the market as the best and only arbiter of economic decisions that affects the peoples of the world and those who see a prominent role for humans, states, and politics in such "economic" decision making. If the period from the end of World War II to about 1973 saw the pendulum swing closer to the Keynesian end of the spectrum (one that saw politics and the state as having a legitimate and ethical role in limiting the often destructive effects of free-market capitalism), since then it has swung over to the market end. When Gordon Gekko, the ruthless finance capitalist in the Hollywood movie *Wall Street* (1987) tells shareholders that "greed . . . is good," he was reflecting a zeitgeist in which a democratically elected prime minister of one of the world's leading countries, Margaret Thatcher, argued that the supposedly ethical commitment to equality often arose from "an undistinguished combination of envy and bourgeois guilt."[29] She went on to observe that "It is our job to glory in inequality and see that talents and abilities are given vent and expression for the benefit of all."[30] Inequality soared in Britain and Reagan's United States, and across the world, and societies ostensibly built on ideas of communal equality and cooperation, namely, the Soviet Union and other centrally planned societies collapsed, adding to the seemingly irresistible sway of market economics. As one society after another (the erstwhile Soviet Union and the East bloc, China,

India, Vietnam, Sri Lanka, Nicaragua, and others) joined in the dismantling of state controls and the liberalizing of their economies, even a figure who epitomized resistance and political agency like Nelson Mandela was moved to remark in July 1998 that "Globalization is a phenomenon that we cannot deny. All we can do is accept it."[31] The pessimism of the organized left in the developed world was summarized by Perry Anderson, Marxist intellectual, historian, and longtime editor of its premier journal the *New Left Review*, who observed that "neoliberalism as a set of principles rules undivided across the globe: the most successful ideology in world history."[32]

As the decade-long resistance to neoliberal globalization inaugurated by the Seattle protests against the World Trade Organization Ministerial Conference in November 1998 has shown, the pessimism of Mandela and Anderson is perhaps misplaced. The theoretical and ideological underpinnings of such movements resistant to neoliberal globalization are truly diverse, and their members vary greatly, ranging from ecological groups in first- and third-world countries, to unionized workers, anarchists, migrant laborers in different parts of the world, economic nationalists of various hues, indigenous peoples, to those committed to fair trade as distinct from free trade, the antisweatshop movement, reformers of international institutions such as the IMF, the World Bank, and the World Trading Organization, farmers, and a wide variety of others. At first glance, there seems to be little in common to these various movements that oppose some or all aspects of neoliberal globalization. Yet, one could argue, as will be presented later in this book, there is a common platform underlying them, a refusal to allow the "logic of the economy," or of market fundamentalism, to be the final arbiter of matters pertaining to the well-being of people and the environment in different parts of the world. The chapters that follow will examine the relationship between such a postcolonial perspective as apposed to the relations between politics and economics, as well as the ways in which that perspective has enabled resistance to, and has itself been enabled by, neoliberal globalization.

Chapter 3

Genealogies of the Postcolonial

Our commonsense understanding of the term genealogy is that it is akin to a family tree: it traces an individual's ancestry through parents, grandparents, great-grandparents, and so forth. The French thinker Michel Foucault, drawing on the work of the philosopher Friedrich Nietzsche, however, uses the term genealogy quite differently. He sees genealogy as the series of interpretations of reality by humans who have sought to corral its meaning. He argues that we can never truly and finally know something; all we can do is conduct an archaeology that plumbs the series of meanings that humans have attached to that something over the ages. Whether it is our concepts of madness, illness, crime, "normal" sexual behavior, the individual, or political agency, for Foucault, the meanings that humans attach to these aspects of reality, in other words, interpretations, are indissociable from issues of power. They are forms of epistemic violence that we impose on a reality that is in no way obliged to "turn towards us a legible face." Foucault describes the genealogical method in the following way:

> Genealogy . . . seeks to reestablish the various systems of subjection: not the anticipatory power of meaning, but the hazardous play of dominations . . . if interpretation is the violent or surreptitious appropriation of a system of rules, which in itself has no essential meaning, in order to impose a direction, to bend it to a new will, to force its participation in a different game, and to subject it to secondary rules, then the development of humanity is a series of interpretations. The role of genealogy is to record its history.[1]

This chapter will excavate a series of meanings of the term postcolonial to help us understand the term. In the spirit of Foucault, the aim here is not to offer the definitive meaning of the term, its truth, but to show its genealogy over time, its imbrications with issues of power and political action, and most centrally, how these various sedimented meanings of the term postcolonial relate to the process of globalization. Each of these interpretations has a stake in the matter: each seeks to bend understanding of the term postcolonial to a particular end and to a certain form of political engagement with the forces of neoliberal globalization. The second half of this chapter will look at four exemplary instances of postcolonial theory in our time: the works of Edward Said, Homi Bhabha, Gayatri Chakravorty Spivak, and that of the Subaltern Studies Collective of historians. I should emphasize that the purpose of this chapter is to delineate the main contours of postcolonial theory in its present form. It therefore does not get into a detailed critique of this body of work, which is the point of the succeeding chapter.

POSTCOLONIALISM AS THIRD-WORLD MARXISM

One of the first usages of the term postcolonial was by the Marxist scholar Hamza Alavi. In a landmark essay in the *New Left Review*, Alavi used the term to describe societies such as India, Pakistan, and Bangladesh.[2] He does not explain how or why he arrives at that term, and at first gloss, it seems to have a straightforward meaning: it refers to societies that were once colonized and are now independent, in other words, ex-colonial countries. In this sense, like third world, the term is primarily geographical. Alavi argues that the effects of colonial rule were enduring and did not simply disappear with decolonization or independence. Analyzing the state in Pakistan and the then newly emergent Bangladesh, he made three crucial points: (1) The state in such societies was "overdeveloped" in relation to civil society. It employed a far greater number of people within it, its economic role as direct producer was quite formidable, the bureaucracy penetrated all aspects of the economy and society, its coercive apparatuses (police and armed forces) were relatively well organized and out of proportion with that of the overall population, and positions within the state bureaucracy were sinecures that were part of the patronage politics in such societies. This "overdeveloped" state emerged during colonial rule when needs were different from that of the independent state that followed it. The primary function of the colonial state was to maintain law and order, extract taxes, favor foreign capital, and rule these countries for the benefit of the metropolis (in this instance, of Britain). This "extraverted" character of the state continued in important ways after decolonization. (2) Unlike Western capitalist societies, in such postcolonial societies, no single class exercised domination or hegemony over the state. In the case of Pakistan, there were "three propertied exploiting classes" vying for control over the state: an indigenous or national bourgeoisie, a landed oligarchy, and a neocolonial bourgeoisie whose economic interests were more consonant with that of the erstwhile colonial power (Britain) and the West in general. This standoff between the three competing propertied classes enhanced the power of the postcolonial state, as it could act with "relative autonomy" from each of these classes, even as it functioned overall in their joint interests.[3] (3) Such postcolonial societies were prone to military bureaucratic dictatorships and the collapse of democracy because of the militarized and overdeveloped character of the state and the relative weakness of the propertied classes. This vulnerability was enhanced by selective aid and support given to the armed forces in such societies by external powers during the decades of the Cold War.

Although the details of Alavi's highly influential theses on the postcolonial state are no doubt important,[4] in the context of this book, a few salient points need to be highlighted. The first explicit use of the term postcolonial emerged from a self-consciously Marxist standpoint and engaged in a serious effort to explain why newly independent third-world countries were prone to veer from both egalitarian economic development and electoral democracy. The story of third-world underdevelopment, detailed in the first chapter, and the emergence of a bifurcated world under modernity form the indispensable backdrop for Alavi's thesis. Alavi engages Marx critically, that is, he uses the Marxian method to analyze postcolonial societies, but he adapts and modifies Marx's writings as they do not work quite as

well in explaining developments therein as they may have done in expli-
cating Western societies.

Second, the "post" in postcolonialism did not signify a leaving behind
of colonialism, but rather emphasized the continued relevance of its impact on the state, politics, class formation, military, bureaucracy, economy,
and other crucial parts of a third-world country's development after decolonization. Here, a crucial distinction needs to be made between Alavi's use
of postcolonialism and the term neocolonialism, which had already gained
considerable popularity by then in Marxist analysis. As used by African
leaders like Kwame Nkrumah (of Ghana) in the mid-1960s, neocolonialism emphasized the fact that Western colonial powers continued to exercise political and economic control over their former colonies, even after
independence. Neocolonialism assigned the primary blame for the economic and political woes of newly independent third-world countries on
the erstwhile colonial powers, and it minimized the role of third-world
leaders, states, and propertied classes in the collapse of development and
democracy in their nations. Alavi's description of postcolonial societies, on
the other hand, emphasizes the interaction between states and elites within
third-world nations, on the one hand, and Western powers and corporate
interests, on the other, in their ongoing underdevelopment. It is, in that
sense, a more radical and politically charged explanation for third-world
developments in the decades after decolonization: it does not exculpate the
local or the domestic forces in the continuance of exploitation and underdevelopment. In crucial ways, Alavi's use of the term postcolonial anticipates the disenchantment with the nation that would become endemic in
postcolonial novels and scholarly works from the 1970s onward. The
choice of the term postcolonial thus simultaneously does two things: it
does not minimize the importance of independence or the moment of decolonization, and Alavi explicitly dissociates himself from those leftists in
the Indian subcontinent who dismissed 1947 as a false dawn, but it is also
not satisfied with merely blaming the West for the third world's descent
into military authoritarianism and the inability to deliver on development.

Befitting a Marxist, Alavi's idea of postcolonialism is tied to an explicit
political project. By emphasizing the international and domestic linkages
that produce and reproduce underdevelopment, he suggests that the way
forward for postcolonial societies is through a socialist or communist revolution that organizes all those outside this charmed circle and captures
state power. The true meaning of decolonization or independence will be
achieved only when the peasantry and working classes, rather than just the

elites, assume state power and reorder the economy, polity, and society to represent the nation in its entirety. In other words, the global problem is world capitalism, and the global alternative is socialism; this Marxist and revolutionary impulse is central to Alavi's conceptualization of the term postcolonialism.

Alavi's essay came at the height of three decades of tremendous communist and socialist activity across the third world. Vietnam was still very much an ongoing struggle, and the Maoist revolution in China continued to inspire millions of young men and women all across Afro-Asia and Latin America. The Naxalite movement was at its peak in India, and Cuba seemed to offer an alternative model for development in Latin America and southern Africa. In the West, the United States was the site of civil rights, feminist, Native American, and antiwar movements, as well as those articulating an alternative lifestyle to that of consumerist capitalism. Across the Atlantic, similar movements were sweeping across Europe as well. Alavi's work on the postcolonial state and society has to be placed within this regional and international context: it represents a third-world Marxist understanding that development under capitalist auspices is inherently underdeveloped, limited, and prone to reversals through military interventions and elite domination in collaboration with Western powers. Another way of stating this is that the inaugural take on the term postcolonial already marked a critical engagement with globalization at its Keynesian apogee and found the latter severely wanting in most respects.

POSTCOLONIALISM AS "TRICONTINENTALISM"

In his encyclopedic work titled *Postcolonialism*, Robert Young accentuates the links between postcolonial theory and Marxist thought that is there in Alavi, but develops it in very intriguing ways.[5] To Young, postcolonialism is the political, cultural, economic, and intellectual resistance of people in the third world to Western domination. He argues that such resistance was coeval with the very discovery of the Americas by Christopher Columbus in 1492 in whose wake emerged both the genocide of the indigenous populations and the slavery of Africans brought to work in the New World. For Young, postcolonialism is not post as in "after the *end* of colonialism," but rather post as in "after the *onset* of colonialism." He argues that the anticolonial tract written by the Iberian Catholic bishop Bartolomé de Las Casas in 1542, "A Short History of the Destruction of the Indies," inaugurates the intellectual tradition out of which postcolonialism emerges.

Young's list of critics of imperialism and colonialism, and therefore part of the intellectual genealogy of postcolonial thought, includes Adam Smith and Edmund Burke as well as Karl Marx and Friedrich Engels. It encompasses the writings and actions of early twentieth-century communist revolutionaries like Lenin, Trotsky, Rosa Luxemburg, and Antonio Gramsci. It includes third-world nationalists like Nehru, Gandhi, Nkrumah, Senghor, and Cabral, as it does third-world revolutionaries such as Mao Zedong, Ho Chih Minh, Che Guevara, Frantz Fanon, and Fidel Castro. Young points out that third-world nationalists like Gandhi or revolutionaries like Fanon drew their political and intellectual inspiration from diverse sources in both East and West; what is crucial is that they used these for the decolonization of third-world peoples.

In the last part of his book, Young details the work of Homi Bhabha, Gayatri Spivak, and Edward Said, widely regarded as the most influential troika in the field of postcolonial studies today, and sees them as intellectual inheritors of this genealogy. Throughout his text, Young emphasizes that the intellectual, philosophical, and political content of postcolonial thought is truly global; what makes it postcolonial is the political project that seeks to liberate the third world from Western domination. Thus he suggests that the neologism "tricontinentalism" better captures the essence of postcolonialism because ultimately the latter is about the resistance of people in the continents of Africa, Asia, and Latin America to Western domination.[6]

Young's genealogy dovetails with Alavi's in that both regard Marxism as the critical tradition that is indispensable for postcolonial thought. They see Marxism not so much as a text that has to be faithfully adhered to, but as a provisional blueprint that needs to be constantly and creatively engaged with and transformed to explain third-world realities and to inform its future politics. Marx was simultaneously progressive and Eurocentric, a bitter critic of capitalism but also a believer in its ability to destroy what he called the Chinese walls of superstition and backwardness in Asia and Africa. He believed men made their own history, but also had a firmly teleological view of social change. To him, societies had to experience the full brunt of capitalist transformation before they could, through a social revolution, ascend to the utopia that was communism.[7] Marx entertained the view that capitalism would promote industrialization, bourgeois freedoms, and development everywhere it went and did not see that in the third world it might instead produce underdevelopment that would render a transition to capitalist modernity very difficult. Young and Alavi regard Marx's legacy as complex and contradictory but always indispensable to the politics of resistance that animates postcolonial thought.

Young's emphasis on postcolonialism as a form of resistance to Western domination, and yet as having always combined Western and non-Western thought, is sustained throughout his book. He argues that the work of poststructural and postmodern thinkers such as Michel Foucault and Jacques Derrida, who have deconstructed the very fundamentals of Western theories of knowledge (epistemologies) and practice (methods), are themselves emergent from and significantly shaped and reshaped through their encounters with the postcolonial world. Rather than arguing (as many do, as described later) that postcolonial thinking reflects the impact of an already existing and analytically distinct Western thought on the non-Western world, Young argues that such categories as Western and non-Western thought were always already in conversation with each other throughout the centuries and cannot be seen as distinct entities, but rather as dialectically related and mutually constitutive.

Compared to Alavi, there is a definite temporal and spatial enlargement of postcolonialism in Young's work. Although for the former the postcolony describes ex-colonial territories after the attainment of independence, for Young, temporally postcolonialism began as far back as 1492 and spatially it covers the whole world in that Western and non-Western knowledge forms have always been in conversation and developed dialectically. If one regards neoliberal globalization as a variation on a theme that really began in 1492 with the "discovery" of the New World by Columbus (as a number of authors do), then Young situates postcolonialism as the resistance that has shadowed the project of Western domination over the world ever since. It is, in this sense, both temporally and spatially, vastly more encompassing than the views of Alavi. As discussed in later sections of this chapter, Young's expansion of the term postcolonial jives with that of many other authors who use that term today.

Let us turn now to a third gloss on the term postcolonial; this one emerging from white settler colonies like Australia in the 1980s, and its significantly different understandings of the very terms colonialism and resistance.

POSTCOLONIALISM AS A LITERARY MOVEMENT AND CULTURAL FORMATION

A crucial moment in the ongoing effort to corral the meaning of the term postcolonial was the publication of *The Empire Writes Back* by Bill Ashcroft, Gareth Griffiths, and Helen Tiffin.[8] At the time all three authors were professors working in Australia: Ashcroft specialized in Australian writing in English and Australian cultural studies, Griffiths in East and West African Anglophone literature, and Tiffin on Caribbean writing. The expansion of the British empire over the eighteenth and nineteenth centuries, itself an instance of globalization, had made English a world language. The canonical primacy of English writing from England was unquestioned within departments of English literature the world over, and yet its links to the very process of colonialism rarely explored.[9] Ashcroft, Griffiths, and Tiffin used the term postcolonial to describe all writing in English that originated outside England itself, that is, from the "colonies." Irish and American writing in English (think James Joyce and Herman Melville), that of Canadians, Australians, or South Africans, and the Anglophone writings of South Asians, East and West Africans, the Caribbean, or Singaporeans, were all regarded within departments of English literature as ineffably mimetic, variants on an original theme doomed to inferiority and provincial status at best. *The Empire Writes Back* was written as the story of the authenticity of such postcolonial literature as an equal, if not better, of canonical English literature. Ashcroft et al. argued that the oppositional impulse of such postcolonial literatures emerged from their colonization, and they could not but question the status of England's literature in the first place. They argued that such postcolonial Englishes were literatures of resistance almost by origin, and the book's title and message was about the long overdue and progressive pluralization of the discipline of English literature.

Yet, for all the apparent attention to colonialism, the authors seemed curiously myopic about a whole host of differences on issues such as race, class, and indigenousness that separated Australia, Canada, and the United States (often termed settler colonies) on the one hand, from India, Trinidad, and Kenya (often referred to as territorial colonies) on the other. A brief analysis of one of the introductory passages in this book reveals some of the problems. The authors note at the outset:

> So the literatures of African countries, Australia, Bangladesh, Canada, Caribbean countries, India, Malaysia, Malta, New Zealand, Pakistan, Singapore, South Pacific Island countries, and Sri Lanka are all postcolonial literatures. The literature of the USA should also be placed in this category. Perhaps because of its current position of power, and the neo-colonizing role it has played, its post-colonial nature has not been generally recognized. But its relationship with the metropolitan centre as it evolved over the last two centuries has been paradigmatic for postcolonial literatures everywhere.

What each of these literatures has in common beyond their special and distinctive regional characteristics is that they emerged in their present form out of the experiences of colonization and asserted themselves by foregrounding the tension with the imperial power, and by emphasizing their differences from the assumptions of the imperial centre. It is this which makes them distinctively postcolonial.[10]

This passage equates the colonial experience of places like India or Africa or the South Pacific islands with those of white settlers in the United States, Australia, and Canada. As proposed in the next chapter, such equivocation between what one might call settler colonialism (in the United States, Canada, Australia, and New Zealand) with the territorial colonialism that occurred across much of Africa and Asia drew sharp critiques from many who were not enamored of postcolonial theory to begin with.

In a second edition published a decade later in 2002, Ashcroft et al. do not significantly modify their position on such equivocation. They aver that drawing distinctions between the colonial experiences of white settlers or indigenous peoples or black slaves does not serve useful analytical purpose, and they remain wedded to the idea that tensions of empire between metropolis and colony constituted a sufficient common condition to warrant the term postcolonial to cover these diverse spaces.

[They] . . . argued that the term post-colonial might provide a different way of understanding colonial relations: no longer a simple binary opposition, black colonized vs. white colonizers; Third World vs. the West, but an engagement with all the varied manifestations of colonial power, including those in settler colonies. The attempt to define the post-colonial by putting barriers between those who may be called "post-colonial" and the rest, contradicts the capacity of post-colonial theories to demonstrate the complexity of the operation of imperial discourse. We have suggested . . . that we need to ground the post-colonial in the "fact" of colonial experience. But it is probably impossible to say absolutely where that experience and its effects begin or end.[11]

The next chapter will examine the critique of this geographical expansion of the term postcolonial to include the settler colonies and the equation of various forms of colonialism into a singular "fact" of being colonized. We now turn to the work of Edward Said and specifically the publication of his *Orientalism*, which may be termed an important turning point in the consolidation of postcolonial theory.

EDWARD SAID, *ORIENTALISM,*
AND POSTCOLONIAL STUDIES

A commonly accepted inaugural moment of the field of postcolonial studies was the publication of Edward Said's book *Orientalism* in 1978.[12] Said
was a professor of English and comparative literature at Columbia University in New York for much of his career, and the publication of *Orientalism*
made him one of the most prominent literary critics and public intellectuals of the past three decades. He was an erudite spokesman for the cause of
the Palestinian people and their right to the recovery of their homeland,
which was gradually and often forcibly occupied by Jewish peoples from all
over the world in the early decades of the twentieth century, a process that
culminated in the creation of the State of Israel in 1948. Said was a forth-
right critic of the excesses of various Israeli regimes, with respect to their
treatment of the Arabs in Palestine, and a trenchant critic of U.S. foreign
policy in the Middle East. Both in his scholarship and his public interventions, he fought against the belittling stereotypes of Islam and Arabs that
have been longstanding in the United States and the West in general, but became even more prominent from the 1970s onward. To Said, the creation of
Israel was coeval with and parallel to the destruction of a longstanding State
of Palestine, and he regarded these events as understandable only in a
framework that included British colonialism in the Middle East, an enduring Western/Christian hostility to Islam, and the guilt of many Western governments and peoples over the horrendous culmination of their own longstanding anti-Semitism in the Holocaust of the Jewish people during the
Third Reich, a guilt expiated through dispossession of the Palestinians.[13]

Edward Said was born in Jerusalem, Palestine, in 1935 to a prosperous
mercantile family and was an Arab Christian. (In one of many ironies of his
life to come, he was delivered by a Jewish midwife in the hospital!)[14] He
lived much of his early life in Egypt and Lebanon and went to elite prep
schools in Cairo and New England, before completing his undergraduate
degree at Princeton University and his doctorate at Harvard University. Although he had already published a well-received work in literary theory
before *Orientalism,*[15] it was the publication of the latter that launched him
on a career as a public intellectual and the (perhaps unwitting and unwilling) forebear of the field of postcolonial studies.[16]

One way of understanding the argument made by Said in *Orientalism*
would be to focus on the two epigraphs that open his book. The first is
from Karl Marx in his *Eighteenth Brumaire of Louis Napoleon,* wherein he
notes regarding the French peasantry of the mid-nineteenth century that

"They cannot represent themselves; they must be represented." The second is a quote from *Tancred*, a novel written, also in the mid-nineteenth century, by Benjamin Disraeli (who would later become the British prime minister): "The East is a career." What both these quotations refer to is the fact that knowledge, or representation, is always inextricably intertwined with issues of power, social class, and materiality. The social world is not an inert object that awaits its objective and impartial description by disinterested and scientific observers or scholars. Rather, how it is seen, understood, and described depends a great deal on who is doing the describing, where they are from, what their interests are, and what they stand to benefit or lose from such descriptions. In mid-nineteenth-century England, Disraeli's "East"—referring presumably to all of England's colonies and empire—was a place where a young man could go and make a life for himself. He could find a place within his nation's far-flung empire, work his way up colonial bureaucracies, acquit himself in colonial armies, apprentice himself to various trading companies, explore the inner realms of Africa, and do any number of things in a world that was his oyster. The East was not so much a geographic direction or an inert space as it was a landscape that enabled generations of English youth to make their mark on this world. It was a "career" in the sense that it afforded them the canvas on which to inscribe a life, to earn wealth and fame, to become men of consequence. From this perspective, the actual content and "reality" of the East and its people mattered less than that it was a space earmarked for the coming of age of young Englishmen (and vastly less so, for English women). The East also mattered less in the sense that what people in the East themselves felt about or thought about being was not of much import. As with the French peasantry of the mid-nineteenth century that Marx referred to in the quote above, the East did not have the power to represent itself in its own words; there were more powerful and consequential others who would represent it.

In *Orientalism*, Said argued that for over two centuries, Western knowledge about Oriental societies,[17] especially of Islam, was indissociable from the fact of Western conquest and colonization of such societies, and of its belief in the innate superiority of its own civilization and religion over those whom it conquered and administered. This Orientalist knowledge collected by Western scholars was presented in various disciplines—history, religion, philology, literature, linguistics, philosophy—as objective facts, or the truth, about the Orient. But they were less interesting as empirically verifiable or accurate observations about such societies and more interesting as (a) observations that enabled—ethically and materially—the conquest, exploitation, and domination of such societies, and (b) as representations that in constituting the Oriental "other" in specific ways, also helped constitute the Western "self" in specific ways. In other words, the discourse of Orientalism was not so much about the verifiable truth of Eastern or Oriental societies, their religions, economy, politics, languages, grammars, and texts, but rather a rhetoric of Western self-fashioning and enabling of its dominance and control over the rest of the world.

Although it would be impossible to summarize the breadth and detail of Said's book, the following extended excerpt comes close to capturing the core of his argument:

My principal operating assumptions were—and continue to be—that fields of learning . . . are constrained and acted upon by society, by cultural traditions, by worldly circumstances, and by stabilizing influences like schools, libraries, and governments; moreover, that both learned and imaginative writing are never free, but are limited in their imagery, assumptions, and intentions; and, finally, that the advances made by a "science" like Orientalism in its academic form are less objectively true than we often like to think. In short, my study . . . has tried to describe the *economy* that makes Orientalism a coherent subject matter. . . . The result for Orientalism has been a sort of consensus: certain things, certain types of statement, certain types of work have seemed for the Orientalist correct. He has built his work and research upon them, and they in turn have pressed hard upon new writers and scholars. Orientalism can thus be regarded as a manner of regularized (or Orientalized) writing, vision, and study, dominated by imperatives, perspectives, and ideological biases ostensibly suited to the Orient. The Orient is taught, researched, administered, and pronounced upon in certain discrete ways. The Orient that appears in Orientalism, then, is a system of representations framed by a whole set of forces that brought the Orient into Western learning, Western consciousness, and later, Western empire. If this definition of Orientalism seems more political than not, that is simply because I think Orientalism was itself a product of certain political forces and activities. . . . It is therefore correct that every European, in what he could say about the Orient, was consequently a racist, an imperialist, almost totally ethnocentric. Some of the immediate sting will be taken out of these labels if we recall additionally that human societies, at least the more advanced cultures, have rarely offered the individual anything but imperialism, racism, and ethnocentrism for dealing with "other" cultures. So Orientalism aided and was aided by general cultural pressures that tended to make more rigid the sense of difference between the European and Asiatic parts of the world. My contention is that Orientalism is fundamentally a political doctrine willed over the Orient because the Orient was weaker than the West, which elided the Orient's difference with its weakness.[18]

Said is quite explicit that in understanding Orientalism as a discourse, rather than a truthful description of the Middle East, he was not saying that all Western scholarship on such societies during the colonial period was simply lies and falsehoods. As he notes:

> One ought never to assume that the structure of Orientalism is nothing more than a structure of lies or of myths which, were the truth about them to be told, would simply blow away. . . . Orientalism, therefore, is not an airy European fantasy about the Orient, but a created body of theory and practice in which, for many generations, there has been considerable material investment. Continued investment made Orientalism, as a system of knowledge about the Orient, an accepted grid for filtering through the Orient into Western consciousness, just as that same investment multiplied—indeed, made truly productive—the statements proliferating out from Orientalism into the general culture. . . . It is hegemony, or rather the result of cultural hegemony at work, that gives Orientalism the durability and strength I have been speaking about so far.[19]

Said argues that Orientalism was a discourse about the non-West in which issues of power were inextricable from those of knowledge. Scholarship was not innocent of material interests and the drive to power and domination; indeed it can be understood only in its relationship to such factors. Rather than regarding power as something that is oppressive and an imposition, Said, following Foucault, sees the power of Orientalism as productive, in the sense that it enables people to make careers, find a role for themselves, and make sense of the world. What is particularly seductive about the power of Orientalism as a discourse is not only that it comes to stand for all respectable or scientific knowledge about the Orient, but that it also comes to dominate the self-understanding of many in the Orient about their own societies and selves. Their internalization of Orientalist "truths" about their own societies is a crucial part of their colonization and their continued subjection to the hegemony of Western understandings of the world. In other words, the "truth" about representations hinges more on the power inhering in the locus of enunciation—who is describing whom, who is representing, and who is being represented. Knowledge thus enables, and is enabled by, the establishment of political domination; it enables careers in various fields and the acquisition of "expertise" in specific areas, and it puts into play narratives that one can enter talking. These practices are intimately related to material enterprises and the ways by which the dominant societies go about governing the world.

Said, in his understandings of "truth" as linked to discourse, that is, emergent from the nexus of power/knowledge, clearly reveals his debt to Michel Foucault and to Friedrich Nietzsche here. However, he also explicitly parts company with them because he is willing to entertain the possibility of scholarship that is less tainted by proximity to political power, more impartial and neutral, even as he discounts the possibility of either truth or objectivity in any final or totalizing sense of those terms. As he notes in this regard:

> Orientalism calls into question not only the possibility of nonpolitical scholarship but also the advisability of too close a relationship between the scholar and the state. It is equally apparent, I think, that the circumstances making Orientalism a continuingly persistent type of thought will persist: a rather depressing matter on the whole. Nevertheless there is some *rational* expectation in my own mind that Orientalism need not always be so unchallenged, intellectually, ideologically, and politically, as it has been. *I would not have undertaken a book of this sort if I did not also believe that there is scholarship that is not as corrupt, or at least as blind to human reality*, as the kind I have been mainly depicting.[20]

Although Said is here pessimistically optimistic about the prospects for a more impartial and less biased form of scholarship about non-Western societies, he is quite clear that he does not buy into the idea that somehow those native to such societies are inherently more likely to be closer to the "truth" or reality of such areas. One might say that he does not believe in the prospects of ethnophilosophy and is in that sense very much a universalist.[21] He notes in this regard that:

> It is not the thesis of this book to suggest that there is such a thing as a real or true Orient (Islam, Arab or whatever); nor is it to make an assertion about the necessary privilege of an "insider" perspective over an "outsider" one. . . . On the contrary, I have been arguing that "the Orient" is itself a constituted entity, and that *the notion that there are geographical spaces with indigenous, radically "different" inhabitants who can be defined on the basis of some religion, culture, or racial essence proper to that geographical space is equally a highly debatable idea.* I certainly do not believe the limited proposition that only a black can write about blacks, a Muslim about Muslims, and so forth.[22]

This suspicion of Said about the superiority of an "insider's" perspective (which is a critique of essentialism) also forms the bridge to his larger humanism, which again distinguishes him from the tradition of thought that Foucault emerges from. Said's belief in the possibility of a more engaged, humanist, and emancipatory politics is hinted at in the concluding pages of *Orientalism* (some of which can be found in the italicized sections of the quotes above), but he is more explicit about it in various essays published thereafter, and especially in his *Culture and Imperialism*, published nearly fifteen years after *Orientalism*.[23]

In this later work, Said focuses to a far greater extent on the discourses of resistance that animated authors and nationalists from the third world as they opposed Western imperialism and Orientalism, but did so without descending into an essentialist understanding of the nation, or "nativism." Third-world nationalists like Frantz Fanon, Amílcar Cabral, Aimé Césaire, C. L. R. James, Iqbal, and Rabindranath Tagore saw antiimperialism and nationalism as necessary way stations on the path to a more liberatory and inclusive cosmopolitanism rather than as destinations themselves.[24] Said recognizes that imperialism and colonialism of the past few centuries have contributed to an irreversible intermixing of cultures, populations, and ideas and enriched them in incomparable ways. In the present world, any claims to either Western civilizational superiority or to nativist essences are seen by him to be racist and untenable, given the history of miscegenation of peoples and ideas and the intermixing and irreversible enriching of populations and cultures over the past few centuries. He prizes someone like the black Caribbean Marxist C. L. R. James who regarded Goethe, Beethoven, Marx, and Shakespeare to be as much a part of the intellectual heritage he could claim as his own as any native Caribbean author or philosopher.

Said is explicit in his excoriation of authors such as Foucault, Habermas, as well as traditions of Western Marxism (including the Frankfurt school), much of Anglo-Saxon cultural theory, and variants of postmodernism (particularly the works of Lyotard and Baudrillard), for what he regards as their claustrophobic Western centeredness, their refusal to deal with issues such as the ongoing neocolonialism, racism, and exploitation of third-world societies by the first, their political pessimism after the so-called defeats of the West in Vietnam or Iran, and their resignation after the end of the era of active protests over civil rights.[25] He sees in many variants of contemporary Western theory an escape from an engagement with the politics of the here and the now and an obsession with "the individual as dissolved in an ineluctably advancing 'microphysics of power' that is hopeless to resist."[26]

While recognizing and accepting the theoretical tensions in his own work, which combines Gramsci with Foucault, Said remains doggedly committed to the idea of the intellectual as a secular, skeptical wet-blanket who, while refusing to become a camp follower of any particular political or academic creed, retains a sense of ethics, of desirable outcomes in political struggle, and of fighting for those with tenacity. As he notes in *Culture and Imperialism*:

> I keep coming back—simplistically and idealistically—to the notion of opposing and alleviating coercive domination, transforming the present by trying rationally and analytically to lift some of its burdens, situating the works of various literatures with reference to one another and to their historical modes of being. What I am saying is that in the configurations and by virtue of the transfigurations taking place around us, readers and writers are now in fact secular intellectuals with the archival, expressive, elaborative, and moral responsibilities of that role.[27]

Said quite explicitly affiliates himself with a humanist political project, and in the context of his own impending mortality,[28] he notes:

> I have called what I try to do "humanism," a word I continue to use stubbornly despite the scornful dismissal of the term by sophisticated postmodern critics. By humanism I mean first of all attempting to dissolve Blake's mind-forg'd manacles so as to be able to use one's mind historically and rationally for the purposes of reflective understanding and genuine disclosure. Moreover, humanism is sustained by a sense of community with other interpreters and other societies and periods: strictly speaking, therefore, there is no such thing as an isolated humanist. . . . Humanism is centered upon the agency of human individuality and subjective intuition, rather than on received ideas and approved authority . . . humanism is the only, and I would go so far as to say, the final resistance we have against the inhuman practices and injustices that disfigure human history.[29]

Said's work articulates a triangle of appealing ethical positions: one, resisting the seductions of an essentialist and nativist nationalism or narrow identity politics as a response to colonialism and racism; two, steadfast critique of any scholarship premised on notions of Western civilizational superiority, exclusive claim to rationality or objectivity; and three, a humanist commitment to a politics of engagement and struggle for progressive change in the here and now, but without ever dissolving one's identity as a relatively skeptical, detached, and secular wet-blanket.

Few academic books attain the status of best sellers; yet, Said's *Orientalism* comes close to one. In some part, this may have had to do with the overall international context into which his work emerged—that of the late 1970s. Here is an excerpt from an essay on the very topic of Orientalism written fully fifteen years prior to Said's work. Writing in 1963, Anwar Abdel Malek anticipates Said's argument almost in its entirety:

> According to the traditional orientalists, an essence should exist—sometimes even clearly described in metaphysical terms—which constitutes the inalienable and common basis of all the beings considered; this essence is both "historical," since it goes back to the dawn of history, and fundamentally a-historical, since it transfixes the being, "the object" of study, within its inalienable and non-evolutive specificity, instead of defining it as all other beings, states, nations, peoples, and cultures—as a product, a resultant of the vection of forces operating in the field of historical evolution. Thus one ends with a typology—based on a real specificity, but detached from history, and, consequently, conceived as being intangible, essential—which makes of the studied "object" another being with regard to whom the studying subject is transcendent; we will have a homo Sinicus, a homo Arabicus (and why not a homo Aegypticus, etc.), a homo Africanus, the man—the "normal man," it is understood—being the European man of the historical period, that is, since Greek antiquity. One sees how much, from the eighteenth to the twentieth century, the hegemonism of possessing minorities, unveiled by Marx and Engels, and the anthropocentrism dismantled by Freud are accompanied by europocentrism in the area of human and social sciences, and more particularly in those in direct relationship with non-European peoples.[30]

Yet Malek's critique of *Orientalism* published in a by-no-means obscure journal failed to have anything near the seismic impact of Said's work, and the difference was primarily one of political context.[31] The publication of *Orientalism* in 1978 was sandwiched by a decade that saw the first and second oil price hikes, the 1973 war between Israel and Egypt, the 1982 Israeli invasion of Lebanon, the rise of the PLO (Palestinian Liberation Organization) in the global mediascape, especially after their massacre of the Israeli athletes at the Munich Olympics of 1972, and an overall climate of hysterical anti-Arab sentiment all over the Western world. Said's demonstration that Western attitudes toward the Arab/Muslim Orient were underlain by centuries of scholarship inextricably intertwined with the colonial enterprise, that it essentially froze and stereotyped the diverse peoples of this region and came as a welcome antidote and resource for left-liberal academics and intellectuals everywhere. These decades also marked the rising tide of multiculturalism in the U.S. academy. *Orientalism* was a powerful text that articulated the linkages between Western knowledge about third-world societies and the historical processes of colonialism and imperialism that underlay them. It rapidly became a central text in courses on third-world politics, world literature, ethnic studies, cultural anthropology, the history of ideas, media studies, feminism, and a whole range of fields and subdisciplines that were themselves newly emerging at this time.

In some ways the emergence of *Orientalism* as a foundational text in postcolonial studies underlies the intimate relationship between scholarly or representational practices and the wider sociopolitical milieu of the time. In earlier chapters it was argued that the 1970s marked the end of the Keynesian experiment in global economic development and inaugurated a still-ongoing period of neoliberal capitalism. It is perhaps unsurprising that the onset of the widespread changes in the world political economy that we today call globalization should have been shadowed from its very beginnings by the rising influence of a work such as *Orientalism* with its attentiveness to Western power in the production of knowledge about the non-Western world. Many events and processes that we associate with globalization—the emigration of significant numbers of peoples from the third world to the first; the "shrinking" of the world in terms of the rapidity of the movement of intellectual ideas and fashions across the world; and the desire of Western capital to know more about societies and markets elsewhere in the world—all interacted to produce the material conditions that made the reception of Said's argument about Orientalism vastly more influential than that of Malek in the early 1960s. The example of *Orientalism* is a powerful indicator of the intertwined nature of globalization as a world economic and sociopolitical cultural process and of postcolonial studies as a body of work that both emerges alongside globalization and is in many ways deeply critical of it.

SUBALTERN STUDIES: FROM POLITICAL CRITIQUE TO CRITICAL METHOD

Another foundational text of postcolonial studies is the work of the Subaltern Studies group of historians, with their distinctive approach to the writing of the history of the non-Western world. In 1982 a group of historians (who called themselves the Subaltern Studies Collective [SSC]), led by Ranajit Guha, argued that a true history of India in the colonial and post-colonial period, a history of ordinary people in their everyday life, had never been attempted hitherto for a number of reasons having to do with the sociology of knowledge.[32] The literal meaning of the word subaltern is someone of "inferior rank," which was commonly used in the British Indian army. It was also used by the Italian Marxist Antonio Gramsci to refer to the lowermost classes in his writings on the southern question there.[33] Guha used the term subaltern to mean "a name for the general attribute of subordination in South Asian society whether this is expressed in terms of class, caste, age, gender and office or in any other way."[34] More specifically, Guha equated the term subaltern with "the people," and argued that it refers to the *"demographic difference between the total Indian population and all those whom we have described as the elite."*[35] Guha made it clear that the precise definition of subaltern and elite was a contextual matter and determined empirically rather than a priori or in theory. The term could be broadly interpreted to refer to landless and small peasants, workers, lower castes, and others at the bottom of the socioeconomic ladder, although in specific cases it might include small landlords, middle peasants, or others with some property.

Guha argued that two forms of elitism had dominated the writing of Indian history until that point in 1982: colonialist elitism and bourgeois-nationalist elitism. The former saw the emergence of the Indian nation and the nationalist movement in general as primarily the work, intended or otherwise, of British colonial rulers, administrators, policies, institutions, and culture. It was in response to the gradually widening set of opportunities to collaborate and share power with the colonial elite that the Indian national movement arose and gradually attained self-government. The Indian nationalist movement was, therefore, largely the work of a self-interested collaborator elite interested in gaining bureaucratic and political office, quite bereft of any ideology or idealism. Their actions are more comprehensible as factional elites competing with one another for colonial crumbs than as a mass upsurge for independence.[36] The bourgeois-nationalist narrative, on the other hand, names the native elite as its protagonists and imputes to them patriotism and self-sacrificing idealism, as they sought to overthrow the yoke of foreign rule and "led the people from subjugation to freedom."[37] In doing so, such nationalist historiography exaggerated the native elite's antagonism to colonial rule, diminished their role

as collaborators with the Raj, and portrayed them as "exploiters and oppressors" within domestic society.

Guha argued that neither variant of elite historiography was capable of
explaining Indian nationalism because they both left out "the contribution
made by the people *on their own*, that is, *independently of the elite* to the
making and development" of this nationalism.[38] Focused as they were on
the organized domain of politics—constitutions, parties, elections, power
sharing in legislatures, provincial governments, and the like—these elitist
forms of historiography were blind to "*the politics of the people*. . . . This
was an *autonomous* domain, for it neither originated from elite politics nor
did its existence depend on the latter. It was traditional only insofar as its
roots could be traced back to pre-colonial times, but it was by no means archaic in the sense of being outmoded."[39] Guha argued that while elite politics mobilized vertically, relied on colonial institutions, was legalistic and
constitutionalist in its form, and largely circumspect and deferential in its
demeanor, subaltern politics mobilized horizontally through kinship, ter-
ritoriality, and rumors; was more violent and thoroughly disruptive in its
expression; and often spontaneous in its emergence. Neither form of elitist
history could adequately analyze instances of mass protest and agitation,
be they the various peasant rebellions, insurrections, riots, and protests
that were endemic to British India from the late eighteenth to the early
twentieth centuries, or movements like those of Non-Cooperation or Quit
India in the first half of the twentieth century, which saw extensive popular participation.

This schism between elite politics and the politics of subaltern classes
was never bridged in the case of India and constituted the reason for the
"*failure of the Indian bourgeoisie to speak for the nation*. There were vast areas in the life and consciousness of the people which were never integrated
into their hegemony."[40] Although the elitist national movement often took
opportunistic advantage of subaltern energy to press its case against colonial rule, it was careful to ensure that a thorough reordering of domestic
caste hierarchies and class oppression never made it onto the political
agenda. In this, the idea of national unity against colonial or foreign oppression, as well as Gandhian insistence on nonviolence, proved to be a
conservative and deradicalizing force that was fully utilized by native elites
to endlessly defer issues like landlordism, oppression of peasants and
workers by Indian upper-caste elites, and bonded labor or untouchability,
into the distant future.[41] The lack of unity and leadership among subaltern
classes rendered them unable to go beyond a form of localism. It was

against this understanding of the limits of both elitist historiography and elitist politics that Guha defined the task for future historians:

> It is the study of this *historic failure of the nation to come into its own*, a failure due to the inadequacy of the bourgeoisie as well as of the working class to lead it into a decisive victory over colonialism and a bourgeois-democratic revolution of either the classic nineteenth-century type under the hegemony of the bourgeoisie or a more modern type under the hegemony of workers and peasants, that is, a "new democracy"—*it is the study of this failure which constitutes the central problematic of the historiography of colonial India.*[42]

In outlining such a manifesto for research, Guha and the rest of the Subaltern Studies historians were clearly writing out of a Marxist tradition, one heavily inflected with the ideas and terminology of Antonio Gramsci.[43] The very categories of revolution used by Guha (bourgeois-democratic and working class) reflected this Marxist genealogy. There was, moreover, a national cartography underlying its spatial understanding of the world, as reflected in phrases like the "failure of the nation to come into its own." Both the teleological narrative of Marx and the spatial narrative of the nation would change in later years as the Subaltern Studies project evolved.

Much of Guha's thoughts regarding Subaltern Studies emerged from his work on the history of peasant movements and rebellions, and before that, of revenue settlements in British India. In *Elementary Aspects of Peasant Insurgency in Colonial India*, published in 1983, he analyzed the hundreds of peasant rebellions, riots, and jacqueries that were so frequent in the period from the late eighteenth to the early twentieth centuries. Here he found that a reliance on the colonial archive was deeply problematic, as British administrators, whose main concern was law and order, had compiled them. They were not interested in peasant insurrections as social or religious or political economic movements and were written from a perspective that did not see the world through the subaltern's eyes. Often, such peasant rebellions were naturalized through metaphors that likened them to forest fires, storms, floods, waves, and tornadoes. The lack of detailed knowledge about subaltern lives and minds was essentially overcome through either dismissal as incomprehensible or as insensate natural phenomena. Hence, Guha described the colonial archive on peasant rebellions as constituting a "prose of counter-insurgency" that had to be read against the grain in order to discern within it the intent and worldview of the subaltern.

Indian historians, when using this archive, either internalized the biases of the colonial administrator for law and order and its dismissal of the subaltern as ineffably opaque and irrational or were preoccupied with assessing if these peasant rebellions advanced anticolonial nationalism. This literally robbed peasant movements of their politics and agency. The twin abstractions of "law and order" and "making the nation," both elitist in their own way, disparaged the political consciousness of the peasant and denied it autonomy and reality. Among Marxist historians, such views of the peasantry had a long pedigree, and peasant ideology, with its invocations of religion, tradition, and kinship, was seen as a false consciousness to be overcome by genuine (working) class identity.[44]

Guha argued subaltern consciousness could not be dismissed as spurious or millenarian or somehow prepolitical but was a distinctive form of the political in conditions of colonial modernity. This, among other things, required historians to go beyond the archive and abstractions like the nation to look at folk songs, ballads, proverbs, myths, legends, rumors, pamphlets, religious symbols and leaders, and a wide diversity of sources in the vernacular languages. Most importantly, one had to read peasant actions during riots, rebellions, and protests (and Guha offered codifications of such actions in a lexicon) as texts in order to understand the subaltern mindset. This innovative use of new historical sources and the emphasis on reading actions as dynamic texts exemplified the intellectual energy of some of the early Subaltern Studies works.[45] At their best, such works from Subaltern Studies make us "ponder the fragility of the notion of nation and democracy when the elite, foreign and indigenous alike, intervene against the emergence of a demos."[46]

Although it would be impossible (and arbitrary) to single out specific articles, the sources referenced here indicate the type of contributions that demonstrated this tension between democracy as a form of governance and democracy as demos, to use Spivak's terms. In his essay on peasant revolts in Awadh, in the years 1919–1922, Gyanendra Pandey showed how the movement arose and acquired an idiom that was autonomous from middle-class nationalist concerns and came from within the peasantry. At its height, it envisaged a radical restructuring of Awadhi agrarian relations that opposed the Raj as much as it did domestic landlords who were seen as having broken with a moral idea of community at this time. The radical nature of the movement was tamed and contained by the Congress leadership of Gandhi and Nehru as it was folded into the nationwide Non-Cooperation movement against the British. It was an instance of subaltern excess or energy that was defused by the bourgeois nationalist emphasis on orderly politics, distinctions between "native" landlords and alien colonial rulers, the primacy of "national unity" (which came, inevitably, at the expense of subaltern interests), and nonviolence.[47]

Shahid Amin, in his essay on "Gandhi as Mahatma," analyzed the rumors circulating among subaltern classes of Gorakhpur district in the United Provinces at this same time of agrarian unrest. He found that these rumors attributed supernatural powers to the figure of Gandhi, and that the peasantry was primed for a moment of rapture that would dramatically reorder their society when Gandhi arrived. The subalterns' "Gandhi" vastly exceeded the man's own program and intent: they saw in his name and figure a license for forms of social radicalism, reversal of hierarchies, and renegotiation of their moral economy that he himself would find violent and unacceptable. Amin's essay reverses the usual focus on authorial intent or charisma in the rise of Gandhi to the status of Mahatma and instead looks to the subaltern construction of him in these terms.[48]

Finally, Partha Chatterjee frames the distinctive optic of Subaltern Studies very well when he observes in the context of the historiography of peasant movements in India that the point is "to write an Indian history of peasant struggle. In principle, this is a different project from that of a history of peasant struggles in India."[49] The reversal is crucial: the latter sees India as a "case" of a wider, more general (universalist) phenomenon that has already happened elsewhere (i.e., a modal European story of proletarianization of the peasantry as society transitions from feudalism to capitalism). The former, however, argues that "theory" or generalization should be built from below, or the ground up: Indian peasant struggles occurred in a specific historical context and were not obliged to replicate modal patterns found elsewhere. Or, as Chatterjee notes, "The framework of this other history does not take as given its appointed place within the order of universal history, but rather submits the supposedly universal categories to a constant process of interrogation and contestation, modifying, transforming, and enriching them."[50]

Subaltern Studies' contestation of received theory and the universal categories of the narrative of world history essentially understand modernity not as something that originated in Europe and was then "exported" elsewhere, be it through nineteenth-century colonialism and conquest or the spread of capitalism or twentieth-century developmental aid and assistance. Rather, it regards modernity as a process that was global and simultaneous, that colonialism and conquest were integral to modernity and constitutive of it. Colonial India was not an aberration from an original and hermetically sealed process of modernization that occurred first in Europe; rather, colonialism *is* the form that modernization took in India, just as slavery and the invention of tribes was the form that modernity took in Africa, and genocide and slavery were the forms that modernity took in the New World of the Americas. To subsume the Indian "case" within a universal theory of a global transition toward modernity that had already occurred elsewhere is precisely what Eurocentrism is about. Thus, by privileging a form of history writing that took subaltern recalcitrance seriously, by insisting on querying so-called universalist but in reality Eurocentric theory at every turn, and by its consistent emphasis on the coeval nature of East-West relations, the Subaltern Studies Collective was engaged in a process that Dipesh Chakrabarty memorably described as tantamount to *Provincializing Europe*.[51]

From its inception in 1982, Subaltern Studies rapidly emerged as an influential, if also very controversial, academic movement within South Asian historiography. Although details on critiques of Subaltern Studies are presented in the next chapter, a brief discussion of these is necessary here as the work of the collective evolved in response to these critiques as well. Early critiques focused on the fact that in overemphasizing subaltern consciousness and its alleged opacity, the group was itself contributing to Orientalist essentializations of the inscrutable "native." Some noted that by imputing so much agency and autonomy to the subaltern the school was empirically on weak ground as well as in danger of romanticizing such so-called resistance, which may have been little more than a struggle to survive in adversity. Still others argued that the figure of the autonomous, agentive subaltern looked suspiciously close to the self-making, empowered "individual" of the modern, Western liberal tradition. The group was also critiqued for its inattention to issues of gender, reflected both in the all-male membership of the collective as well as their forms of analysis, which seemed, at best, to add gender and stir, and, at worst, oblivious to the issue. There were also somewhat predictable Marxist critiques of the shift away from materialist structures to modes of religious and cultural expression as sites of resistance.[52]

This early debate regarding Subaltern Studies in the period 1982–1988 was largely confined to India specialists. But soon Subaltern Studies became a prominent theoretical force to reckon with in the global academy due to a variety of factors that underline the link between postcolonial scholarship and the political economy of globalization. It was the publication, in 1988, of *Selected Subaltern Studies*, by Oxford University Press in New York and England, edited by Ranajit Guha and Gayatri Chakravorty Spivak, with a foreword by Edward Said, that launched Subaltern Studies on an international career.[53] It gained rapid acceptance into the curricula of universities in Western Anglophone universities, especially the United States, Canada, Australia, and England, and a visibility that transcended Indian historiography. In disciplines such as history, cultural studies, anthropology, English, ethnic studies, and indigenous studies, references to the work of the Subaltern Studies Collective became common. For example, a Latin American version of Subaltern Studies emerged, and a radical questioning of historical relationships between indigenous peoples, mestizos, and (Euro-American) Creole elites in South America began in its wake. A rewriting of South American history from the perspective of its genuine subalterns (i.e., the indigenous peoples) was the task this group set for itself.[54] Subaltern Studies was one of those rare instances of a set of theoretical formulations that emerged from a third-world society having a palpable intellectual impact on the first-world academy.

It is in this post-1988 period that Subaltern Studies became folded in as an indispensable component of something called "postcolonial studies." A similar set of social and intellectual forces (as had propelled *Orientalism* a decade earlier)—the growing multiculturalism of the academy, the emergence of disciplines and trends that questioned the canonicity of Euro-American literatures and theory and were based on specific identity groups striving for a presence in the academy, the rise of postmodernism and poststructuralism, the increasing presence of graduate students and young faculty in Western universities who were of third-world origin or second-generation immigrants from such societies, and a much greater awareness of the political economic underpinnings of scholarship in general—accounted for the sudden visibility of Subaltern Studies in an international academic marketplace.

Three related debates have profoundly shaped the reception of Subaltern Studies from this point onward. First, a number of themes present in Subaltern Studies from its very outset converged rather well with those that were prominent in postmodern and poststructural scholarship. For example, the critique of abstractions like the nation and its role in defusing subaltern energy, or the refusal to write Indian history as a later and aberrant "case" of the more general history of capital or modernity, dovetailed with a postmodern suspicion of grand narratives, teleological reasoning, and essentialist arguments. There was a whiff of a postnational imagination that characterized both Subaltern Studies and the poststructural and postmodern approaches at this time. Similarly, the emphasis in Subaltern Studies on forms of resistance that were local and fragmentary resonated with a Foucaldian emphasis on the microphysics of power, that is, power in its capillary rather than arterial or structural form. Both these trends emphasized the fragmentary and the ephemeral over the structural and shared in a certain critique of essentialism. This led to the work of Subaltern Studies being recognized as part of a larger global intellectual moment of deconstruction of received wisdom, of categories and narratives that constituted the meat of modernity. Subaltern Studies was swept along, and lumped with, a wave of critical deconstructive scholarship under the sign of Nietzsche, Foucault, and Derrida.[55]

Second, the arrival of Subaltern Studies to global prominence seemed, especially to Marxist critics, to accentuate a shift in concern from issues of the structural logic of capitalism, class exploitation, and the creation of a new democracy, to that of theoretical aporia, the limits of knowledge, and an overattention to cultural dominance. With the rise of politically conservative and economically neoliberal globalization in the post-1975 world order, Subaltern Studies' critique of the narrative of capitalist modernization as Eurocentric, essentialist, and teleological, Marxists argued, incapacitated political mobilization and resistance. It further obfuscated the ways in which a reenergized transnational capital was breaking all barriers to investments in and exploitation of the third world. The plea for writing "post-foundational histories of the third world" (as made by the Subaltern historian Gyan Prakash) that were unencumbered by essentialisms like the nation, class, modes of production, and capital, it was argued, was ultimately complicit with global capitalism and guilty of confusing representation with reality.

Third, and perhaps unsurprisingly, as Subaltern Studies reached the West, it was found interesting more for its theoretical innovations in methods of inquiry rather than what it had to say about the actual details of subaltern life in colonial and postcolonial India. Critiques of Subaltern Studies noted that their writings had transitioned from politically engaged criticism to research method, or shifted from revolutionary science to normal or paradigmatic science (as discussed in the next chapter). In India itself the group was under attack for its diminishing relevance to the most important political issues of the 1990s—the rise of Hindu fundamentalism, the decline of the organized left, the renewed salience of caste privilege, women's inequality, and the rapid ascent of neoliberal ideology within the country. Its general critique of modernity and the hegemony of Enlightenment values (folded within its critique of Eurocentrism) seemed misplaced in a context of rising Hindu and Muslim fundamentalisms, reassertion of patriarchy, the attacks on the left, and the thoroughgoing insertion of India into neoliberal globalization. It was as if Subaltern Studies were more focused on its relevance to a transnational academic public sphere centered in Berkeley or New York and less concerned with the politics of contemporary India.

The (still ongoing) story of Subaltern Studies is exemplary of the intertwined careers of postcolonialism and globalization. The rise of Subaltern Studies within the academic canon of the West had a great deal to do with a process we would recognize as globalization. The promise of that body of work in resisting the process of globalization, like the promise of postcolonial studies in general in this regard, remains an open question, one that is investigated in the remaining chapters of this book.

HOMI BHABHA: ON AMBIVALENCE, MIMICRY, AND HYBRIDITY

Hazarding a summarization of an author as difficult as Bhabha might seem foolish to say the least, but in this section such an effort is both worthwhile and has profound implications for our understanding of the contemporary moment in globalization. This foray into Bhabha begins somewhat obliquely, first through the work of Gyan Prakash on colonial science to understand Bhabha's notion of ambivalence, and second through Jean Baudrillard's demonstration of the role of social desire in the production of value.

In his book *Another Reason*, Gyan Prakash zeroes in on a central contradiction in the enterprise of colonialism.[56] The British justified their rule over India in some part at least by their claim to a superior scientific rationality. The success of their science was continuously presented to the bewildered and awed native as spectacle: railways that shrank distance, impressive dams that channeled unruly rivers, cantilevered bridges that spanned them, electricity that turned dark night into bright day, and so forth. The contradiction within colonialism was this: at one level, the rationality and grandeur of colonial science had to presume an intelligent and discerning native capable of comprehending the magnitude of what was being achieved. But at another level, colonial rule and its attendant racism, violence, and domination over the native rested on the assumption that he was incurably unscientific and irrational and therefore incapable of being a truly discerning and appreciative audience. It was this inherent inferiority of the native that necessitated colonial rule in the first place and justified its continuance in the second. In other words, *in order to be understood and appreciated for what it was really worth*, colonialism had to deny one of the foundational premises of its civilizing mission, namely, the fundamental unworthiness of the native. Prakash's work on colonial science offers a clear explication of one of Bhabha's central insights into the whole enterprise of colonialism, the *ambivalence* at its core.

For Bhabha, colonialism is a deeply conflicted and contradictory enterprise. The confidence of the colonizer in his racial and civilizational superiority is constantly undercut by an ambivalence that seeks recognition of this superiority in the eyes of the colonized, a recognition that could be neither fulsome nor reliable given the colonizer's firm belief that the native was sly, untrustworthy, and a congenital liar to begin with. The desire for this recognition from the despised native made the colonizer hate himself, a hatred that is then displaced onto the native and constitutes a form of paranoia. As Bhabha notes in this regard, "The frustrated wish 'I want him to love me,' turns into its opposite 'I hate him' and thence through projection and the exclusion of the first person, 'He hates me.'"[57]

Ambivalence lies at the heart of the colonial encounter, and it informs both colonizer and colonized. If the former is rendered paranoiac because of his desire to be loved by one whom he ought to despise, and cannot ever be sure that such love is forthcoming or real or authentic, the colonized goes through a related process of ambivalence in his relations with the colonizer. Drawing heavily on the work of Frantz Fanon in this regard, Bhabha argues that the colonized native self is split in its relations of desire vis-à-vis the colonizer. On the one hand, the native wants to occupy the station of the colonizer, to become him, and to invert their roles. On the other hand, however, even as the native desires such a reversal of roles, his self is split because "the fantasy of the native is precisely to occupy the master's place while keeping his place in the slave's *avenging* anger."[58] To become the colonizer while remembering the pain and the righteous anger that emanates from having been colonized is the impossibly ambivalent desire of the native, and this splits his self irrevocably.

This ambivalent and split desire of the native to become the colonizer is often incompletely and damagingly satiated by the latter, whose highest form of praise for the native runs something like: "you are okay, you are different, you are not like the rest of them, you are more like one of us." As Bhabha notes:

It is precisely in that ambivalent use of "different"—to be different from those that are different makes you the same—that the Unconscious speaks of the form of otherness, the tethered shadow of deferral and displacement. *It is not the colonialist Self or the colonized Other, but the disturbing distance in-between that constitutes the figure of colonial otherness*—the white man's artifice inscribed on the black man's body. It is in relation to this impossible object that the liminal problem of colonial identity and its vicissitudes emerges.[59]

Identity is neither the secure space of the colonial self nor that of its complete negation, the colonized self, but instead a third space of otherness. Notions of ambivalence as constitutive of colonialism run through the length of Bhabha's work, and what is offered here are merely a couple of exemplary instances, no more.

In thinking of these and related themes, we move to the relationship between desire, value, and sociality, as found in Baudrillard, for it helps elucidate Bhabha's understanding of the political as presentist and performative, rather than oriented toward the transcendent or an overcoming. In his brilliant *For a Critique of the Political Economy of the Sign*,[60] Baudrillard invites us to contemplate a hypothetical scenario in which the doors of a supermarket are thrown open and everyone is invited to help themselves to anything they want, need, or desire. Far from inciting a frenzy of consumption, Baudrillard argues, such an act would possibly produce paralysis and bafflement, with people either not picking up anything or worthless rubbish they could have had any day. No one would know how to behave in this new economy that suddenly took away assigned values, prices, and other insignia that help us make choices.

> The more or less experimental and limiting case of the department store shows that once exchange value has been neutralized, use value disappears with it. When the demand for always more utility and satisfaction is confronted with the possibility of its immediate realization, it evaporates. The whole package of motivations, needs and rationality that is so conveniently supposed to constitute human nature simply flies apart. Beyond the transparency of economics, where everything is clear because it suffices to "want something for your money," man apparently no longer knows what he wants.[61]

Baudrillard's point here is that value emerges from a process in which desire is central. It is however not merely individual desire, predicated on the satisfaction of needs, that is somehow regarded as natural or presocial, but rather a desire that is always governed by the fact that the same object is desired by others as well and contains the possibility that it may not be fulfilled. Thus value, and the intersubjective desire that constitutes value, is embedded in a social economy that exceeds the fulfillment of supposedly natural or biological needs and is always accompanied by the shadow of interdiction or thwarting. In contrast to the traditional Marxist narrative about value as emanating from the use that a certain object has in fulfilling human needs, Baudrillard argues that use-value is itself a social fact and not a pure a priori that is thereafter corrupted by exchange-value and the mystifications of money, capitalism, social relations, the market, and the commodity form. The entire Marxian narrative is predicated on a critique of the obfuscations and mystifications of capitalism and the possibility of recovering the transcendent domain in which only use-value reigns. With its emphasis on socially mediated desire as constitutive of both use-and exchange-value and the significance of thwarted desire in this, Baudrillard draws our attention to the sociality of consumption and production of value itself.

In his conception of ambivalence, and his understanding of both colonizer and colonized in terms of the impossible desire that animates them, Bhabha clearly locates value as emanating from thwarted desire. For the former, it is the desire to finally and fully know the native that is thwarted, which leads to a question mark over one's self-worth; for the latter, it is the (impossible) desire to replace the colonizer but remain the avenging native that splits any sense of selfhood. By emphasizing the transactional nature of value, that is, the sociality of so-called use-value, by refusing it that transcendent and suprasocial a priori status, Bhabha may be read as arguing for a politics that is not about overcoming in the hereafter but about survival in the here and now. It is an understanding of politics that is intensely presentist and performative.

Bhabha seems unenamored of a politics of transcendence or overcoming, be it that of third-world nationalism or Marxist social revolution. Although he is deeply insightful about Fanon's writings on the split self of the colonized native, he does not spend much time in discussing Fanon's intense nationalism, along with his notion that such a nationalism, in order not to descend into pathology, had to become both universalized and humanized as it transcended its own local context. Bhabha is endlessly fascinated by the detail of everyday negotiations between colonizer and colonized and the highly ambiguous and split selves that emerge from that encounter. Culture, for him, is the manifestation of the effort of the split self of the colonized to render themselves whole through aesthetic practices. Culture and aesthetic practices, then, are products of interdicted desire, and by their very nature, bound to be different and irreconcilable with domination. Bhabha's refusal to dwell on emancipatory narratives, because they constitute a negation of politics through an act of overcoming, positions him as a cultural critic who is devoid of "structural" analysis in Marxian terms. Bhabha's reasons for his refusal to lift his analysis beyond the quotidian and the performative to the realm of the transcendent and of overcoming cut to the heart of his take on the postcolonial. As someone who learned his Marxism even as he was writing his dissertation at Oxford on the work of the Indo-Trinidadian writer V. S. Naipaul, and increasingly steeping himself in Lacanian psychoanalysis, he could not see the postcolonial self, not here and not in the future, as a sovereign being. As Bhabha notes in an interview:

> In the Seminar room [at Oxford] I learnt that the "interpellative" function of ideology was to produce a subject in a posture of coherence, straddling the fissures, the cracks, and constitutive contradictions of bourgeois, capitalist society. To become conscious of oneself as an agent or an "individual" one had to experience oneself in this illusion of a self-fulfilling, plenitudinous personhood. Working on Naipaul reminded me of the fact that, in literature at least, no colonized subject had the illusion of speaking from a place of plenitude or fullness. The colonial subject was a kind of split-subject and "knew" it both phenomenologically and historically. Whereas I was being taught that such a splitting of the subject was the general condition of the psyche (Lacan), or the act of enunciation itself (Benveniste), there was a much more specific or "local" historical and affective apprehension of this which was part of the personhood of the postcolonial subject. The "decentering of the self" was the very condition of agency and imagination in these colonial or post-colonial conditions, and it becomes more than a theoretical axiom; it becomes a protean, everyday practice, a way of living with oneself and others while acknowledging the "partiality" of social identification; it becomes part of one's ethical being in the sense that such a "decentering" also informs the agency through which one executes a care of the self and a concern for the "other," in the late Foucauldian sense . . . being colonial or postcolonial is a way of "becoming modern," of surviving modernity, without the myth of individual or cultural "sovereignty" that is so central a tenet of liberal individualism and its sense of serial progress or cultural evolution.[62]

What is central to Bhabha's thinking is not merely that the postcolonial self was irretrievably fractured, but that the source of creativity, writing, politics, and engagement with one's social world lay precisely in this fracture.[63]

The political project of overcoming, to arrive as a self-assured and sovereign being, that is to say, either decolonization or successful socialism, is not one that is open to such an understanding of postcoloniality as a condition whose very productivity emerges from its eternally thwarted desire of becoming white while being not quite. It alters the vision from that of mastery or dominance over life and reality to that of surviving the day. For the split self of the colonized, a sense of agential sovereignty is probably forever impossible, and yet, surviving modernity through the gritty, stubborn, everyday refusal to be broken is itself a form of success. As Bhabha notes in an evocative passage in this regard, "Survival continually haunts the dream of sovereignty with the possibility that *failure is not the other side of success or mastery; it is its lining,* an intimate and proximate mode of being or living in the midst of what we think needs to be done afresh or anew and what requires repeatedly to be repaired, revised, or reassembled."[64]

At some level, colonialism is about knowing: knowing that one has rendered the colonized completely transparent to one's surveillance, or knowing that one's translation of their idiom is authentic and accurate, or knowing them well enough to govern them successfully and eternally. It is the veracity of this knowledge that justifies the enterprise in many ways. On this basic point, the British in India, as colonizers everywhere, were wracked by self-doubt.

To use one of Bhabha's more persuasive examples, consider the predicament of the missionary Alexander Duff in early nineteenth-century India. Duff was constantly besieged by doubt as to the efficacy, or even the possibility, of converting Hindus to Christianity because "translating" the gospel into a domestic idiom imperiled the text. For instance, when Duff uses the idea that conversion to Christianity represents a form of rebirth for the native, this is immediately deciphered by him as a variation on the idea of the twice-born Brahmin, alongside notions of reincarnation and rebirth as a form of reward or punishment for previous lives, and other ideas that the scientific and rational Duff found abhorrent. The possibility of conversion is derailed by the fact that the colonizer is not inscribing on a tabula rasa but rather on "preoccupied" native terrain within which all attempts at translation contain the dangerous possibility of misrecognition.

In a terse passage, Bhabha clearly delineates the critical components of his take on colonialism:

> The grounds of evangelical certitude are opposed not by the simple assertion of an antagonistic cultural tradition. The process of translation is the opening up of another contentious political and cultural site at the heart of

colonial representation. Here the word of divine authority is deeply flawed by the assertion of the indigenous sign, and in the very practice of domination the language of the master becomes *hybrid—neither the one thing nor the other*. The incalculable colonized subject—half acquiescent, half oppositional, always untrustworthy—produces an *unresolvable problem of cultural difference* for the very address of colonial cultural authority. The "subtle system of Hinduism," as the missionaries of the early nineteenth century called it, generated tremendous policy implications for the institutions of Christian conversion. The written authority of the Bible was challenged and together with it a postenlightenment notion of the "evidence of Christianity" and the historical priority, which was central to evangelical colonialism. The Word could no longer be trusted to carry the truth when written or spoken in the colonial world by the European missionary. Native catechists therefore had to be found, who brought with them their own cultural and political ambivalences and contradictions, often under great pressure from their families and communities.[65]

It is noteworthy that Bhabha's definition of "hybrid" is not that of a combination of two or more entities reflecting their attributes partially, that is, a synthesis, but as something qualitatively different, a third space that is "neither the one thing nor the other." A number of critics of Bhabha, especially those who allege his work amounts to an "emollient retrospect" on colonialism, see his idea of hybridity as anodyne synthesis, a concept that minimizes or mitigates the violence of the colonial encounter. Linked as it is in Bhabha's schema to ambivalence and the resultant impossibility of any form of successful colonialism,[66] hybridity becomes something other than synthesis. Hybridity is a third space that is neither one nor the other because the translation or encounter between different cultural forms occurs in a context where both these spaces are already preoccupied. Translation, or attempted domination, or colonialism, thus always carries with it the possibility that the "original" is subverted, rendered inauthentic, and followed in form but altered in content. The encounter between the colonizer and the colonized thus produces a third space that represents neither the decisive victory of one over the other nor a combination of the two, but a third entity (the hybrid) that is itself the productive and aesthetic space of a new cultural formation and consists of all the doubts, split selves, and ambivalences that constitute the colonial encounter itself.

Bhabha contrasts this parlous notion of the hybrid space with the more widely accepted view regarding "the noisy command of colonialist authority or the silent repression of native traditions,"[67] which is characteristic of conventional analyses of colonialism. Colonial authority requires the willing acceptance of its superiority by the native. Yet the very terms of translation that allow for its possible internalization by the native also constitute its corruption, its rendition into an idiom and worldview that is either incommensurable to that of the colonial power, or, at minimum, rarely fully comprehensible to it. Hybridity, for Bhabha, refers to that third space where this impossible negotiation between authority and its supposed supplicants occurs and endlessly recurs. In fact, that is what culture is for him. Cultures are not constituted prior to the encounter with difference and thereafter pacifically contained by nations, civilizations, states, regions, or whatever, but are themselves formed and enunciated in that encounter with difference.

Ambivalence, hybridity, and mimicry are closely interrelated in Bhabha's analyses. The fact that colonial power needs to be acknowledged, and more importantly, understood, as a superior form of rationality or civilization constitutes the condition that allows the native, in all his sly civility, to destabilize authority. The native's excessive submissiveness, exaggerated forms of deference, and overenthusiastic appreciation of the "master's" power and dominance, in other words his mimicry, continuously threatens to slip into both mockery and parody. The edifice of colonial rule comes to rest upon the seriousness with which colonizer and colonized play their roles. In other words, successful colonialism requires the willing, comprehending, and genuine acceptance by the colonized: a venture whose impossibility is palpable when stated in such terms. On this issue, Bhabha parts company with someone such as Fanon who averred the native had a binary choice (to turn white or disappear), and instead, emphasizes the presentist and performative mode in which ambivalence, mimicry, and camouflage constitute the third space of hybridity. The impossibility of colonialism, requiring as it does an unverifiable but complete acceptance of the terms of rule by the colonizer, is captured perfectly in the anxious lamentation of a missionary in 1815 who had worked on conversions for a quarter of a century in southern India: "in embracing the Christian religion they never entirely renounce their superstitions towards which they always keep a secret bent . . . there is no *unfeigned, undisguised* Christian among these Indians."[68]

In preference to a politics of transcendence or of overcoming, one that sees decolonization as a possibility, Bhabha emphasizes a presentist and performative politics of resistance, which, in a colonial context of highly unequal power, is often oriented toward survival. Culture is a crucial component of such strategies of survival in colonial times, and this carries over with greater intensity, if anything, into contemporary or postcolonial time, according to him. Bhabha's emphasis on culture as a product of injury, alienation, nostalgia, as the intellectual life-worlds of a people being out of joint with their own time and place, and as a form of self-defense, somehow rings truer than archaic notions of culture as the highest forms of aesthetic representation in relatively enduring, settled, and pacific spaces with uncontested borders and a united populace.

Critics allege that Bhabha's use of the term postcolonial implies a world in which colonialism is over and done with and charge him with a willful neglect of continuing North-South inequalities and the continued salience of neocolonialism under the regimes of globalization. Benita Parry, for instance, points to Bhabha's preference for the term agonism rather than antagonism to characterize relations between colonizer and colonized. She points that in its Greek origin, agonism referred to forms of debate and athletic contests between putatively equal members of a shared community in order that such competition may evoke the best in each of them. Parry thinks antagonism, with its connotation of enmity across a chasm that divides oppressors and the subjugated, would seem to be the more accurate term to describe colonizer-colonized relations. Such a preference for agonism over antagonism is reflective of a more general tendency within Bhabha toward quiescence, according to her, and the result is that "conflictual nature of the colonial encounter [is] occluded."[69]

Although it is neither my place nor intent to defend Bhabha against such critique, my thinking is that it is not so much that he is inattentive to the "conflictual nature of colonialism" or its continued salience (one can easily cite chapter and verse from his writings showing an acute empirical-historical knowledge of North-South inequality and neocolonialism within globalization),[70] but rather that his interests lie elsewhere. His is a viewpoint closer to that of someone like Ashis Nandy, who sees colonialism as an implicit pact between the elites of both colonizing and colonized societies, which came at the expense of the marginalized groups in both of them and produced psychological conditions like split selves, paranoia, and forms of creativity always burdened by doubts about originality and authenticity. It is an optic that is more sensitive to the psychological aspects of domination for both conqueror and conquered, of the ultimate impossibility of knowing an other. It embodies a skepticism regarding our ability to transcend injury and arrive at an unalienated sense of selfhood. In terms of an academic division of labor, or in terms of chosen analytical foci, this leads to a different set of emphases, those perhaps traduced by seeing it exclusively as an alibi of neoliberal globalization that negates the violence of colonialism.

SPIVAK AND TARRYING WITH THE DOUBLE NEGATIVE

Gayatri Chakravorty Spivak is often cited, along with Said and Bhabha, as constituting the indispensable troika of postcolonial theorists. Her self-description is someone whose work straddles feminism, Marxism, and deconstruction.[71] Upon completing her undergraduate degree (in English literature) from Presidency College in Calcutta, India, she came to the United States for her doctorate, which she completed under Paul De Man. She was still a relatively young academic when she translated Jacques Derrida's *Of Grammatology* from the original French into English (along with a seventy-plus-page translator's preface that is regarded as a crucial philosophical text in its own right). Her work has ranged across an awe-inspiringly wide variety of disciplines, methodologies, and spatiotemporal contexts, while revealing a degree of mastery over the urtexts of Marx, Freud, Hegel, Kant, Heidegger, Benjamin, Derrida, and literally innumerable other thinkers in the Western canon that is formidable, to say the least. She has critiqued French feminist theory, reread seminal texts within the English literary oeuvre from the perspective of third-world feminism, and shown the crucial ways in which a "worlded" reading of such texts vastly enhances our understanding of them. She is more recently part of the Subaltern Studies Collective of historians, and her translations and analyses of the Bengali woman author Mahasweta Devi (whose novels and stories depict the lives of tribal women living in conditions of virtual slavery in India) are read both in India and in Western academia.

It would require an intellect at least as formidable as Spivak's to summarize her work effectively, and it is not with false modesty that I bequeath that task to others. In this section the focus will be on a certain circumlocution that continuously appears in Spivak's various writings. It will be argued that this circumlocution, here described as "tarrying with the double negative," can be interpreted as Spivak's distinct take on a politics of postcoloniality in times of globalization.[72] In bald terms, this is a viewpoint that sees hegemonic structures, be they economic or cultural, as simultaneously empowering and impoverishing. These structures are to be resisted, opposed, and bent to one's ethical concerns for equality and humanity, but one cannot do that from without; rather, it is by inhabiting them intimately and working from within that one tries to change them. Spivak repeatedly articulates this insight through a double negative: she talks of these hegemonic cultures and structures as spaces *one cannot not want* to inhabit but which one is obliged to critique or change.

Spivak sees the postcolonial as someone who is a product of what she calls the culture of imperialism. What she means by this is that the modern intelligentsia or middle class of decolonized countries, among whom she counts herself, is constituted into a situation of power, even as they are colonized, because of their felicity with the language, culture, politics, institutions, and ideology of the colonizer (i.e., the West). This class's opposition to imperialism and colonialism, which was articulated in the movement for national sovereignty and independence, could never be something that broke with the culture of imperialism completely because of the very nature of its formation and content. Conversely, the subaltern is the person who is outside this "culture of imperialism" and whose position is literally inaudible to those who are postcolonial.

In the case of India, the idea of the future as articulated by this postcolonial elite in the name of the people included parliamentary democracy; a secular state; civil rights such as equality of opportunity, freedom of expression and religion; industrialization; and a host of other desires that were, in important ways, derivative from the colonial encounter itself, even as it reversed many of their valences. As we have seen with the work of Partha Chatterjee in an earlier section of this chapter, at an ideational level, independence or decolonization in the third world came perilously close to the notion that one should have the right to autonomously imitate what other (Western) nations had already ostensibly achieved elsewhere. That is, there was a mimetic aspect to third-world nationalism (a derivative discourse, in Partha Chatterjee's terms) that was inescapable. Further, there is no prelapsarian and authentic nation to return to or recover through decolonization because history, time, and the colonial encounter are, fundamentally, irreversible.

For Spivak, postcoloniality is a condition that recognizes the privilege of being conversant with the culture of imperialism, knows it as an instance of one's own colonization, and yet cannot disown it: "This impossible 'no' to a structure, which one critiques, yet inhabits intimately, is the deconstructive philosophical position, and the everyday here and now named 'post-coloniality' is a case of it."[73] Colonial modernity, then, is the vexed inheritance of the postcolonial: it is a structure that, according to Spivak's circumlocution, *one cannot not want to inhabit.* The double negative indicates that for the postcolonial, even as modern values, institutions, and culture are indispensable elements of a desired future, they are also discomfiting insignia of one's erstwhile and continued colonization and are further (as we will see soon) frustratingly incomplete in their vision of who is included in the nation and who is not.

As Spivak notes:

> [T]he political claims that are most urgent in decolonized space are tacitly recognized as coded within the legacy of imperialism: nationhood, constitutionality, citizenship, democracy, even culturalism . . . what is being *effectively* reclaimed is a series of regulative political concepts, the supposedly authoritative narrative of the production of which was written elsewhere, in the social formations of Western Europe. They are being reclaimed, indeed claimed, as concept-metaphors for which no *historically* adequate referent may be advanced from postcolonial space. That does not make the claims less urgent. A concept-metaphor without an adequate referent may be called a catachresis by the definitions of classical rhetoric. These claims to catachresis as foundations also make postcoloniality a deconstructive case.[74]

In a series of instances, Spivak returns to the double negative as a way of describing postcoloniality. For example, she considers the situation of Muslims in Britain during the height of the crisis over the publication of Salman Rushdie's *Satanic Verses*. She notes that the issue was framed by the mainstream English media almost exclusively in terms of the liberal right of an author to free speech versus the backward, book-burning fundamentalists of the Islamic faith. This was both inadequate and polarizing, according to Spivak. The British Muslims (who are overwhelmingly of South Asian, especially Pakistani and Bangladeshi, origin) were constantly treated like second-class citizens in a racist and neoliberal society. They were protesting against the publication of *Satanic Verses* not because they were opposed to freedom of speech or the authorial right to creativity, but because they saw in it yet another Orientalist caricature of Islam, and this time, engaged in by someone whom they had regarded as one of their own, no less. The support accorded to Rushdie from the political establishment, the majority culture, and mainstream media arose, from the British Muslim point of view, not merely from the liberal tenet of freedom of speech, but also because it reconstituted Britain as a white, liberal society with a "minority problem." Some noted that the liberal right to free speech in England stopped short of the right to publish materials that might compromise national security, for instance, while others noted restrictions in representations of the majority faith (Christianity). The point they were making is that the authorial right to freedom of speech was not something above pol-itics but was itself premised on extant definitions of what constituted ap-propriate use of that freedom. The insult to the Prophet Mohammad in the *Satanic Verses* was seen as part of the enduring habitus of a society yet to accept the Muslim minority as a part of itself. The way the debate was framed it was obvious that the defense of the liberal right of freedom of speech became, for many, an alibi for the worst forms of racist stereotyp-ing of British Muslims.

For a postcolonial activist in Britain at this time, committed to the idea of a color-blind, egalitarian society and minority rights, the issue was: How does one contest such racial stereotyping while also not giving up on the liberal right to freedom of speech, a right that is often a crucial resource precisely in combating such racism in the first place? Spivak notes in this context, "It is only if we recognize that *we cannot not want* freedom of ex-pression as well as those other normative and privative rational abstrac-tions that we on the other side can see how they work as alibis."[75] In other words, while recognizing the limits of liberal privative freedoms, and re-membering the important role they have played historically in justifying British colonialism of distant lands in past centuries, and contemporarily in justifying white racism toward the Muslim minority in Britain, a post-colonial activist has to also remember that this freedom is too valuable an asset to toss away in the heat of the moment: It is a freedom that one can-not not want in order to survive another day.

In similar fashion, the British Muslim or minority member more gener-ally has to energetically claim a place within the category of nation as well, even as he or she recognizes that the content of that nation has always been coded white, and has always—culturally, historically, economically, and in multiple other ways—privileged the male, Christian, property-owning cit-izen as its "normal" referent. As Spivak observes in yet another turn of the double negative for the postcolonial activist fighting on behalf of minori-ties within England:

> It is only if we acknowledge the heterogeneous desire for that great rational abstraction, agency in a nation, that we postcolonials will be able to take a distance from it. It is here that the transgressor must persistently critique that transgressed space, *which she cannot not want to inhabit*, even if coded another way.[76]

Throughout her various writings, Spivak returns to this idea of post-coloniality, and more generally deconstruction, as marking a space that one "cannot not want to inhabit" but that one has to energetically critique and transform at the same time. In a fashion similar to Bhabha, the understanding of politics that informs Spivak's work is not one of transcendence or overcoming, but that of intimately critiquing from within:

> As far as I can understand, in order to intervene one must negotiate. If there is anything I have learnt in and through the last 23 years of teaching, it is that the more vulnerable your position, the more you have to negotiate. . . . I mean by negotiation here . . . that one tries to change something that one is obliged to inhabit, since one is not working from the outside. In order to keep one's effectiveness, one must also preserve those structures—not cut them down completely.[77]

Spivak here follows what Young has described as a "fifth-column politics," one that derives from Derrida's notion of deconstruction as an enterprise based on the "necessity of lodging oneself within traditional conceptuality in order to destroy it."[78]

In a similar vein, Spivak's critique of essentialism is one that is careful, cognizant that anchoring oneself in an essentialist position may be sometimes politically valuable and a crucial weapon in mobilizing a constituency (whether it is the category "woman" in feminism; or "native" in indigenous movements for sovereignty; or ethnicity or race in the struggle against a majoritarian state bent on assimilation/annihilation). Her critique of essentialism is not derived from an a priori abstract philosophical or moral commitment but rather is situational. She charts her view in the following quote, which once more exemplifies her use of the double negative:

> So long as the critique of essentialism is understood not as an exposure of error, our own or others', but as an acknowledgment of the dangerousness of *something one cannot not use*, I would stand by it as one stand among many. The critique of essentialism should not be seen as being critical in the colloquial, Anglo-American sense of being adversely inclined, but as critique in the robust European philosophical sense.[79]

Spivak's work has a keen eye for the situation of the subaltern/tribal woman as the figure doubly oppressed by discourses of both imperialism and nationalism. The culture of imperialism that produces both the colonizer and the middle-class nationalist is one that excludes the subaltern for whom the discourse of postcolonial development and nation building appears as no more than the latest form of domination. Similarly the discourse of the working class, and its emancipatory narrative of socialism, is one that excludes the subaltern tribals, especially their women. Existing in a peripheral economy characterized by bonded labor, forced migration, and patriarchy, the subaltern tribal woman emerges as the lowest substratum of all. Drawing on the works of the Bengali author Mahasweta Devi, Spivak notes that the violence exercised upon this group is outside the purview of the conventional empire-nation dyad. For example, amid all the focus on religious violence between Hindu and Muslim in contemporary India, Spivak observes that we fail to notice that "tribal animism does not even qualify as a religion"[80] in our optic.

This theme of resistance from within structures one cannot not want to inhabit informs Spivak's understanding of postcoloniality in the era of neoliberal globalization. She is careful to dissociate postcolonial intellectuals in the West (whom she regards, including herself, as mainly economic migrants) from the role of native informants, which a distracted metropolitan academy is only too keen to bestow upon them. Nor does she wish to speak from some "subaltern" status, something that she reserves for those, such as tribal women in the poorest districts of India, who are outside what she calls the cultures of imperialism. Yet she recognizes that both these dissimulations often do characterize postcolonial intellectuals in the metropolitan academy.

Spivak refers to herself as "an academic in a trivial discipline in the United States"[81] and describes one of her most recent works as "a trivial book"[82]—forms of self-effacement that sound exaggerated at times and hollow at others—and often her politics can be difficult to discern.[83] When asked directly about the political implications of her work, her answer confines herself to the persona of a teacher in a classroom, as seen in the following exchange during an interview:

> Q: Would you like to discuss the pragmatic political usefulness of your own recent work which has focused on the subaltern gendered subject?
>
> GCS: *I cannot get a hold of what is meant by a direct pragmatic political usefulness which might be unrelated to the classroom.* In America, some people say their pedagogy is their politics—I think it can be a kind of alibi. In the long run, and I am sorry if I seem too reactive here, I would like to learn about the political usefulness of my work, whatever it might be, from the outside, and from an outside which I inhabit myself. *If you ask me directly what its pragmatic political usefulness is, I would say very little . . . as little as anyone else's.*[84]

Although Spivak is quite clear and insightful about the connections between historical forms of colonialism and contemporary neoliberal globalization and the racism and sexism that the current New World Order is predicated upon, when it comes to either outlining what might seem to be a desirable politics of resistance to such globalization or what the role of the academic might be in this regard, her thinking, like that of Bhabha, is less easily classifiable into any of the available genres of the political. An example might illustrate this: "I have been consistent in my insistence that the economic be kept visible under erasure. What good will it do? Who knows? Marx's books were not enough and the text of his doing remained caught in the squabbles of preparty formation and the vicissitudes of his personal life. You work my agenda out."[85]

On a literal reading, such a quote would seem to suggest that notwithstanding Marx's intellectually robust and insightful critiques of capitalism, neither was he able to live up to his own revolutionary ideals in his personal life nor was the onward march of capitalism through our planet ultimately deflected despite his work. What Spivak seems to offer in this context is a politics of deconstruction, of exposing the contradictions and silences of hegemonic discourses, showing the absences around which they cohere, without claiming a transcendent position from which one can escape one's own complicity in structures of domination. Hence, the constant refrain of the double negative: to critique from within what one cannot not want to inhabit. As in Bhabha's case, this is most emphatically not a politics of overcoming or transcendence. It is not about the grand mobilization of oppositional constituencies oriented toward the capture of the political apparatus and the installation of a form of social democracy thereafter. It is, where articulated at all, a politics of resisting structures of domination and privilege that one also inhabits, and of critiquing them from within.

There is, perhaps, a certain honesty in Spivak's admission that the "pragmatic political usefulness" of her work is very limited. However, as with Bhabha and the Subaltern Studies Collective, it has certainly left her open to the charge that her politics lacks a programmatic vision or a resounding telos, and that the emphasis on textual deconstruction comes at the expense of an engagement with the "real." Such critiques of the postcolonial standpoint abound, and it is to some of these that we turn our atten in the next chapter.

CHAPTER 4

CRITIQUES OF POSTCOLONIAL THEORY

This chapter will look at the vigorous critiques of postcolonial theory as they have emerged in recent decades. There have always been critiques of a postcolonial *perspective*, especially from those committed to modernization theory and its latter-day variant of neoliberal globalization. They argue that the emphasis on the history of colonialism and underdevelopment as explanations of third-world poverty is misplaced, and suggest that free markets, scientific rationality, and individualist ideology in the rise of the West were more important. That encounter between the modernization and postcolonial perspectives was examined at length in Chapters 1 and 2. In this chapter the focus is instead on a more limited domain, that is, critiques of postcolonial *theory* as they have emerged in the past two or three decades. In the context of this book, then, the focus is on critiques of the works of theorists such as Said, Spivak, and Bhabha, and bodies of work such as the Subaltern Studies Collective. Although we occasionally look at responses by postcolonial theorists, the focus is more on the critique. The last section of this chapter will take a detailed look at one particular variant of critique of postcolonial theory, that emanating from the perspective of indigenous politics, and use it as a way of understanding where postcolonial theory stands at this juncture in its engagement with globalization.

POSTCOLONIAL STUDIES AS SANITIZING IMPERIALISM

One of the earliest and most robust critiques of postcolonial studies emerged in the wake of the publication of Ashcroft, Griffiths, and Tiffin's *The Empire Writes Back* in 1989. As indicated in the previous chapter, these authors had argued postcolonial space included countries marked by what one might call white settler imperialism: Australia, Canada, the United States, and South Africa. They suggested these societies too had been once colonized by Britain, and that experience had crucially inflected their literatures and national cultural formation. Critics of such an expansive definition of the postcolonial would point out to the millions of nonwhite natives killed in the white settler colonies the systematic underdevelopment of the territorial colonies. Nothing remotely comparable happened to white settlers in the United States, Canada, Southern Africa, Australia, or New Zealand; in fact they were primarily perpetrators and beneficiaries of such colonialism. From the vantage of the third world, the American war of independence of the settler colonies from Britain looks more like an intraelite skirmish between the English and their kinsmen in the New World, rather than the anticolonial wars of the mid-twentieth century in places like Vietnam or Algeria. Similarly, to equate the "tensions" between England and places like Canada and Australia, and the latter's feelings of cultural cringe, with the decolonization struggle in places like India or Kenya seems incredible. To aver that the United States became a colonizing power *after* its emergence as an industrialized and developed nation, as the authors do, is to miss the central point that from the very outset the establishment of white settlements in the United States was an act of colonialism marked by genocide and slavery.

Despite its mildly progressive argument in the context of a deeply conservative and England-centric discipline such as English literature, critics saw *The Empire Writes Back* as popularizing a definition of the "postcolonial" that conflated too much within its ambit. They argued that it was precisely the anodyne reduction of postcolonialism to tensions between literary productions emanating from England and its ex-colonies (especially white settler colonies) that made the term "postcolonial" so rapidly influential and popular within Western academia in the 1990s. For example, in the United States, universities had been besieged by the civil rights, antiwar, feminist, indigenous, and ethnic studies movements from the 1960s onward. Such movements questioned the self-representation of the United States as a democracy and argued it was a neoimperial power with its own history of colonization of indigenous peoples within and outside its territory. In the context of the study of literature, such movements were critical of the tendency to regard literature as an aesthetic practice somehow "above" politics, colonialism, racism, and other facts of history. Scholars and students radicalized by such movements were impatient with the hostility of such "humanities" departments to insights drawn from Marxism, feminism, and studies of colonialism (the dependency school and the world-systems approach, for example) in analyzing literary or cultural forms of representation. English departments were also under pressure to pluralize the literary canon to reflect a changing population that was increasingly non-Euro-American in ethnicity. Such departments had been loath to seriously engage the imperial colonial underpinnings of so-called aesthetic disciplines, such as English literature, and they found in the expansive yet milquetoast idea of the "postcolonial," as articulated in *The Empire Writes Back*, a way to remain conservative while appearing progressive.

In a widely cited essay, Ella Shohat notes:

> My recent experience . . . at one of the CUNY branches illustrates some of the ambiguities . . . the generally conservative members of the college curriculum committee strongly resisted any language invoking issues such as "imperialism and Third Worldist critique," "neocolonialism and resisting cultural practices," and "the geopolitics of cultural exchange." They were visibly relieved, however, at the sight of the word *postcolonial*. Only the diplomatic gesture of relinquishing the terrorizing terms *imperialism* and *neocolonialism* in favor of the pastoral *postcolonialism* guaranteed approval.[1]

Shohat argues this is exemplary of why postcolonialism gained rapid popularity within Western, especially American, academia in recent decades. Its equivocations served as an alibi to avoid dealing with the interlinked histories of colonialism, imperialism, racism, and genocide on the one hand and the rise of English literature to a canonical status on the other. Postcolonial theory's focus on literary analysis, matters of representation, tensions between metropolitan and ex-colonial Englishes, and related disciplinary issues, rather than the history of colonialism, was the source of its appeal to such departments.

Unlike Young and Alavi, the work of Ashcroft et al. does not foreground the Marxist and underdevelopment legacy of the term, and indeed pushes that to the very margins of its constitution. The word capitalism is not there in the index of *The Empire Writes Back*, or in another highly influential book written by the same authors, *Key Concepts in Post-Colonial Studies*.[2] Neither book contains any detailed discussion of either Marx or Marxism, or for that matter, of the multifarious process of underdevelopment, which Chapter 1 examined at length. Marxist concepts and ideas are briefly referred to in discussions of class and of national liberation movements, but ideas such as the capitalist mode of production, development and underdevelopment as simultaneous and dialectical products of capitalism, socialist revolution, peasant-based insurgencies, Maoism, and other concepts that play a major role in the works of authors like Alavi and Young, are notably absent. In effect, this means socialist struggle is not seen as the means to overcome postcoloniality.

Second, by equating radically different colonialisms (white settler colonial experience and that of underdeveloped third-world societies) it focuses more on forms of literary representation and psychological states of being of both colonizer and colonized, rather than on the structural and epistemic violence of colonialism itself.

Third, postcoloniality has now come to refer to much more than the third world; it is a generalized condition that affects cultural, especially literary, representations across any divide between metropolitan and provincial, and thus includes many first-world countries like the United States, Canada, Australia, New Zealand, and others. And finally, the popularity of this literary definition of postcolonial in first-world academia owed very much to a specific moment in neoliberal globalization. It occurred at a time when the metropolitan university and academy was itself undergoing a pronounced pluralization in terms of ethnicity, race, and gender; when global capital was suffusing an expanding global market economy with new waves of investment, and literary production in English was becoming truly global.

THESES ELEVEN: POSTCOLONIALISM AS THE ALIBI OF NEOLIBERAL GLOBALIZATION

Many critiques of Ashcroft et al. focus on what is called the cultural turn of their work, that is, an overattention to issues of literary and aesthetic representation in comparison to a "real" or material history of colonialism and inequality. In making this distinction between representation and reality, such critics were consciously or otherwise speaking from a Marxist vantage that regards cultural forms (literature, poetry, the arts, and so forth) as dependent on and ultimately derivative of more basic and fundamental material factors of human existence: the economy defined in the widest sense of how people use and exploit nature and one another to fulfill their existential needs. This is often described as the base-superstructure model, and it regards cultural, artistic, religious, and ideological expression or representation as the superstructure that is dependent on and derived from the economic or material base of human existence.

From this viewpoint, the crucial flaw in efforts such as that of Ashcroft et al. was that they were seeking changes in the representational realm ("how to change the second-class status attached to English literatures emanating from ex-colonies") without adequately addressing the basic economic structures that produced such inequalities in the first place (the legacy of imperialism and colonialism in economic terms, and the crucial difference between settler and territorial colonialisms). In other words, demanding equal status for all English literatures when they were so divided in terms of economic status and power was utopian and unrealistic. In Marxian language, Ashcroft et al. could be charged with "idealism," that is, the tendency to regard changes in the representational realm as real and consequential, when in actuality, they are merely epiphenomenal (or superficial) if they were not accompanied by more basic, fundamental, and consequential changes in the economic or material realms.[3]

In many ways, this critique of Ashcroft et al. constitutes the modal form of critique that is leveled against postcolonial theory more generally in the period from the 1980s onward. The likes of Alavi and the long pantheon of writers that Young enlists in his genealogy of the postcolonial—spanning Bartolomé de Las Casas to Fanon, Mao, Che, and Castro—are essentially removed from the story, and postcolonialism, now more sharply and narrowly defined as "postcolonial theory" or "postcolonial studies," is seen as the third-world version of postmodernism and poststructuralism. Prominent among these critics of postcolonial theory are Arif Dirlik, Aijaz Ahmad, Neil Lazarus, Benita Parry, Ella Shohat, Anne McClintock, Timothy Brennan, Sumit Sarkar, and Keya Ganguly. The crucial and related points that many of these authors have made about postcolonial studies can be summarized in the eleven theses that follow.

1. The rise of postcolonial theory in the Western, especially American, academy coincides with the rise of neoliberal globalization in the period

since 1980. It also parallels the diminution in the hopes and ideals of various radical movements of the 1960s and 1970s—for civil rights, women's rights, indigenous peoples, a transfer of resources to the global South, for world socialism, and the Green movement. Postcolonial studies or theory is not merely coeval with these conservative trends; it is causally related to them. Indeed, to stay with the base-superstructure model for the moment, postcolonialism is one of the ideational forms that neoliberal economic globalization and rising conservatism takes at the present time in Western societies. Or, as a preeminent critic puts it:

> [T]here is a parallel between the ascendancy in . . . the idea of postcoloniality and an emergent consciousness of global capitalism in the 1980s . . . the appeals of the critical themes in postcolonial criticism have much to do with their resonance with the conceptual *needs* presented by transformations in global relationships due to changes within the capitalist world economy. . . . "Postcolonial" . . . as a term mystifies both politically and methodologically a situation that represents not the abolition but the reconfiguration of earlier forms of domination. The complicity of "postcolonial" in hegemony lies in postcolonialism's diversion of attention from contemporary problems of social, political, and cultural domination and its obfuscation of its own relationship to what is but a condition of its emergence: a global capitalism that, however fragmented in appearance, serves nevertheless as the structuring principle of global relations.[4]

2. Notwithstanding protestations to the contrary, the appeal of postcolonial theory is in no small part due to the fact that the very word "post" means past, over, done with. This is the reason why postcolonial theorists themselves prefer the term postcolonial over "third world" or "South" or "neocolonial"—the latter reminds the powers-that-be of the uncomfortable and still ongoing inequality of relations between the West and non-Western societies. Thus Benita Parry observes that the meaning of "post" as found in a Marxist text, like that of Alavi, is distinct from that in postcolonial theory where we find a

> manifestly unsustainable contemporary use of the word "postcolonial" as a temporal category where "colonial" is understood to have been superseded or left behind and the "postcolonial" establishment of formally independent regimes is perceived as signaling the end of North/South inequalities.[5]

3. With its focus on hybridity and ambivalence in the colonial encounter, its critique of "binarisms" (such as development/underdevelop-

ment, first/third world, metropolis/satellite, core/periphery, West/non-West), and its disavowal of essentialisms (like class, race, nation, territory, gender, or the capitalist mode of production), postcolonial theory equivocates about the racism, genocide, and economic exploitation that has characterized the world under capitalism and colonialism, and continues today under globalization. It is this alleged equivocation that accounts for the sudden and rising popularity of postcolonial studies within Western academic circles, and its dominant form is reconciliatory rather than resistant.[6]

4. Postcolonial scholars like Spivak and Bhabha mystify and obfuscate global inequalities and racism through incredibly dense and convoluted prose. Perhaps no postcolonial theorist has evoked stronger reaction than Homi Bhabha in this regard. While Arif Dirlik describes him as a "master of political mystification and theoretical obfuscation,"[7] Benita Parry avers that his equivocations about colonizer and colonized were through "the dissemination of emollient retrospects, lacking in conceptual credibility and amenable to neither intertextual confirmation nor empirical validation."[8] Spivak's prose can be formidably dense, and like Bhabha, has evoked much criticism for its opacity. Further, critics have argued, the "cultural turn" within postcolonial theory has meant overattention to fragments of history, to plumbing the depths of individual psychology in assessing the impact of colonialism, and to narrative and rhetorical devices in colonial discourses, at the expense of empirically verifiable structures of exploitation, institutions of power, and the need to mobilize people as social beings for political purposes and struggles. In the words of Keya Ganguly, postcolonial theory has for too long been "locked in an endless embrace of ideals of difference, deferral, and constitutive paraphrasis that inform myriad readings in the literature about hybridity, liminality, mimicry, and so on."[9]

In other words, postcolonial theory is too caught up in a linguistic and cultural turn to be of much relevance to real history. It seems theoretically radical and avant-garde, but studiously ignores the present world situation, its contradictions, and their origins in the history of capitalism and colonialism. Or to put it in Parry's summary:

> In the realm of postcolonial studies . . . discussion of the internal structures of texts, enunciations, and sign-systems became detached from a concurrent examination of social and experiential contexts, situations, and circumstances. A theoretical position wholly neglectful of political economy has had the effect of disengaging colonialism from historical capitalism and re-presenting it for study as a cultural event. As the Marxist analysis of

colonialism and imperialism was set aside, the economic impulses underlying territorial expansion, the military appropriation of geographical space and physical resources, the exploitation of human labor and institutional repression, all receded from view . . . the effect of [postcolonial] scholars' one-sided concern with the constitution of "otherness"/alterity/difference, or with the production of silenced subject positions, has been to cause matters of discourse undeniably to take precedence over the material and social conditions prevailing during colonialism and in the post-independence era. The postcolonial shift away from historical processes has meant that discursive or "epistemic" violence has tended to take precedence in analysis over the institutional practices of the violent social system of colonialism.[10]

5. The national and class origins of most postcolonial scholars prevent them from undertaking a thorough and searching critique of contemporary forms of Western, especially American, imperialism and neoliberal globalization. Most of them are from third-world countries like India and migrated to the first world not because of any oppression in their home countries, where they are often from upper-caste and socioeconomically privileged backgrounds, but for scholarly advancement and better economic opportunities. Both these facts uncomfortably implicate them in a form of careerism that is quintessentially capitalist and individualist. This locus of their enunciation as economic migrants who have turned their backs on their still underdeveloped original societies disenables them from launching any truly radical critique of either contemporary capitalism or the imperialist foreign policy of Western nations. If they were to do so, they would immediately beg the question: "Well, if you dislike American/Western society and what it stands for so much, why don't you go back where you came from?" As Neil Larsen notes, their quiescent politics emerges from the

> typically petty bourgeois origin and metropolitan location of the postcolonial intelligentsia itself as well as of its metropolitan sympathizers. With labor in general retreat, this intelligentsia, like others, knows with instinctive precision how far it can go before its own material interests become endangered—[it is] . . . not so much what this intellectual thinks as of what, for him or her, is unthinkable.[11]

Postcolonial theorists do not subject their own class origins and the histories of their own emigration to the West to the critical gaze they routinely train on other social processes. This amnesia is deliberate, according to some critics, and uncomfortable truths are sanitized by careless and expansive use of concepts such as diaspora and exile. This point is made with characteristic vigor by Aijaz Ahmad as he observes:

> What we have witnessed, however, is that the combination of class origin, professional ambition and lack of a prior political grounding of stable socialist praxis predisposes a great many of the radicalized immigrants located in the metropolitan university towards both an opportunistic kind of Third Worldism as the appropriate form of oppositional politics and a kind of self-censoring, which in turn impels them towards greater incorporation in modes of politics and discourse already authorized by the prevailing fashion in that university. . . . The fact that some of these intellectuals actually were political exiles has been taken advantage of, in an incredibly inflationary rhetoric, to deploy the word "exile," first as a metaphor, and then as a fully appropriated descriptive label for the existential condition of the immigrant as such; the upper-class Indian who chooses to live in the metropolitan country is then called "the diasporic Indian," and "exile" itself becomes a condition of the soul, unrelated to facts of material life. Exile, immigration, and professional preference become synonymous and, indeed, mutually indistinguishable.[12]

6. Although many postcolonial theorists may have once had strong intellectual foundations in Marxism, in recent decades they have clearly been more inspired by the antihumanist thought of Foucault and Derrida, drawing as the latter do from Nietzsche. The critique of essentialism is now accompanied by a suspicion of emancipatory and teleological thought. Together these have been combined into a larger critique of the project of modernity and of "Enlightenment values" in general. All this has incapacitated the struggle against religious fundamentalism, political authoritarianism, and the forces that drive neoliberal globalization in places like India. When ideals like secularism, social democracy, tolerance, the environment, and human rights come under attack by antihumanist philosophies on grounds that they are essentialist, teleological, Eurocentric, and overly enamored of Enlightenment values, it can have a disastrous effect on a progressive politics.

The Indian historian Sumit Sarkar makes these points in his critique of the work of the Subaltern Studies group of historians on India of which he was originally a part. The initially strong Marxist-Gramscian underpinnings of this collective changed in the mid-1980s as their works became more explicitly inspired by the works of Said, Foucault, and Derrida, among others. Sarkar summarizes the political consequences of such a turn in the work of the collective thus:

> The spread of assumptions and values associated with late *Subaltern Studies* can have certain disabling consequences. . . . The organized Marxist left in India remains one of the biggest existing anywhere in the world today, while very recently the forces of predominantly high-caste Hindutva have been halted in some areas by a lower-caste upthrust drawing on earlier traditions of . . . protest. *Subaltern Studies*, symptomatically, has ignored histories of the left and organized anti-caste movements throughout. . . . Movements of a more innovatory kind have also emerged in recent years: organizations to defend civil and democratic rights, numerous feminist groups, massive ecological protests . . . and very new and imaginative forms of trade-union activity. . . . Any meaningful understanding of or identification with such developments is undercut by two kinds of emphasis quite central to late *Subaltern Studies*. Culturalism rejects the importance of class and class struggles, while notions of civil, democratic, feminist and liberal individual rights—many of them indubitably derived from certain Enlightenment traditions—get delegitimized by a repudiation of the Enlightenment as a bloc. . . . Words like "secular," "rational" and "progressive" have become terms of ridicule, and if "resistance" . . . can still be valorized, movements seeking transformation get suspected of teleology. The decisive shift in critical registers from capitalist and colonial exploitation to Enlightenment rationality, from multinationals to Macaulay, has opened the way for a vague nostalgia that identifies the authentic with the indigenous, and locates both in the pasts of an ever-receding community, or a present that can consist of fragments alone. . . . There is not a word . . . about that other rationality of the "free" market, derived at least as much from the Enlightenment as its socialistic alternatives, which is being imposed worldwide today by the World Bank, the IMF and multinational firms. The claim . . . to an adversarial relationship to the dominant structures of scholarship and politics resounds oddly in the midst of this silence.[13]

Sarkar's point about the declining, and indeed counterproductive, impact of postcolonial theorists on their "home" societies is one that is echoed by many others, and we will return to it in the last of the eleven critiques summarized here.[14]

7. Postcolonial theorists energetically proclaim their resistance to Eurocentrism and the importance of provincializing Europe as a step toward genuine decolonization. Yet, in their own obsession with the colonial period; in their tendency to see secularism, scientific rationality, bourgeois freedoms, human rights, and other such values as emergent from the Eu-

ropean Enlightenment; their continuous theoretical engagement with the latest in Western philosophical and intellectual movements; and their disinterest in ways in which Europe (and Euro-America) plays such a central role in contemporary neoliberal globalization, postcolonial theorists are themselves complicit in the continued hegemony of Eurocentrism. As Neil Lazarus notes:

> Eurocentrism has typically been viewed [by postcolonial writers] not as an ideology or as a mode of representation but as itself the very basis of domination in the colonial and modern imperial contexts. Setting out from this strictly idealist[15] conceptualization, postcolonial theorists have sought to produce an anti-Eurocentric . . . scholarship. . . . But to the extent that a plausible account of the structurality of the modern world order has necessarily eluded them, postcolonial theorists have been unable to situate Eurocentrism as an historical problematic, to understand how it has been able to achieve its momentous effects.[16]

Lazarus argues Eurocentrism was historically powerful and endures today because this particular form of ethnocentrism was underlain by capitalism and colonialism. To analyze Eurocentrism outside these structural accompaniments is to repeat the errors of idealism laid at the feet of Ashcroft et al.[17] Furthermore, it leads to an ahistorical fetishization of Europe, attributing a singularity and perniciousness to it that is, in its own way, racist and guilty of crude stereotyping.[18]

8. Postcolonial theory is basically an unoriginal derivative of the other posts of our time, poststructuralism and postmodernism, both of which celebrate the ephemeral, the fragmentary, and are suspicious of grand narratives of emancipation, be they of class, race, gender, national solidarity, or liberal democracy. In joining poststructuralism and postmodernism in the critique of grand narratives, postcolonial theory is nothing but the translation of these problematic ideas into the domain of what used to be called third-world studies. In the words of Arif Dirlik:

> [A]s a progeny of postmodernism, postcolonialism is also expressive of the "logic" of this phase of capitalism, this time on Third World terrain. . . . If postcolonialism is a progeny of postmodernism, then these developments within capitalism are also directly or indirectly pertinent to understanding postcolonialism. Postcolonial critics readily concede the debt they owe to postmodernist poststructuralist thinking; indeed, their most original contribution would seem to lie in their rephrasing of older problems in the study of the Third World in the language of poststructuralism.[19]

9. The antiessentialism and antipathy to teleological forms of reasoning that characterize postcolonial studies have left it incapable of challenging capitalism in its current form in neoliberal globalization, according to its critics. One clear instance of such critique and response is found in the exchange between Arif Dirlik and Gyan Prakash, a historian from the Subaltern Studies Collective. Prakash made his case for writing "postfoundational" histories of the world on the basis of a critique of abstractions, like the nation and its role in defusing subaltern energy, and in refusing to write Indian history as a later and aberrant "case" of the more general history of class, capital, or mode of production as found in the "original" case of the European transition to modernity. He notes in his essay critiquing foundational histories, especially of the Marxist variety, that

> when I call this form of historical writing foundational, I refer to this assumption that history is ultimately founded in and representable through some identity—individual, class or structure—which resists further decomposition into heterogeneity. From this point of view, we can do no better than document these founding subjects of history, unless we prefer the impossibility of coherent writing amid the chaos of heterogeneity. . . . Take, for example, the narrativization of Indian history in terms of the development of capitalism. How is it possible to write such a narrative, but also contest, at the same time, the homogenization of the contemporary world by capitalism? How can the historian of India resist the totalizing claims of the contemporary nation-state if their writings represent India in terms of the nation-state's career? . . . India, which is seen in this history as trapped in the trajectories of global modernity, is doomed to occupy a tragic position in these narratives. Such a vision cannot but reproduce the very hegemonic structures that it finds ideologically unjust in most cases, and occludes the histories that lie outside of the themes that are privileged in history.[20]

In response, critics like Dirlik argue that Prakash and others were throwing the baby out with the bathwater in their supposedly postfoundational critiques of capitalism and Eurocentrism. To give importance to analytical terms like capital, modes of production, class, or nation, in trying to understand contemporary capitalism was not the same as reifying these same entities, or being unable to critically analyze capitalism, or succumbing to the homogenizing forces of world capitalism. Nor were they instances of an unthinking Eurocentrism. The critique of essentialism as reflected in the quote from Prakash above is attacking a straw man, from the perspective of someone such as Arif Dirlik. The latter notes that the alternatives offered by Prakash to such foundational history writing, namely, emphasizing heterogeneity, the local, or the fragment (as distinct from to-talizing forces or structures), the hybrid (as distinct from so-called essences), the relational (as opposed to dominant binaries), all end up in a form of individualistic culturalism or lifestyle politics that simply obscures the tremendous organizational innovations and exploitative structures that characterize global capitalism in its latest neoliberal variant.

Just as post-Fordist capitalism decentralized production and spread it out over multiple sites the world over, reduced the power of nation-states to regulate movement of capital, and targeted niche markets through a dizzying array of products, subaltern and postcolonial studies too empha-sized the demise of grand or unifying narratives, focused on the fragment at the expense of structural analysis, and celebrated postnational and dias-poric forms of being. In Dirlik's blunt formulation, drawn directly from a base-superstructure understanding of reality and representation, "post-coloniality is designed to avoid making sense of the current crisis and, in the process, to cover up the origins of postcolonial intellectuals in a global capitalism of which they are not so much victims as beneficiaries."[21]

Prakash justifies postfoundational history on grounds that it allows one to write histories that are not Eurocentric. But Dirlik responds that Euro-centrism is not an idealistic preference that can simply be wished away or changed through new forms of writing. The intimate connection between the rise of Eurocentrism in recent centuries and that of capitalism/colo-nialism is underlined by Dirlik when he observes:

> Without capitalism as the foundation for European power and the motive force of its globalization, Eurocentrism would have been just another eth-nocentrism. . . . An exclusive focus on Eurocentrism as a cultural or ideo-logical problem, which blurs the power relationships that dynamized it and endowed it with hegemonic persuasiveness, fails to explain why this partic-ular ethnocentrism was able to define modern global history, and itself as the universal aspiration and end of that history, in contrast to the regional-ism or localism of other ethnocentrisms.[22]

10. The physical emigration to the West of many postcolonial theorists has been accompanied by a subtle shift in the audiences they primarily ad-dress and politics of constituency and affiliation that sustains their work. Increasingly, critics argue, their work is seen more in terms of its relevance to metropolitan concerns, academic debates, and politics than as an osten-sible source of affiliation with the third world or the ex-colonial countries. In the West, postcolonial theory is found to be interesting more for its

theoretical innovations in methods of inquiry rather than what it had to say about the actual details of subaltern life in colonial and postcolonial India. In India, as we saw in Sumit Sarkar's critique earlier, the group was under attack for its diminishing relevance to the most important political issues of the 1990s: the rise of Hindu fundamentalism, the decline of the organized left, the renewed salience of caste privilege, women's inequality, and the rapid ascent of neoliberal ideology within the country. Its general critique of modernity and the hegemony of Enlightenment values (folded within its critique of Eurocentrism) seemed misplaced when Hindu and Muslim fundamentalists were both actively discrediting the women's movement in the name of tradition. It was as if Subaltern Studies were more focused on its relevance to a transnational academic public sphere centered in Berkeley or New York and less concerned with the politics of contemporary India. It was ironic that a movement that began with the quest to rewrite an authentic Indian history from below, to study *"the historic failure of the nation to come into its own,"*[23] was now more popular and visible in the West than in its home country.

11. The dominant mood produced by postcolonial theory is one of ironic resignation and apathy, rather than militancy and third-world solidarity. This plays into the hands of neoliberal globalization and militarism. Noting the ubiquity of terms like neocolonialism and imperialism and the absence of the term postcolonialism in the various oppositional movements to the Gulf War of 1991, Ella Shohat pointedly asks, "Was this absence sheer coincidence? Or is there something about the term *postcolonial* that does not lend itself to a geopolitical critique or to a critique of the dominant media's Gulf War macronarratives?"[24] Clearly, her answer is that postcolonial scholarship is disengaged from the politics of resistance to globalization or militarism in the West and, if anything, is complicit with it. Shohat's point is made with regard to the first Gulf War of 1991, but critics argue it remains as true of the American interventions in Afghanistan and Iraq beginning in 2003 and ongoing to this day. Further, it is also obvious that postcolonial theory did not serve as one of the rallying cries for those who protested against neoliberal globalization in Seattle in 1999, or in the World Social Forum meetings at Porto Allegre and other flashpoints of antiglobalization protests in recent years. Although the critique of capitalist development and its inequality has long depended on a postcolonial or underdevelopment perspective, as outlined in the initial chapters, these movements of resistance to globalization have not found anything useful or inspirational in postcolonial theory in its latest forms.

At the risk of oversimplification, one could argue that the eleven theses outlined above together constitute a Marxist or materialist critique of postcolonial studies: such critique sees it as an ideational derivative of the materiality of neoliberal globalization at the present time.

POSTCOLONIAL THEORY AS MELANCHOLIA

David Scott has recently argued that postcolonial theory has lost much of its relevance because the questions it once sought to answer are no longer the key questions. According to him, postcolonial thought emerged in the aftermath of the hopes and idealism of the anticolonial movements of the post–World War II decades and coincided with the rise of interpretive rather than positivist methods in social inquiry. It effectively demonstrated the limits of conventional anticolonial thought, especially those variants that saw in political decolonization and nationalism the answer to all the problems of the third world. The crucial point about postcolonial studies was that ideas such as antiessentialism, the critique of teleology, and the demonstration of the epistemic continuities between Western nationalism and anticolonial nationalist thought contributed to a richer understanding of the limitations of third-world national movements and of decolonization.[25]

However, once such insights were achieved, Scott argues, postcolonial thought transitioned from "criticism to method" and became, as it were, the deployment of ideas such as antiessentialism, the critique of teleology, the ambivalence that informed colonial encounters, and the nuances that governed their relations, to more and more historical instances. In other words, the same methods were used to generate similar insights, but in newer historical and geographical contexts. Scott analogizes this to the conduct of "normal science" in Thomas Kuhn's terms—that is an incremental and predictable *extension* of findings to newer domains—rather than "revolutionary science" in the sense of a radically new way of seeing and conceptualizing things. In large part, the sense of diminishing relevance that characterizes the field of postcolonial theory, in Scott's view, is due to the fact that it has lost sight of the political point of its scholarship. What, ultimately, animates our study? What is it that we wish to change in the world out there through our inquiry? Scott's phrasing of these concerns is:

[H]ow colonialism ought to be understood for the present we live in has always to be a question we formulate and argue out rather than something we generate abstractly on the basis of theoretical inclusiveness or ethnographic broadmindedness. It seems to me that unless we persistently ask what the point is of our investigations of colonialism for the postcolonial present, what the question is to which we are fashioning an answer, what the argument is in which we are making a move and staking a claim, unless we systematically make this part of our strategy of inquiry, we are only too likely to slide from a criticism of the present to "normal" social science.[26]

I read Scott as arguing that postcolonial theory has to redefine for itself the political point of its scholarship. What is it there for? If the answer is "to constantly refine and nuance our understandings of past colonial encounters," that will push it in a certain direction, one that Scott sees as having only a limited utility. However, if the answer is that the point of postcolonial scholarship is a criticism of the present, then we need to ask ourselves what in the present represents the greatest threat to that which we hold dear?

In a recent compendium on postcolonial studies that foregrounds precisely this question, Ania Loomba, Suvir Kaul, Matti Bunzl, Antoinette Burton, and Jed Esty argue that in the post–9/11 world, the vocation of postcolonial studies unmistakably should be that of resisting neoliberal globalization or what they call "contemporary neo-imperialism" under U.S. auspices.[27] They argue that the rise of globalization, both as a form of academic inquiry and a process that is changing the world, has "eclipsed" postcolonial studies. In response, they suggest that the future of postcolonial studies is inextricably tied to its critique of globalization:

> [I]n its insistence on the structural links between colonial and neocolonial forms of global hierarchy [postcolonial studies] has only now begun—in the age of globalization—to find its real, critical vocation . . . as . . . the historical conscience—and consciousness—of the discourse of globalization . . . our intellectual priorities must respond not only to the search for historical clarity about the making of the modern empires but also to the continuing and bloody ambition of neo-imperialism. As postcolonial intellectuals, we have to be responsible also to the cultural and political struggles that define the social being of once-colonized nations today. Faced with these circumstances, we see postcolonial studies reasserting its vocation in coming to terms with the contemporary shape of neoliberal global institutions.[28]

What unites critics like Scott, Loomba et al., and Seshadri-Crooks is their clear understanding that postcolonial studies is both a product of a longer process of globalization and simultaneously a political resource that is potentially invaluable in resisting it, even if that potential remains, to some extent, either unrealized or sidetracked at the present time. In this, they are quite different from authors like Dirlik, Parry, Ahmad, and others who regard postcolonialism as the ideological alibi of neoliberal globalization, and far from resisting it, they are actually complicit with its hegemony.

POSTCOLONIAL THEORY AND INDIGENOUS CRITIQUE

Recent decades have seen the tremendous rise in what one might call indigenous politics, that is, the resistance of various first peoples in different parts of the world to their colonization and dispossession. Native Americans, Maoris, Hawaiians, Australian aborigines, the first peoples of Canada, the Dalits and so-called untouchables of India, the indigenous peoples of Latin America, the Pacific Islands, and elsewhere have embarked on political struggles to reclaim lands and sovereignty, revive languages, histories, and cultural practices, and regain independence from nation-states built on expropriation and genocide. The rise of such indigenous movements is inseparable from the struggle for decolonization and independence across Afro-Asia in the aftermath of World War II, and the civil rights, antiwar, feminist, and ecological movements of the 1960s and 1970s.

In more recent years, globalization and various movements that oppose its spread have also energized indigenous politics the world over. On the one hand, the technologies of globalization such as the Internet have enabled indigenous movements in various parts of the world to learn from and about one another. Websites and cyber communities that link indigenous populations have spread throughout the world, raising awareness of legal precedents, rights of aboriginal populations in different contexts, strategies of struggle, and the like. Similarly, critiques of neoliberal globalization, and especially its destructive impact on the environment, have found in indigenous worldviews and cosmologies an alternative to the modern view of nature as an endless basket of resources placed by divine providence purely for consumption by humans. The forces propelling neoliberal globalization and movements resisting its spread have both had deep impacts on the rise of indigenous movements in various parts of the world.

At a general level, resistance to colonialism and imperialism represented by centuries of postcolonial thought has been an invaluable intellectual and historical resource for the struggles of indigenous peoples, just as the resistance of indigenous societies has constituted so much of the material that is today marked as postcolonial. Whether it was the first oppositional tracts written by the likes of Bartolomé de Las Casas in the New World in the sixteenth century, or the ideas of Karl Marx in the nineteenth, or that of Lenin, Fanon, Mao, Said, and Césaire in the twentieth, anticolonial writings have profoundly influenced and energized movements for indigenous resistance.

However, there have also emerged a number of recent critiques of some aspects of postcolonial theory that view it as either amnesiac or hostile to indigenous politics. To summarize this literature broadly, the following points are made: (a) notwithstanding disclaimers, postcolonialism seems too focused on societies that were once formally colonized and are today independent. This focus does not account for the situation of various first peoples or aboriginals, in both settler and territorial colonies, whose colonization is still ongoing and far from over. (b) Postcolonial theory constantly foregrounds movement of peoples across the planet through colonialism and globalization: diaspora, exiles, refugees, indentured labor, migrants, "skilled" emigrants to Western countries, and so on. None of these categories, however, captures the situation of indigenous peoples rendered homeless minorities in their own lands through genocide, denial of citizenship, influx of a large number of migrants to work plantations or mines, and racist exclusion. That postcolonial theorists sometimes do not even mention, let alone intellectually and politically engage with, first peoples of the countries into which they are the newest immigrants makes them more like Western colonizers than progressive opponents of Eurocentrism. (c) Postcolonial intellectuals of third-world origin have gained positions of power and prestige within Western academia, have sought to pluralize its content, and provincialize its Eurocentrism. However, their vision of a non-Eurocentric Western academy has not been inclusive enough of the literature and philosophy of first peoples, even as it has shown remarkable facility with philosophies and theories of the West. Postcolonialism has often been energetic about including the literature of the former colonies—both white settler nations, like Australia or Canada, and others such as the Indian subcontinent or Kenya and Uganda in Africa or Trinidad in the Caribbean. But it has not shown a comparable energy regarding literatures, philosophies, and worldviews of aboriginal peoples of the countries to which they have emigrated. (d) Postcolonial theory's antiessentialism may wind up complicit with denial of claims to land, identity, and sovereignty made by various first peoples. If identities such as the nation or ethnicity, or notions such as "traditional homelands" of native peoples, can be shown to be historical and social constructions or fictions, governments and elites can use such ideas to deny their responsibility for past crimes or to oppose current claims for reparation or redress.

In a fairly representative critique, Ella Shohat details the limits of postcolonial theory from the perspective of the indigenous:

> Postcolonial theory's celebration of hybridity risks an antiessentialist condescension toward those communities obliged by circumstances to assert, for their very survival, a lost and even irretrievable past. In such cases, the assertion of a culture prior to conquest forms part of the fight against continuing forms of annihilation. If the logic of the poststructuralist/postcolonial argument were taken literally, then the Zuni in Mexico and the United States would be censured for their search for the traces of an original culture and the aborigines in Australia criticized for their turn to aboriginal language and culture as part of their own regeneration. The question, in other words, is not whether there is such a thing as an originary homogenous past, and, if there is, whether it would be possible to return to it, or even whether the past is unjustifiably idealized. Rather, the question is who is mobilizing what in the articulation of the past, deploying what identities, identifications, and representations, and in the name of what political vision and goals.[29]

In similar fashion, the indigenous theorist Linda Tuhiwai Smith observes:

> [P]ost-colonial discussions have also stirred some indigenous resistance . . . to the idea that colonialism is over, finished business. This is best articulated by Aborigine activist Bobbi Sykes, who asked at an academic conference on post-colonialism. "What? Post-colonialism? Have they left?" There is also, amongst indigenous academics, the sneaking suspicion that the fashion of post-colonialism has become a strategy for reinscribing or reauthorizing the privileges of non-indigenous academics because the field of "post-colonial" discourse has been defined in ways which can still leave out indigenous peoples, our ways of knowing and our current concerns.[30]

In a recent essay on the experience of Hawai'i, Cynthia Franklin and Laura Lyons take postcolonial studies as their object of critique for its "complicity . . . in the erasure of indigenous cultural forms and political struggles."[31] Franklin and Lyons argue variants of postcolonial theory that emphasize "hybridity" are especially guilty of such erasure, and cite Homi Bhabha in this regard. They argue that he

> collapses the different material circumstances that characterize migration, diaspora, social displacement, exile, and refugee status to describe "the new internationalism." He then opposes these conditions to national identity, historical tradition, and "'organic' ethnic communities," *all of which* potentially represent, for him, "a psychosis of patriotic fervor" that belies the "overwhelming evidence of a more transnational and translational sense of hybridity of imagined communities." Bhabha celebrates hybridity in order to critique—indeed, to denounce—nationalist and/or nativist politics and identity.[32]

Franklin and Lyons aver that hybridity theory à la Bhabha rests upon the construction of "binary oppositions" (between hybridity and essence, in this case) and is itself "predicated on a reactionary and politically conservative form of essentialism."[33] The notion of hybridity as found in postcolonial theory, according to them, "tend[s] to see all elements of any particular cultural mixing . . . as equal and so to level the differences in power among vastly divergent national and cultural traditions." Furthermore, Franklin and Lyons assert that "postcolonial critics often interpret any attempts to enlist or to recover parts of a pre-colonial culture as a search for a pristine past, nostalgia for lost origins, or an appeal to unreconstructed nativist authenticity."[34]

It is true that Bhabha (and many other postcolonial theorists) is critical of efforts to discipline hybrid histories into univocal nationalist essences. In this he follows Edward Said who opposes Léopold Senghor's construction of an essentialist "negritude" or Wole Soyinka's quest for an Africa purified of both Arabs and Islam, even as he celebrates their resistance to colonialism.[35] Both Said and Bhabha would aver that supporting the rights of indigenous peoples to the recovery of their lands, sovereignty, cultural practices, and language does not entail supporting constructions of indigenous identity and history through discourses of purity. The latter shares too much with precisely the sort of pseudo-scientific racism, claims to civilizational superiority, and social Darwinism that characterized European nationalisms of the nineteenth century and powerfully underwrote their colonization of the non-Western world. The claim to a transcendent and historically pure essence cannot be sustained by any society—colonizer or colonized—and the argument that a colonized society or the movement for indigenous rights needs such a form of essentialism for contingent or "strategic" reasons seems wrong-headed.[36] The consequences of such essentialism are often the same: they serve as a principle of discrimination, they array individuals in terms of their approximation to authenticity, and their gradual slippage into blood counts, litmus tests of linguistic mastery or knowledge of indigenous cultures, and other modes of exclusion seems inevitable.

It is important to emphasize that neither Bhabha nor Said is against nationalism, especially the nationalism of the colonized. Indeed, the latter's entire career may be seen from a certain perspective as animated by the desire to recover his lost homeland of Palestine. They are, however, opposed to the idea that different cultures or nationalities embody essences that are unique to a people or a region or a nation. In this regard, the critique of Bhabha by Franklin and Lyons, that his critique of essentialist nationalism equates vastly different historical contexts and is insensitive to power differentials between colonizer and colonized, seems difficult to sustain if one looks more fully at the specific quotations from Bhabha through which they make their case. For example, the phrases "psychosis of patriotic fervor" and "'organic' ethnic communities," critiqued by them, are used by Bhabha not to decry nationalism *tout court*, but to discredit highly problematic forms of nationalism in a very specific context, namely, Serbian nationalism at the apogee of its annihilatory ethnic cleansing in the mid-1990s. I reproduce the fuller quote from Bhabha to elucidate my case:

For the demography of the new internationalism is the history of postcolonial migration, the narratives of cultural and political diaspora, the major social displacements of peasant and aboriginal communities, the poetics of exile, the grim prose of political and economic refugees. It is in this sense that the boundary becomes the place from which something begins its presencing in a movement not dissimilar to the ambulant, ambivalent articulation of the beyond that I have drawn out. . . . The very concepts of homogenous national cultures, the consensual or contiguous transmission of historical traditions, or "organic" ethnic communities—*as the grounds of cultural comparativism*—are in a profound process of redefinition. The hideous extremity of Serbian nationalism proves that the very idea of a pure, "ethnically cleansed" national identity can only be achieved through the death, literal and figurative, of the complex interweavings of history, and the culturally contingent borderlines of modern nationhood. This side of the psychosis of patriotic fervour, I like to think, there is overwhelming evidence of a more transnational and translational sense of the hybridity of imagined communities. Contemporary Sri Lankan theatre represents the deadly conflict between the Tamils and the Sinhalese through allegorical references to State brutality in South Africa and Latin America; the Anglo-Celtic

canon of Australian literature and cinema is being rewritten from the perspective of Aboriginal political and cultural imperatives. . . . The "middle
passage" of contemporary culture, as with slavery itself, is a process of displacement and disjunction that does not totalize experience. Increasingly,
"national" cultures are being produced from the perspective of disenfran-
chised minorities. The most significant effect of this process is not the pro-
liferation of "alternative histories of the excluded" producing, as some
would have it, a pluralist anarchy. What my examples show is the changed
basis for making international connections. The currency of critical comparativism, or aesthetic judgment, is no longer the sovereignty of the national culture conceived as Benedict Anderson proposes as an "imagined
community" rooted in a "homogenous empty time" of modernity and
progress.[37]

There are a number of points of critical import in this excerpt for the
encounter between postcolonial theory and indigenous politics. First, it
has to be reiterated that Bhabha's critique of nationalism is reserved for the
extremism of the Serbs, not a critique of nationalism per se. Second, he opposes the idea of culture as contained within relatively homogenous and
impermeable containers, whether called nations or civilizations. As he
notes, the study of comparative cultures has proceeded all too often by taking this static and ahistorical assumption as given. Instead, he sees culture
as emergent from agonistic and antagonistic encounters between civilizations, states, societies, language communities, or races, in which neither
comes to the encounter already constituted but are both made and remade
through the encounter itself. Each translates its understandings of the
other through concepts that are in important ways already preoccupied,
and their interactions produce a third space that is neither one nor the
other. All this, for him, renders the effort to compare cultures as if they
were already constituted prior to the encounter, and then to evaluate these
relatively enduring and static cultural containers, both futile and ethnocentric. His critique of the very idea of cultural diversity (which is
premised on this idea of culture as prior to the encounter), and his preference for cultural difference, is another clue in this regard.

Third, the passage can be read as Bhabha listing out the multiple loci of
enunciation that characterize a "new internationalism," perspectives of migrants, diaspora, internally displaced peoples, aboriginals and first peoples,
exiles, refugees, and others. These are counterposed to a previous time
when the modal citizen who was authorized to write the biography of the
nation was usually male, propertied, and of the majority community, reli-

gion, and race. It also complicates a contemporary world wherein certain identities are privileged as authentic representatives of a nation's literature and others as provincial, if also exotic, variations. Thus, John Updike is viewed as an "American" author in ways that Jhumpa Lahiri or Lois Ann Yamanaka or Walter Moseley is not. Similarly, John Le Carré or Harold Pinter is regarded as quintessentially British, while Salman Rushdie or Ben Okri or Zadie Smith is a qualified or hyphenated (not unmarked) British author. Bhabha's list is not so much an equivocation between the emerging spaces from which authors can write the nation today, but rather one that complicates previously regnant notions of who can and does represent the nation.

Finally, the target of Bhabha's critique in this passage (the same one from which Franklin and Lyons excerpt to make their case against him, and thereby against postcolonial studies) is the majoritarian and state-sponsored nationalism of the nation-state and its ongoing efforts to establish unitary notions of the canon, or the civilizational/racial center of gravity of a society, or its linguistic purity. That is, the target of the critique here is the triumphant nationalism and anxious disciplining of ambiguity in the likes of Samuel Huntington, Arthur Schlesinger Jr., Allan Bloom, William Bennett, or Lynne Cheney in the United States: those who would regird its identity with English as the national language, a Judeo-Christian and northwest European heritage, and purify its literary canon of third-world, black, Native American, or Hawaiian accretions, and the like.

This critique of essentialism does complicate the idea of indigeneity, but it arguably does so in ways that are enabling and empowering. The nub of the idea here is that indigeneity is not a frozen and static set of values, attributes, and epistemologies awaiting our recovery and retrieval once independence or sovereignty or decolonization is achieved. As noted by Bhabha, the encounter between indigenous and colonizer occurred across preoccupied spaces that resulted in a complex hybridity. To illustrate the complexity and unsustainability of claims to a pure and prelapsarian indigeneity, brief forays into two prominent works in postcolonial theory may be useful.

In her *Masks of Conquest*, Gauri Viswanathan demonstrates that the provocation for the first English literature syllabi, and thence the consolidation of something called the canonical works of the English language into a discipline called literature, was the training of a corps of civil servants to administer Britain's empire from the late eighteenth century onward.[38] Until this moment of encounter in which England was called upon (interpellated, to use an Althusserian term) to represent itself as a civilized power due to colonialism, there had been no need to define itself in terms of its heritage or claims to a canonical literature. Thus, the colonial encounter with the other produces notions of English essence, selfhood, its antiquity, classical civilization, and culture.

A second example is Lata Mani's work on the debate over Sati in colonial India.[39] Mani demonstrates, among other things, British legislation against the practice of widow burning was an act of self-making as a civilized society in opposition to a barbaric and uncivilized India worthy of colonization. Definitions of the practice of Sati emerged by a process of interlocution between British civil servants and Brahmin priests who now become the authoritative interpreters of something called "Hindu" tradition and scripture. In the process, there occurred a freezing and codification of the practice of Sati itself, besides locating it in the interpretive traditions of one caste of Indians, namely, the Brahmins. We know little of the practice in precolonial society, and it may have actually varied enormously across the time and space of this region now named India. The entire "debate" over Sati takes place between colonial officials, Hindu priests, and native elites, and yet the (Hindu) woman has no say whatsoever in the debate. She is but a site for the production of patriarchy in both colonizer and colonized, and, in this context, for the production of notions of "indigenous" Indian or Hindu culture and civilization. Claims about the indigeneity of Sati and its iconic role as a signifier of Indian or Hindu culture and civilization are rendered dubious, given our inability to recover an Indian past that predates the arrival of colonial rule.

These two encounters should suffice to illustrate postcolonial studies' view that antiessentialism is not just a fashionable philosophical stance that one adopts, irrespective of its political consequences for "real world" situations. Rather, opposing the idea that cultures have ahistorical essences is a profound reminder that cultures are always already a cauldron of prior and ongoing encounters between entities constantly in the making and being remade. Recovering a pure indigeneity located somewhere in the past runs the danger of resurrecting past practices of discrimination, patriarchy, and hierarchy. By the same token, the postcolonial theorist's opposition to Eurocentrism is more than just an "idealistic" reversal of polarities, simply asserting the superiority and primacy of the East, or the native, or the authentic indigene, over the West. It is rather a worldview that regards all these antinomies—East and West, native and colonizer, periphery and core, underdeveloped and developed, provincial and cosmopolitan, satel-

lite and metropolis, indigenous and outsider—as analytical distinctions
that are coeval, co-constituted, and dialectically informing each other. As
the introduction to a recent collection on how citizens, migrants, and
states produce sovereignty in the postcolonial world reminds us:

> [T]he colonial world was integral to the formation of law, public institu-
> tions, cultural identities, and ideologies of rule in Europe. Technologies of
> public health, management, crowd control, and urban planning were devel-
> oped and experimented with in the colonial world; consolidation of unitary
> sovereign rule in the European nation states was informed by experiments
> with sovereignty in the colonial world; the disciplining and management of
> sexuality was prompted by encounters with what was seen as an excessive
> sexual culture in the colonial world that would corrupt especially the lower
> classes in Europe; and notions of the self-restrained Western self, of litera-
> ture, of "true" religion, and of the necessity of a cultural canon was
> prompted by the desire to present the West to the colonized people through
> modern education and missionary work.[40]

Ironically, much of Bhabha's argument in the passage quoted by
Franklin and Lyons and in the rest of his essay is convergent with what
they establish about the movement for Hawaiian sovereignty in recent
decades. They argue that the sovereignty movement is not about the "recovery" of a putatively authentic past, nor is its construction of identity
based on blood counts and other essentialist notions. Hawaiian identity
emphasizes genealogy, respect, and familiarity with Hawaiian culture, practices, and history. It is performative and girded around "discourses and cultural practices that are produced by and for Native Hawaiians" in the present.[41] They point out the centrality of issues such as access to lands and
other resources for native Hawaiians. They detail the complex mixing and
interweaving of forms of poetry and music that constitute "Hawaiian" productions today and the ways in which they range across spatial, temporal,
and racial boundaries, even as they articulate a sense of identity and a demand for justice. All of these forms of representation and identity query
the idea of a unitary national citizenship and narrative. They are ways of
being and thinking that are transverse or orthogonal to a geopolitical
modernity based on settled notions of territory and citizenship. This is
convergent with Bhabha's point that contemporary culture is the act of migrants, exiles, first peoples, and multiple others that destabilize unisonant
notions of identity and represent ways of thinking and being that are "otherwise" with the geopolitics of modernity.

In the end, as with many matters of academic debate, the encounter between postcolonial theory and indigenous politics is ongoing and will remain a fraught arena. Although the two arenas of thought have greatly informed and enriched each other, it is undeniable that postcolonial theory has been more attentive to metropolitan theory and often less explicitly concerned with the movement for indigenous rights and sovereignty—both in the third world and in the settler societies of the first world—than it could be. As the various critiques of postcolonial theory have pointed out at length, intellectual formations reflect the material conditions of their own emergence and reproduction. Postcolonial theory, in that sense, reflects the power structures of the world, one dominated by metropolitan or Western theory, even as it tries to critique and overcome it. In the era of globalization, this has made for an engaged, productive, and yet uneasy relationship with the politics of the indigenous.

CHAPTER 5

POSTCOLONIAL ENCOUNTERS: ISLAMIC "TERRORISM" AND WESTERN CIVILIZATION

The initial chapters of this book argued at length that the rise of the West to a hegemonic position in both economic and cultural terms was a process that was violent and coeval within the third world. Contemporary globalization is as dependent on the visible fist of military power as it is on the invisible hand of the market. Viewing the rise of the United States to global eminence in the second half of the twentieth century from a postcolonial perspective, the consistent use of military power and the tactics of destabilization of autonomous regimes in third-world countries are inescapable facts. This chapter focuses on the discursive links between so-called Islamic terrorism and the idea of postcoloniality as resistance to Western dominance. To a surprising degree, it appears that the discourse of Islamic militancy stems not from religious doctrine but from a secular understanding of the emergence of American/Western domination and third-world subjection in the past century. In other words, this chapter, somewhat counterintuitively and controversially, argues that the all-too-moralistic discourse about Islamic terrorism, increasingly referred to in the United States as Islamofascism, that characterizes much of the Western media needs to be leavened by an understanding of history as seen from a postcolonial perspective. This may not only be indispensable to "combat" international terrorism, but it may be vital to the survival of democratic norms and practices the West regards as central to its own identity and formation.

EVERYDAY ORIENTALISM
AND AMERICAN FOREIGN POLICY

In the "Letters" section of the *New York Times Sunday Magazine* dated November 19, 2006, there was a response from a reader named Carol Haskill in San Francisco to a cover story on the Iraqi dissident and exile Ahmad Chalabi that had appeared a couple of weeks prior. Chalabi, a naturalized U.S. citizen, had long lobbied various U.S. administrations to overthrow Saddam Hussein and had finally gotten his wish during the George W. Bush regime. He had, at one time, envisioned himself returning to Baghdad, cheered by welcoming crowds and triumphantly leading a post-Saddam regime. Haskill wrote:

> The adjectives that Dexter Filkins [the author of the cover story] uses to describe Chalabi—"enigmatic," "brilliant," "nimble," "unreliable," "charming," "narcissistic," "finally elusive"—apply to both the man and the country. In that part of the world, nothing is as it seems. Allegiances [sic] are made, then broken, while the ground shifts in an instant, as unstable as the sands.

In three sentences, Haskill epitomizes a worldview that Edward Said described at length in his book *Orientalism*. A set of adjectives effortlessly moves from describing one individual (Chalabi) to generalizing about a country (Iraq) to an entire region ("that part of the world") comprising approximately 200 million people. The fact that Chalabi had been living for close to three decades in the United States and had made no more than a few brief trips back to Iraq had clearly done nothing to alter his essential character. There, where "nothing is as it seems" and the ground is "as unstable as the sands," an equation is drawn between nature, in the form of shifting sands, and culture, in the form of shifty people. Haskill avers Chalabi (and therefore Iraqis and Middle Easterners) as enigmatic, elusive, unreliable, and as frequently breaking "allegiances," qualities that would presumably make him/them hard to understand. Yet that does not come in the way of her belief that they can be quite completely understood and forever summarized in just three sentences by someone who is, as far as I could discern, no student of Middle Eastern affairs or politics or culture in any sense of the term.[1]

Haskill's "knowledge" of people in a distant place, and her distillation of their essential character, is an instance of what one might call the everyday Orientalism of many Americans. By everyday Orientalism I mean the illusion a large number of Americans have that they "know" what Muslim Middle Easterners are like and what their essential characteristics are, and the fact that these characteristics have endured, without much change, for centuries. This secure knowledge about the Middle East is accompanied by a startling ignorance on the part of most Americans of the most basic facts about the region—the location of many of these countries on a map, the fact that Iran is not an Arab country, that there are Christians, Jews, and people of other religions who have lived for centuries in the region, that the vast majority of the world's Muslims do not live in the Middle East but in South and Southeast Asia, and so on. Although Americans would hesitate to describe Europeans or their own society in terms of such an unchanging essence, they have no problem doing so when it comes to Middle Easterners, Asians, blacks, and various other minorities or non-European peoples.

Haskill's prose in this brief letter is very similar to that of one of the most influential commentators on both globalization and Middle Eastern affairs, Thomas Friedman, whom we have encountered earlier in this book. Writing in December 2006, after the U.S. invasion of Iraq, which he had enthusiastically supported at the outset, had gone horribly wrong, Friedman offered President Bush fifteen "Mideast Rules to Live By." Although nearly every one of them is an instance of what I have called everyday Orientalism, the following are especially worthy of note:

> Rule 2: Any reporter or U.S. Army officer wanting to serve in Iraq should have to take a test, consisting of one question: "Do you think the shortest distance between two points is a straight line?" If you answer yes, you can't go to Iraq. You can serve in Japan, Korea or Germany—not Iraq. . . .
> Rule 3: If you can't explain something to Middle Easterners with a conspiracy theory, then don't try to explain it at all—they won't believe it. . . .
> Rule 6: In the Middle East, the extremists go all the way, and the moderates tend to just go away. . . .

Rule 8: Civil wars in the Arab world are rarely about ideas—like liberalism vs. communism. They are about which tribe gets to rule. So, yes, Iraq is having a civil war as we once did. But there is no Abe Lincoln in this war. It's the South vs. the South.

Rule 9: In Middle East tribal politics there is rarely a happy medium. When one side is weak, it will tell you, "I'm weak, *how* can I compromise?" And when it's strong, it will tell you, "I'm strong, *why* should I compromise?" . . .

Rule 11: The most underestimated emotion in Arab politics is humiliation. The Israeli-Arab conflict, for instance, is not just about borders. Israel's mere existence is a daily humiliation to Muslims, who can't understand how, if they have the superior religion, Israel can be so powerful. . . .

Rule 13: Our first priority is democracy, but the Arabs' first priority is "justice." The oft-warring Arab tribes are all wounded souls, who really have been hurt by colonial powers, by Jewish settlements on Palestinian land, by Arab kings and dictators, and, most of all, by each other in endless tribal wars. . . . For us, democracy is all about protecting minority rights. For them, democracy is first about consolidating majority rights and getting justice.[2]

Like Haskill, the distinguished foreign affairs correspondent of the *New York Times* moves seamlessly between "the Arabs," Iraqis, Muslims, and Middle Easterners as if they were all equivalent categories. Irrespective of whether they are Shi'a, Sunni, or something else, Muslim or Christian, religious or atheistic, no matter what their levels of education or the sorts of professions they are engaged in, whether rural or urban, men or women, from oil exporting countries or not, whether from a sizable nation or a tiny entrepôt, none of it matters: these are "rules" that govern the behavior of "these people." Moreover, they all share these static and enduring characteristics, which are, to put it plainly, variations of untrustworthiness, making them unfit for democracy. These "rules" that Friedman outlines are also a classic illustration of Said's insight that Orientalism is as much about constituting the "self" as it is about describing or representing the "other." Friedman is constantly talking about how "we" differ from "them," and how we are committed to democracy, while they prize justice (that is, vengeance), and so on. A set of rules that ostensibly describes Iraqis is also inescapably an act of self-fashioning and the reproduction of the idea of the United States as a bastion of democracy, equality, trust, freedom, rationality, and pragmatism.[3]

Friedman's "Rules" draw upon, and reinforce, the scholarship of someone like Bernard Lewis who could well be regarded as one of the premier

Orientalists of contemporary times. Lewis notes in his essay "The Roots of Muslim Rage":

> There is something in the religious culture of Islam which inspired, in even the humblest peasant or peddler, a dignity and a courtesy toward others never exceeded and rarely equaled in other civilizations. And yet, in moments of upheaval and disruption, *when the deeper passions are stirred*, this dignity and courtesy toward others can give way to an explosive mixture of rage and hatred which impels even the government of an ancient and civilized country—even the spokesman of a great and ethical religion—to espouse kidnapping and assassination, and try to find, in the life of the Prophet, approval and indeed precedent for such actions.[4]

Lewis's seemingly reasoned prose (note the complimentary packaging within which the Muslims' "deeper passions" lie) regarding their essential character underlies the blatantly racist depiction of Palestinians by a recent Israeli prime minister. Ehud Barak noted:

> They [Palestinians] are products of a culture . . . in which to tell a lie creates no dissonance. They don't suffer from the problem of telling lies that exists in Judeo-Christian culture. Truth is seen as an irrelevant category. There is only that which serves your purpose and that which doesn't. The deputy director of the US Federal Bureau of Investigation once told me that there are societies in which lie detector tests don't work, societies in which lies do not create cognitive dissonance.[5]

For Carol Haskill, Thomas Friedman, Bernard Lewis, and Ehud Barak, every Muslim in the Middle East is an irrational, untrustworthy liar. It is this self-confident "knowledge" about the Middle East, resting as it does on the centuries-long edifice of Orientalism, that energizes and informs policy, including the latest war. In March 2003, the United States launched a horrific war on Iraq, despite the absence of any evidence (a) linking that country to the events of 9/11, (b) that there were any weapons of mass destruction there, (c) that Iraq had the capability of imminently producing nuclear weapons, and (d) that it posed an immediate threat to either its neighbors or the region. All these absences were confirmed by U.S. intelligence reports filed from the region, as well as by neutral organizations such as the United Nations, and by media outlets both inside and outside the United States. Yet, when a neoconservative cabal in Washington, D.C. (more on this below) convinced the president of the United States to launch this war against Iraq, a sizable majority of Americans acquiesced in the decision.[6] Public opinion reports indicated that there was majority support for each of the myths outlined above to justify the war. President Bush did not really need to provide evidence regarding his claims about Iraq's untrustworthiness and its danger to the world, all he needed to do was to activate certain long-held beliefs and prejudices regarding that country. As with Vietnam many decades ago, U.S. opposition to the current war in Iraq has increased because it has not gone according to expectations of a quick and painless (for Americans) victory, not because we now realize that many of the original justifications for launching the war have turned out to be lies.

Orientalist beliefs accompanied by stark ignorance about Iraq and the Middle East are hardly confined to the lay public or influential journalists, but are equally true of decision makers at the highest levels of the government. As the national security editor for the *Congressional Quarterly* Jeff Stein found, those entrusted with intelligence gathering from the Middle East or congressional oversight on the current war did not know the difference between a Shi'a and a Sunni, two of the main religious sects within Islam in Middle Eastern countries. Stein interviewed, among others, Willie Hulon, the chief of the Federal Bureau of Investigation's new national security branch, Representative Terry Everett, an Alabama Republican who is vice chairman of the House Intelligence Subcommittee on technical and tactical intelligence, and Representative Jo Ann Davis of Virginia, who is the head of a House Intelligence Subcommittee tasked with reviewing the Central Intelligence Agency's (CIA) performance in recruiting for and analyzing information about Islamic societies. He asked them a simple question: What was the difference between the Shi'a and the Sunni? None of them knew. Stein was not looking for detailed historical or theological answers, just the very basic difference, and which country was on which side of that divide. He drew a blank with almost everyone he interviewed. He concludes, "as I keep asking it around Capitol Hill and the agencies, I get more and more blank stares. *Too many officials in charge of the war on terrorism just don't care to learn much, if anything, about the enemy we're fighting.* And that's enough to keep anybody up at night."[7]

We now know that such ignorance of basic elements of Middle Eastern history within the highest office in the United States underlay the decision to invade Iraq. One of the key steps in the U.S. decision to attack Iraq in March 2003 was taken long before the events of 9/11. As far back as 1996, during the Bill Clinton administration, a report outlining the desired direction of U.S. foreign policy in the region was written by a group headed by Richard Perle (who later became chair of the Pentagon's Defense Policy Board during the George W. Bush administration until a corruption scandal forced him out of the chairmanship). This Report, titled "A Clean Break: A New Strategy for Securing the Realm," was a set of recommendations made to then newly elected right-wing Israeli Prime Minister Benjamin Netanyahu.[8] It outlined an incredibly hard-line policy to be adopted vis-à-vis the Palestinians and abandoning the ongoing Oslo peace talks. It pushed for a strategy that "rolled back" Syria, Iran, and Hezbollah in Lebanon, through robust military attacks, counteroffensives, and "hot pursuit" of insurgents, and saw the centerpiece for Israeli security and U.S. interests into the future as the removal of Saddam Hussein and engineering a regime change in Iraq.

Besides Perle, others crucial in authoring this document, which was underwritten by the Institute for Advanced Political and Strategic Studies (an Israeli think-tank based in Washington, D.C.), included Paul Wolfowitz (who later became deputy secretary of defense to Donald Rumsfeld), Douglas Feith (undersecretary of defense, a rung below Wolfowitz), I. Lewis Libby (Vice President Dick Cheney's chief of staff), and David Wurmser (Cheney's national security advisor for Middle Eastern affairs). This core group of neoconservative "intellectuals," many of them at this time working in or with close links to think-tanks like the American Enterprise Institute and the Project for a New American Century, had essentially outlined in their report what would become the basis for the U.S. decision to launch a war against Iraq. The events of 9/11 became the reason or the excuse that enabled the implementation of a Report written years earlier. The fudging of intelligence, the insistence (against the facts) of Saddam's culpability in the events of 9/11, the rush to war, the sidelining of Arabists and Middle East experts in the State Department or CIA who were skeptical of the evidence, and the relentless exaggeration of nonexistent Iraqi weapons of mass destruction or its nuclear program become comprehensible in light of the agenda set out in this Report.[9] The translation of its aspirations into reality continues to produce horrendous consequences with at least tens of thousands of Iraqi casualties, over 4,000 U.S. soldiers and hundreds of other soldiers from allied countries killed, tens of thousands maimed and injured, and a civil war that will probably linger for years.

And yet, this Report contained the same glib ignorance combined with plain prejudice that I have described as the everyday Orientalism of the average American. As Rashid Khalidi notes in his detailed analysis:

> Much about this extraordinary document is worthy of comment, not least of all the ignorance of the history, politics, societies, and religions of the Middle East that pervades it. The lack of basic knowledge about the Middle East

exhibited in the report goes beyond the misspelling of names and places to its core recommendations. Thus Perle, Feith, Wurmser, and others, part of a group that often seems to have virtually exclusive access to the top deci-sion-makers in the Bush administration, make the suggestion in this report that putting a member of the Hashemite royal family back in control of Iraq would wean Shi'ites in Lebanon and Iraq away from Hezbollah and Iran. This master stroke is possible, the report claims, since "Shia retain strong ties to the Hashemites." . . . As beginning students of Middle East history would know . . . the loyalty of Shi'ites has as a rule been to one specific lin-eage of the descendants of 'Ali, rather than to all who claim descent from him. The Shi'ites do not venerate . . . the Hashemites. The latter . . . are Sun-nis, and as such are often regarded with suspicion by religious Shi'ites. Moreover the ill will between many Iraqi Shi'ites and the Sunni Hashemite monarchy from its imposition by the British in 1920 until its overthrow in 1958 is well attested. These are among many basic facts about the Islamic world and the Middle East that are well known to experts and even to those not so expert, but which these "prominent opinion makers," as they de-scribe themselves in the introduction to the report, seem to have missed al-together. They appear to have learned nothing in the interim. Virtually all of the thinking that underlay the planning for the Iraq war by these same in-dividuals and their colleagues . . . was blighted by the same enthusiastic ig-norance and ideological blindness.[10]

Khalidi notes that nowhere in this Report does the word "democracy" ap-pear, nor is there any mention of "human rights," except to discredit the Palestinian Liberation Organization (PLO). Yet, once the war in Iraq turned into a military disaster and the cache of weapons of mass destruction and nu-clear weapons were never found because they were never there, such terms became part of the post facto justification for war. It should be apparent by now that the uninformed Orientalism of U.S. policy makers and the general public powerfully propels U.S. unilateralism into the Middle East.

NEOLIBERAL GLOBALIZATION, COLONIALISM, AND THE POLITICS OF TERRORISM

The historical link between gunboat diplomacy and colonial "free trade" is one of the staples of postcolonial thought. In the past few decades, U.S. hegemony and its underwriting of the global capitalist order have been no less reliant on the use of force in the third world. Such a connection is lost on one of the most influential proponents of neoliberal globalization like Thomas Friedman. Having argued that Middle Easterners are essentially untrustworthy liars, as seen in the previous section, Friedman argues neoliberal globalization is the best prophylactic against Islamic terrorism. To him, Muslim youth in the Middle East and in places like Afghanistan, Pakistan, Indonesia, Philippines, Sudan, and Tunisia are fertile recruits for organizations such as Al Qaeda because of a lack of opportunities in education and employment. These countries are inadequately modernized, their governments authoritarian, and these underemployed youth (whom he calls the "Sitting Around People") become soldiers in struggles in Afghanistan, Iraq, Kashmir, Chechnya, and the Philippines. What these countries need, in Friedman's view, is closer integration with a globalizing neoliberal economy and full-scale modernization of their societies. This will force their governments out of their medieval and quasi-feudal authoritarian ways, democratize the political system, create economic opportunities for youth, and reduce the role of religion in public life. Friedman is quite clear that such Muslim-majority societies, steeped as they are in religious orthodoxy, have yet to undergo the transformation into modernity that occurred in the West through the transition to capitalism, parliamentary democracy, and secularism over recent centuries.

In one of his favorite contrasts, Friedman compares India with places like Pakistan, Egypt, Saudi Arabia, or Afghanistan:

> India has the second largest Muslim population after Indonesia. And there is one crying fact that stands out from the year of 9/11 . . . there isn't a single Indian Muslim in Al Qaeda. And there isn't a single Indian Muslim in Guantanamo Bay. Now why is that? I'll tell you why I think that is. I think it's because the richest man in India today is a Muslim software entrepreneur, Aziz Premji, the founder of Wipro. I happen to think it's because the president of India today is a Muslim. I happen to think that one of the few mosques I know where women demanded the right to pray alongside men was in Hyderabad, India, because they were empowered and protected to do so. Guess what folks. This isn't complicated. Give people a context where there is a free enough market for them, if they work hard, to advance themselves. Where there is enough democracy where if they have a grievance they can shout it without being thrown in jail. And where there is enough rule of law that if they have a dispute with someone they can adjudicate it without buying off the judge with a goat. And guess what. They don't want to blow up the world; they want to be part of it.[11]

Free markets, hard work based on individual enterprise, the rule of the law, and democracy: this is Friedman's recipe for success in today's globalizing world, as well as the bulwark against the seductions of Islamic terrorism.

Presented at this level of abstraction and through simplistic contrasts, his analysis is persuasive to the average reader. Yet, as discussed below, the situation is far more complex. When Friedman points out in this essay that none of the twenty-two countries in the Arab League are democratic, he does not mention that some of the most important members of the League have authoritarian regimes that were and are supported by the United States—Saudi Arabia, Egypt, and Kuwait, for example. Other autocratic regimes were either installed with the help of the United States—Jordan and Iraq, for instance—or have benefited from Western support, trade, and aid—the French in Syria and Lebanon, for example. The same Western governments, prominently the United States, have always propped up the autocracy that is rife within the Arab League because such autocracies have been crucial in the maintenance of Western capitalist development and the sustained growth of their economies, whether through import of cheap oil or sale of military equipment or other means. When Friedman sees the West as a bastion of free markets and liberal democracy and the Middle East dominated by authoritarian regimes, he conveniently forgets that Western freedoms have invariably been underwritten by systematic sponsorship of un-freedom in the ex-colonial world. Friedman's smug notion that America is a democracy never faces an elementary question: if a country installs and supports dictatorships elsewhere, does it still deserve to be called a democracy?[12]

What is absent in analyses such as Friedman's is any historical perspective, save a lazy Orientalist prejudice masquerading as scholarship. To understand the reasons why so many Middle Eastern nations are today ruled by religious and royalist autocracies one needs to turn to a work like Rashid Khalidi's *Resurrecting Empire*. He outlines in detail the history of the Middle East from about the mid-nineteenth century and points out that in many parts there were strong movements toward forms of democracy, secular states, constitutionalism, modern education, and the values of liberal society. These movements, while often halting and prone to reversals, were at least comparable to what was going on in Southern and Eastern Europe at this time. It should also be remembered that in the early twentieth century few blacks could vote in the South in the United States, and that in nearly every Western country women still had not acquired the right to vote. In one instance after another, a combination of colonial repression (notably from Britain and France), later hostility from American and multinational interests in petroleum, and thereafter geopolitical factors such as the Cold War and the emergence of Israel, resulted in the negation of efforts by modernizers in Middle Eastern societies. In Egypt, Iran, the Ottoman Empire, Iraq, Tunisia, Sudan, Algeria, Morocco, Syria, Jordan, Kuwait, and Lebanon, popular, middle-class political leaders and their movements managed to achieve significant successes in the modernization of their societies. However, they encountered the active hostility of colonial powers and were marginalized by the support accorded by the latter to authoritarian groups of either a putative royal lineage or religious order or both.

Khalidi points out that, ironically, in late nineteenth century and especially in early decades of the twentieth, the United States was seen by anticolonial nationalists in many of these countries as a beacon of hope. America's tepid attitude toward British and French colonialism before and after World War I, President Woodrow Wilson's advocacy of the rights of self-determination of nations in his Fourteen Points outlined in 1918,[13] and America's own history of noninvolvement in the Middle East until that point were factors that contributed greatly to its positive image. American presence in the Middle East until this point was prominent through the establishment of excellent schools and universities by Protestant missionaries, such as the American University in Beirut and Cairo, for example. However, this would soon change as the United States rose to become the hegemonic power in the post–World War II order. U.S. involvement, along with the British and the Dutch, in oil exploration in Saudi Arabia beginning in the early 1930s, marked an important turning point. After World War II, secular anticolonial nationalists in the Middle East and elsewhere were often seen as communists or sympathizers and drew the ire of the United States. Even at this time, as United States' opposition to the French and English during the Suez crisis of 1956 revealed, it could act in ways different from the erstwhile colonial powers and gain the goodwill of many in the Middle East.

Yet, in an overall sense, the pattern seemed to be set. The sidelining of democratic, secular, and progressive nationalist movements in the various countries of the Middle East, often under the rubric of containment, was invariably followed by the installation of authoritarian and neoroyalist regimes pliable by Western powers. The archetypal example was the overthrow of the democratically elected regime of Mohammed Mossadegh in Iran by the machinations of the English and the Americans, and his replacement by Shah Reza Pahlavi in 1953, as discussed in Chapter 2. When one ponders why the Iranian revolution of 1979 that overthrew the shah was so anti-American, it is necessary to remember the history of their involvement in the overthrow of Mossadegh and the support they gave to the shah for close to three decades. Yet, it is precisely such history that is ignored by columnists like Friedman and the mainstream U.S. media in general. Instead, anti-Americanism is deemed to be an inborn trait of the average Iranian, and emblematic of Muslim hatred of "Western" values such as freedom, democracy, and women's rights, or their jealousy of U.S. prosperity.

Khalidi's main point, drawing on the actual historical experience of countries in the Middle East, is that there is no innate proclivity for authoritarian rule in such societies compared to others. Rather, the fact that the vast majority of them are today dictatorships has to do with the ways in which Western colonialism, world capitalism, and the Cold War have interacted to produce such an outcome in this part of the world. *Far from being incompletely or inadequately modern or strangers to the rule of law, such autocracies are the form that modernity has taken in these ex-colonial countries.* Authoritarian rule in such societies is a thoroughly modern outcome of colonialism and neocolonialism more than anything to do with Islam.

Today, there is an overwhelming tendency to evade understanding and explanation of events such as 9/11 by recourse to the term Islamic terrorism. The constant refrain from the Bush administration and from a pliant media is that "they hate us because of who we are," with the word "they" standing in for Muslims in any part of the world. Yet, knowing the history outlined by Khalidi and others would lead Americans to understand that "they" often hate not us but what we have done and keep doing in their part of the world. Although Americans may be amnesiac about history, colonized peoples everywhere retain an acute memory and draw upon an enduring reservoir of past images and instances of their colonization at the hands of Western powers. The history of such colonialism is part of the education—both formal and informal—of every third-world citizen, and it constitutes a political reservoir of extreme sensitivity to any hint of Western domination, racism, or even patronization. This resistance is, in Young's formulation, the legacy of postcolonialism going back at least two centuries and is the unshakeable shadow of the rise of the West. It is not something unique to a particular region or religion; it characterizes Latin American perceptions of U.S. actions in their continent, African and Asian views regarding English, French, Spanish, Portuguese, Dutch, and German colonialism, and so on. It is this reservoir of third-world resistance that accounts for the enormous popularity of figures as diverse as Yasser Arafat, the boxer Muhammad Ali, Fidel Castro, Malcolm X, and Nelson Mandela in the third world. Despite decades of excoriation by the Western media of many of these individuals as terrorists or traitors or megalomaniacs, across the non-Western world there is an almost instinctive appreciation of them as people who stood up to the West despite enormous personal costs. It is impossible to understand skeptical third-world reception of the ideas of global terrorism and Western innocence outside this habitus of postcolonial knowledge—formal as well as everyday wisdom—that informs it. As brutal and reprehensible as Saddam Hussein was, the idea that U.S. soldiers would be greeted by cheering crowds as liberators seemed ludicrous to everyone in the third world because they were viewing such expectations against the backdrop of this history. As Khalidi notes with characteristic understatement, "As a general rule, people do not want to be ruled by others from far away, even if those rulers are well intentioned. Americans, whose very independence resulted from a similar sentiment, should be able to appreciate this simple fact."[14]

Although the media image of the bearded, fanatical, religiously inspired Islamic terrorists flying planes into buildings and suicide bombing crowds of innocent civilians reigns paramount, such images also close off any conversation with or understanding of one's adversary. They proceed from the typically Orientalist assumption that one already knows all there is to know about "them," and yet, we have already seen the empirical and historical fallacies that underlie such an assumption. In this regard, it may be useful to actually look at what the United States has been doing in various parts of the Middle East in the past two decades as a necessary backdrop to understanding why 9/11 happened.[15] Since it would be impossible to cover such a large canvas, in the sections that follow I focus specifically on U.S. involvement in Iraq and Afghanistan since the late 1970s as exemplary illustrations.

In 1979, two events occurred that would mark a significant shift in the conduct of U.S. foreign policy, with immense consequences. In Afghanistan, the emergence of a pro-Soviet regime in the 1970s created an opportunity for the United States to arm, train, and support the mujahideen as a fighting force against the state. In the Middle East, the Iranian revolution brought into power a theocratic regime hostile to the United States, one that moreover replaced a longstanding ally in the shah. The United States supported Saddam's Iraq in the war that commenced against Iran in September 1980, but never with the event of ensuring its victory. The explicit hope was that a prolonged war would bleed both countries white and result in large-scale destruction of their armies and infrastructure. In supporting Iraq against Iran, and in supporting the Afghan mujahideen against the Soviets, the United States consciously acted on the principle of "my enemy's enemy is my friend."

Americans had trained Iraqis in the use of chemical, biological, and radiological weapons as early as the 1960s and sent strains of anthrax to them in the period between 1968 and 1978. Iraq used poison gas in the war against Iran and in the assault on its own Kurdish minority during this war, the first use of chemical weapons since the United States used them in the Vietnam War, and a clear violation of international law. Not only did the United States provide annual aid to the extent of half a billion dollars a year to Saddam's regime at this time, it repeatedly used its veto in the Security Council of the United Nations to prevent discussions of the use of chemical weapons by Iraq.

When Saddam Hussein miscalculated the extent of the U.S. support for his regime and invaded Kuwait in 1990, it began a series of violent retributions by the United States that has continued until today.[16] These actions amount to nothing short of genocide and have flouted every international convention on the conduct of war, human rights, protection of civilians, treatment of surrendered soldiers, and norms regarding proportionality of violence to military gains sought. The first Gulf War of 1991 commenced with aerial bombing that targeted anything essential to the functioning of Iraqi society. Something of the order of 88,500 tons of bombs were used during this brief war, and in contrast to the U.S. media's hype, nearly 93 percent of the bombs used were not the so-called smart bombs. U.S. bombs were estimated to have missed their targets as much as 70 percent of the time. There is evidence that the United States used cluster bombs, bombs involving depleted uranium, napalm (which was now renamed Mark-77 firebombs), and explosives, all in violation of international law. In less than two weeks of "fighting," anywhere between 100,000 to 200,000 Iraqi soldiers and civilians were killed, and another 300,000 estimated injured. The devastation wrought on Iraqi medical facilities, water, electricity, industry, and agriculture was total. In contrast, the U.S.-led Allied Forces had fewer than 400 casualties, many of them due to "friendly fire." The ground troops under the leadership of General Norman Schwarzkopf, furious at having been cut out of the action by the rapid "success" of the aerial bombarding, pursued a retreating Iraqi army for over two days, overran it, and forced it into an engagement it did not want. The resultant casualties numbered in the tens of thousands, essentially, conscripted Iraqi soldiers in full-scale retreat and intent only on surrendering, not fighting.[17]

Once the "war" was over, for strategic and political reasons, the first Bush regime decided that a weakened Saddam was preferable to the chaos that might follow his ouster. Thereafter, for over a decade Iraq was subject to intermittent aerial bombing, stifling UN-mandated sanctions that disproportionately victimized children and civilians, and repeatedly charged with pursuing a nuclear weapons program for which no credible evidence has ever been produced. To give one example of the continuous assault on a society, between December 16 and 19, 1998, at the height of President Bill Clinton's woes in the Monica Lewinsky scandal, Iraq was bombed around the clock in an attempt to divert the attention of the U.S. public. U.S. and British pilots flew more than 650 strike missions, about 325 cruise missiles were fired at a rapidly diminishing number of targets by the U.S. navy, and another 90 cruise missiles were fired by the U.S. air force.[18]

No country has ever been subject to the stringent and enduring sanctions that Iraq has since 1990. The mortality rate for Iraqi children under the age of five went from 56 per 1,000 births in the 1980s, to 131 per 1,000 births in the 1990s, and the country dropped a hundred places in the United Nations Development Programme's ranking of countries in terms of overall quality of life. In June 2000, the United Nations reported that the total number of deaths that could be directly attributed to the sanctions ranged between half a million to a million and a half, with the majority of the dead being children.[19] These hundreds of thousands of civilian deaths caused by sanctions were aimed at punishing one man, Saddam Hussein, who had not even been elected by the Iraqi people to office, who had been at various times in the preceding decades an ally of the United States, armed by it with weapons of mass destruction, and supported to the extent of billions of dollars of aid through the 1970s and 1980s by them. Throughout this devastation, the United States repeatedly used its veto in the Security Council to block humanitarian goods from reaching Iraq and refused to allow goods that might allow for the reconstruction of electricity, telephone, water, sewerage, and transportation services on grounds that these were dual-use goods that might strengthen the military. Medical supplies, especially those critical to the purification of water systems contaminated by a damaged sewerage infrastructure, were repeatedly denied entry into the country. One UN administrator in charge of the program after another resigned, unable to implement these genocidal sanctions. In September 1998, one of them resigned saying, "We are in the process of destroying an entire society. It is as simple and terrifying as that. It is illegal and immoral."[20]

In March 2003, the United States launched its second official war (although in some senses the first one had never really ended) against Iraq, ostensibly in retaliation for the events of 9/11. As noted earlier, the push for the war came from a neoconservative cabal with a long-term vision of reorganizing the Middle East to further American interests and preserve Israeli security into the future. As with the first Gulf War, this one too began with an incredible and indiscriminate aerial bombing assault (Operation Shock and Awe), and the rapid annihilation of whatever little was left of the Iraqi army from the first Gulf war and the decade of sanctions and aerial bombing. Saddam Hussein's regime was overthrown, his sons killed, and Baghdad occupied by the invading forces. On May 1, 2003, President Bush made his dramatic landing on a U.S. aircraft carrier with a huge banner proclaiming "Mission Accomplished." Given that Iraq had had nothing to do with the events of 9/11, that Al Qaeda's leadership, including Osama Bin Laden, were still at large, one could only wonder what mission had been accomplished. Many warned that toppling a weakened Saddam Hussein and momentarily taking over Baghdad would be the easiest part of the war. Maintaining control, organizing a credible successor regime, restoring oil production, rebuilding the country, and returning it to some semblance of normality were all going to be immensely difficult, if not impossible, tasks. But such historical acumen or even basic intelligence is not the strong suit of the George W. Bush regime. Iraq rapidly degenerated into a civil war, and insurgents from across the world joined various militant groups within the country that began to battle against the U.S.-led troops within the country and with one another. What was naively expected to be a brief operation has now reached its fifth year and shows no signs of a pullout.

Estimates regarding Iraqi casualties from the current war, given the anarchic ground conditions there, are very difficult to come by. Based on its experience in Vietnam, the U.S. military now proclaims that it does not engage in body counts of the number of Iraqi soldiers, insurgents, or civilians killed. On December 12, 2006, President Bush said that 30,000 Iraqis had been killed since the war began. His aides later said that it was an unofficial estimate based on media sources.[21] In January 2007, the Iraqi administration estimated that 16,273 Iraqis, including 14,298 civilians, 1,348 police, and 627 soldiers, died violent deaths in 2006 alone.[22] One of the few organizations concerned with documenting Iraqi civilian deaths since the U.S. occupation is Iraq Body Count, which is comprised mainly of U.S. and British academics. Using largely media accounts of casualties reported in skirmishes between the U.S.-led forces and insurgents, reports of casualties in the civil war, as well as accounts of random bombings, ambushes, and other instances of violence, the group has maintained a continuous count of the deaths. As of May 28, 2008, Iraq Body Count estimates that anywhere between 84,051 and 91,714 Iraqi civilians have been killed as a result of the U.S. occupation.[23] Although it would be impossible to estimate the precise number of casualties, the above numbers are illustrative of the carnage that has gone on since the war was deemed over by President Bush more than five years ago. The vast majority of the Iraqi casualties have been civilians. They had no say in Saddam's rise to power, had nothing to do with 9/11, and are caught between the U.S.-led occupation and various insurgent armies that have overrun the country since the end of the war. Since the first Gulf War of 1991, it would appear that anywhere in the region of 2 million Iraqis have been killed in the past fifteen years. Given Iraq's total population of about 27 million, this means roughly 8 percent of the population has been eliminated.

Turning briefly to Afghanistan, under President Jimmy Carter, the United States embarked on a policy of militarily and financially supporting the mujahideen in their fight against the pro-Soviet regime there. This U.S. support began in July 1979, that is, even prior to the Soviet invasion of that country (which occurred on December 24, 1979). This shift in U.S. policy in actuality did much to precipitate the Soviet invasion. As had happened throughout the Cold War, the two superpowers conducted their foreign policy toward each other largely by supporting proxy wars and insurgent groups in the third world. This support to the mujahideen increased exponentially after Ronald Reagan took over the presidency after Carter. In alliance with the Zia-ul-Haq regime in neighboring Pakistan, and in close association with the Inter-Services Intelligence (ISI) agency in that country, the United States (primarily the CIA) orchestrated what it explicitly hoped would be the Soviet Union's own "Vietnam" in Afghanistan. Although the billions of dollars that the United States and Saudi Arabia poured into the Afghan insurgency was important, as were the over 1,000 shoulder-launched Stinger missiles provided to them, the longer-term consequences of the way the Afghan war was conducted were truly profound, and perhaps unanticipated.

It would take us too far afield to do a thorough analysis of the implications, but in summary form the following are critical: First, the Afghan insurgency was deliberately globalized and outsourced in the sense that the CIA-ISI nexus recruited Islamic warriors for this cause from a number of countries in the Muslim world. This is where the young Osama Bin Laden first cut his spurs as a warrior. Insurgents from Algeria, Egypt, Indonesia, Saudi Arabia, Pakistan, Kashmir, Sudan, Chechnya, Kosovo, and elsewhere were trained in the elements of guerrilla warfare prior to their insertion into Afghanistan, and they in turn trained thousands of other insurgents all across the Muslim world. Second, given various U.S. congressional restraints and oversight on the pursuit of such clandestine warfare (one of the legacies of the Vietnam War), the executive branch sought to circumvent these by financing the war through dubious means. It was during the war against Soviet occupation that Afghanistan went from being an insignificant player in the world drug trade to one of the world's largest producers of opium. Academic studies have detailed the extensive links between the drug trade, the CIA, the ISI, and the means by which the Afghan insurgency was funded. Third, many of the insurgents were schooled into an extremely conservative form of Islamic theology (Wahabi-ism) that the Saudi regime had been proselytizing in other countries for decades. Fourth, the impact of the Afghan war was deeply felt in Pakistan. That country's democracy, always fragile on account of its role in U.S. geostrategic designs in preceding decades, now receded even further into the background. The equation between the military and intelligence branches, on the one hand, and the civilian regime, on the other, turned decisively in favor of the former.[24] Besides the influx of over a million refugees from Afghanistan and the entry of a huge amount of drugs, weapons, money, and other contraband from that war, Pakistan's impoverished rural population now found in many newly established madrassas one of the few avenues for education (or some semblance thereof) or even physical survival. When the Soviet Union was successfully ousted, and soon thereafter collapsed into a number of individual nation-states, the United States, having accomplished what it had set out to do, simply turned its back on Afghanistan and walked away. In the resulting anarchy, the extremist Taliban established their writ over the region.

As more than one commentator has noted, the idea of jihad or a holy war is somewhat peripheral in the history of Islam, and jihad was defined more in terms of an individual's personal quest for salvation, rather than allied to any political goal. The globalization of the idea of jihad owes primarily to the way the Afghan war against the Soviets was conducted by the United States. The deterritorialization of the Islamic struggle against the West and the presence of tens of thousands of trained warriors behind the cause became an important legacy of the Afghan war. When Osama Bin Laden broke with his erstwhile U.S. sponsors in the early 1990s, specifically on the issue of the continued presence of U.S. troops and bases in the Arabian Peninsula, he had the ideological and material means to deliver an unprecedented riposte to state terrorism. In some ways, one could argue that 9/11 represents the inauguration of a new form of war—that between the nation-state and a transnational, borderless entity that is at least its equal.

In contrast to a Western obsession with Islam as the energizing force behind Al Qaeda, when one focuses on what some of the spokesmen for the group have actually said in various forums, one finds a dogged insistence on locating their actions within an historical framework that is recognizably postcolonial, rather than on millenarian ideologies or religious differences. In fact, the long history of Western colonialism and third-world resistance to it figures far more prominently in justifications for the actions of a group such as Al Qaeda than does religion. As Faisal Devji, in his book on the phenomenon of the Jihad, observes, "Very few Al Qaeda operatives . . . have a religious education, most having been trained within secular institutions and in technical fields, and many are as familiar with the infidel West as with any other place."[25] The various Al Qaeda communiqués are not particularly attentive to schisms within Islam, or identifiable with particular traditions of thought and law, and seem even careless in their knowledge of Islamic scripture—not exactly evocative of "religious fundamentalism." Where they do perhaps strike a chord among ex-colonial peoples everywhere in the world, and among various minorities within the United States itself, is when they make explicit connections between their actions and what they regard as the provocations of U.S. imperialism in their region.[26]

The myopia of U.S. observers to such secular and political reasoning on the part of Al Qaeda is often startling. For example, let us consider Thomas Friedman's report on the trial of Ramzi Yousef, a Pakistani who was behind the 1993 bombing of the World Trade Center, which resulted in six deaths and left more than a thousand injured. Although Yousef is meticulously historical and nonreligious in his justification for his act, locating it within a narrative of just retribution for the actions of U.S. foreign policy in the Middle East and South Asia, Friedman (as well as the presiding judge, Kevin Duffy, in his rejoinder to Yousef at his sentencing) persists in seeing him exclusively as a religious warrior. Here is Yousef's comments at his trial:

> You keep talking about collective punishment and killing innocent people. . . . You were the first one who killed innocent people, and you are the first one who introduced this type of terrorism to the history of mankind when you dropped an atomic bomb which killed tens of thousands of women and

children in Japan and when you killed over 100,000 people, most of them civilians, in Tokyo with firebombings. You killed them by burning them to death. And you killed civilians in Vietnam with chemicals, as with the so-called Orange agent. You killed civilians and innocent people, not soldiers, in every single war you went to. You went to war more than any country in this century, and then you have the nerve to talk about killing innocent people. And now you have invented new ways to kill innocent people. You have so-called economic embargo, which kills nobody other than children and elderly people, and which, other than Iraq, you have been placing the economic embargo on Cuba and other countries for over thirty-five years.[27]

In this lengthy passage defending his actions, Yousef does not anywhere enlist Islam or religion. He does not make the case that the murders are justified because the victims were (presumably) Christian, or because the act occurred in a city in a Christian-majority country. He, however, does embed them in a narrative that one can describe, following Robert Young and various others discussed throughout this book, as postcolonial. Yousef is specific about the links between state-sponsored terrorism, attacks that deliberately target civilians (as happened in Japan, in Vietnam, and since 1991, in Iraq), and his own actions. The reference to the Cuban embargo is another clue to the postcolonial or third-world ecumene of his narrative.

Almost a decade later, Osama Bin Laden would be similarly specific in outlining historical instances to justify the events of 9/11. Speaking a month after that event, Bin Laden had this to say:

The killing of innocent civilians, as America and some intellectuals claim, is really very strange talk. Who said that our children and civilians are not innocent, and that shedding their blood is justified? That it is lesser in degree? When we kill their innocents, the entire world from east to west screams at us, and America rallies its allies, agents, and the sons of its agents. Who said that our blood is not blood, but theirs is? Who made this pronouncement? Who has been getting killed in our countries for decades? More than 1 million children, more than 1 million children died in Iraq and others are still dying. Why do we not hear someone screaming or condemning, or even someone's words of consolation or condolence? How come millions of Muslims are being killed? Where are the experts, the writers, the scholars and the freedom fighters, where are the ones who have an ounce of faith in them? They react only if we kill American civilians, and every day we are being killed, children are being killed in Palestine.[28]

There is an historical argument being made here by individuals like Yousef and Bin Laden. The actions of 9/11 were deplorable and horrendous, and the murder of civilians is unjustifiable under any circumstances. Yet, I submit that one has to listen to—not dismiss—this argument of Yousef and Bin Laden when they locate their action within a specific historical narrative of retaliation against what they see as indiscriminate killing in their part of the world as a result of U.S. policy. Just as "communism" became a word that Americans used as a way of refusing to come to terms with legitimate economic nationalism of various leaders and societies in the third world during the Cold War, today, "Islamic terrorism" or "religious fundamentalism" has become a blanket term that indexes the refusal of Americans to listen to the outrage of Muslims everywhere about what is happening to civilians in places like Iraq, Palestine, and Afghanistan. U.S. claims to the high moral ground has been severely weakened by the enormity of civilian casualties in Iraq since 1991 and further compromised by their actions in two spaces that will, in time, become iconic of U.S. humiliation of the non-West, namely, Abu Ghraib and Guantánamo.

Although it is true that the globalization and outsourcing of insurgents for the Afghan war created an indispensable and mobile core of trained warriors capable of what the West calls "terrorism," U.S. actions in Iraq have outraged ordinary Muslims in different parts of the world who are now more sympathetic to the cause of the so-called jihadis than before. An affiliate of the London subway bombers claimed that they had watched hours of television footage showing the carnage of civilians in Iraq before deciding that they had to do something in retaliation. According to Noam Chomsky, Saudi intelligence agencies and an Israeli think-tank concluded that the bulk of the fighters opposing the U.S. occupation of Iraq are not trained terrorists but rather first-time recruits into the war against them who had been radicalized by U.S. intervention more than any other factor.[29] Similar findings have been reported by French intelligence experts and many U.S. studies, including those conducted by the CIA, among others. Similarly, the CIA analyst whose task was tracking Osama Bin Laden from 1996 onward, Michael Scheuer noted:

[B]in Laden has been precise in telling America the reasons he is waging war on us. None of the reasons has anything to do with our freedom, liberty and democracy, but have everything to do with US policies and actions in the Muslim world. . . . US forces and policies are completing the radicalization of the Muslim world, something Osama bin Laden has been trying to do with substantial but incomplete success since the early 1990s. As a result . . . it is fair to conclude that the United States of America remains bin Laden's only indispensable ally.[30]

The discourse of the Islamic terrorists on the issue of the ethics of civilian casualties is worth analyzing. In a consistent way, Osama Bin Laden and a number of other leaders of the jihad have argued that the United States has dispensed with the distinction between regimes and civilians when it comes to the non-Western world. They cite the atomic weapons dropped on Nagasaki and Hiroshima, as well as the firebombing of Tokyo during World War II, and the use of napalm and air power in Vietnam as proof. From there, they point out that both in Israel/Palestine as well as over recent decades in Iraq and in Afghanistan, U.S. aerial bombing and Israeli attacks, economic sanctions, and embargoes have disproportionately impacted children and women in particular, and civilians in general.

Documentary proof for such U.S. policy is not difficult to come by. As far back as 1960, in a series of public pronouncements, various U.S. administration officials, from Presidents Dwight Eisenhower and John Kennedy downward, had explicitly justified the sufferings caused to Cuban civilians due to the economic embargo on grounds that such suffering was necessary to prompt them to overthrow the Castro regime.[31] Although Cuba was a dictatorship, its people were held responsible for the actions of its leader, and their suffering was justified on that grounds.

The absurdity of this "logic" reached its apogee in the fifteen-year-long nightmare that has been visited upon Iraq by the United States because of Saddam's regime, a regime that was never elected and was indeed foisted upon its people by none other than the Americans themselves. In a brilliant reversal of this logic that the people are responsible for the actions of their leaders, Ayman al-Zawahiri, who is Osama Bin Laden's lieutenant in Egypt, argues that if it is permissible to attack civilians on grounds that their ruler is evil, as Americans have done in Iraq or Cuba, this logic should hold even more robustly when one is dealing with a democracy in which people have the power to choose their leaders. He notes:

> It also transpires that in playing this role, the western countries were backed by their peoples, who were free in their decisions. It is true that they may be largely influenced by the media decision and distortion, but in the end they cast their votes in the elections to choose the governments that they want, pay taxes to fund their policy, and hold them accountable about how this money was spent. Regardless of [sic] method by which these governments obtain the votes of the people, voters in the western countries ultimately cast their votes willingly. These peoples have willingly called for, supported, and backed the establishment of and survival of the State of Israel.[32]

As Devji observes regarding this quote, al-Zawahiri is here advocating "the responsibilities of democracy in the most full-blooded way. It is because the United States is a functioning democracy that its citizens can be held responsible for the actions of their government, something that might not apply to people living under dictatorships. Such holding responsible of the U.S. people to the implications of their democracy puts the jihad in the curious position of taking this democracy more seriously than Americans themselves."[33]

Finally, turning to the issue of the suicide bomber, in contrast to Western depictions of him or her as an irrational fanatic, Devji invites us to listen to the words of a Hezbollah fighter from Lebanon as he makes his case:

> The Americans pretend not to understand the suicide bomber and consider them evil. But I am sure that they do. As usual, they are hypocrites. What is so strange about saying: "I am not going to let you rob me of all my humanity and my will?" What is strange about saying: "I'd rather kill you on my own terms and kill myself with you rather than be led to my death like a sheep on your terms?" I know that the Americans fully understand this because this is exactly what they were celebrating about the guy who downed the Philadelphia flight on September 11, the one where the hijackers failed to hit their target. Isn't that exactly what he must have said when he decided to kill himself and everyone else by bringing the plane down? Didn't he say to those hijacking him: "I'd rather kill you on my own terms and kill myself with you rather than be led to my death like a sheep on your terms?" They made a hero out of him. The only hero of September 11. They are hypocrites, the Americans. They know as much as we do that as a human being we all have the capacity to rush enthusiastically to our death if it means dying as a dignified being.[34]

In this paragraph, this unnamed Hezbollah militant rewrites the suicide bomber from irrational fanatic to someone whose sole chance of altering the circumstances of his humiliation lies in coauthoring his own death alongside that of his tormentor. My point is not to valorize such actions for their bravery or to condone the civilian casualties that ensue. Rather, I suggest that we need to move beyond words like "terrorism," "religious fanaticism," and "Islamic fundamentalism" to understand the politics of Muslim resistance to the United States and its foreign policy. And understanding always begins from the premise that one is dealing with a fellow human being, even when one is dealing with an adversary. In listening to what Osama Bin Laden and others have had to say in the preceding paragraphs, it is evident that an historical argument is being made. One need not agree with it, and one can and ought to debate it. But to refuse to listen to it on grounds that its makers are irrational fanatics is to forget the most elementary aspect of politics: To understand an other, one has to accept that we both share a basic humanity. It is the refusal to accept the humanity of the other that the discourse of Orientalism permits in contemporary America.

A set of recurring themes dominates the preceding analyses. These include: (a) the edifice of everyday Orientalism that permits the incredibly violent and ignorant actions of the United States in the Middle East and elsewhere, (b) the intricate ties that bind this Orientalism to a prior history of colonial domination and continued neocolonial exploitation of third-world countries, (c) the centrality of these ties to Western prosperity and affluence, and the immiserization of many in such societies, (d) a politics of resistance from within these nations that focuses precisely on this history and articulates itself in terms of this narrative, and (e) the refusal to accept the linear narrative that equates the West with modernity, rationality, and modernization and the rest with irrationality, emotion, and backwardness. These are all themes that have resounded at the very core of what has been called postcolonialism throughout this book. The issue of "Islamic terrorism" thus indicates the extraordinary salience of what one might call a postcolonial perspective in our time of globalization. If some see in neoliberal globalization an answer to the "problem" of religious terrorism, a postcolonial perspective is invaluable in demonstrating that neoliberal globalization itself has a highly problematic relationship to the history of colonialism in the third world, and that religious terrorism enfolds many aspects of postcolonial resistance to such colonization in its own discourse. Both the exponents of so-called religious terrorism—such as Osama Bin Laden—and theorists who have analyzed this terrorism, not as an unthinking or essentialist characteristic of certain peoples but in historical and political terms—such as Devji, Mamdani, Khalidi, and Barkawi—explicitly use insights drawn from a postcolonial perspective in making their cases.

CONCLUSION

POSTCOLONIALISM AND GLOBALIZATION: TOWARD A POST-COLUMBIAN IMAGINATION

In this concluding chapter, the relevance of postcolonialism to movements that have resisted the onslaught of neoliberal globalization in various parts of the world over the past three decades is examined. Such movements have ranged across the spectrum of ideological positions and thrown together strange bedfellows, from economic nationalists and protectionists to ecological and green parties, from socialists and anarchists to racists and white supremacists, and from those emphasizing indigenous groups and peoples to ideas of world citizenship and a planetary consciousness. There are a number of excellent works that have delineated these antiglobalist movements.[1] It is not the intention here to repeat the details of this resistance and its occasional successes in arresting the onslaught of neoliberalism. It is argued here that despite the diversity of ideologies and movements that have opposed neoliberal globalization, one can discern three important strands in postcolonial thought that converge with progressive aspects of such resistance.

First, there is a refusal to accept the neoliberal worldview that human society is comprised of competitive, asocial individuals out to maximize their consumption of worldly goods, and that out of such competition and consumption there can arise anything bordering a moral order that dignifies either humans or our planet. As stated in earlier chapters, such a refusal has characterized the intellectual genealogy of postcolonial thought from its very outset.

Second, these movements critique what one might call the methodological nationalism that coheres neoliberal thinking. For all the talk of free markets, globalization, a shrinking planet, and the world as a village, the truth is that for accumulation to occur under the auspices of neoliberal globalization, national borders and the continued viability of the nation-state remain paramount. The critique of such nationalism is a critical step in the creation of a planetary democratic consciousness, and in this regard, postcolonial thought has and continues to play an enormously productive role.

Third, the critique of neoliberal globalization is rendered most comprehensive if we regard colonialism as something beyond just physical conquest and material exploitation of some parts of the world by others, or as an imposition by the West on the rest. Ashis Nandy, a leading postcolonial intellectual, has argued that colonialism is tantamount to the corralling of our very imaginations and paralyzing our capacity to conceive of the future in ways other than the modernization project. Through a focus on Nandy's work, this chapter proposes that one of the most enabling and liberatory strands of postcolonial thought is when it dares to imagine a future outside the imperium of modernization and neoliberal globalization.

BEYOND TRUCK, BARTER, AND EXCHANGE

In an internal memo dated December 12, 1991, that was leaked to the Internet, the chief economist of the World Bank, Lawrence Summers, had the following to say about toxic wastes and the third world:

> Just between you and me, shouldn't the World Bank be encouraging more migration of the dirty industries to the LDCs [less developed countries]? . . . I think the economic logic behind dumping a load of toxic waste in the lowest wage country is impeccable and we should face up to that. . . . I've always thought that underpopulated countries in Africa are vastly under-polluted, their air quality is probably vastly inefficiently low compared to Los Angeles or Mexico City. . . . The concern over an agent that causes a one in a million change in the odds of prostate cancer is obviously going to be

much higher in a country where people survive to get prostate cancer than in a country where the under 5 mortality is 200 per thousand. . . . The problem with the argument against all of these proposals for more pollution in LDCs (*intrinsic rights to certain good, moral reasons, social concerns, lack of adequate markets,* etc.) could be turned around and used more or less effectively against every Bank proposal for liberalization.[2]

Although there was brief controversy over Summers's remarks, it clearly did not impact his career adversely. He went on to become secretary of the treasury during Bill Clinton's presidency and then to serve as president of Harvard University. Though the reductio ad absurdum of the logic of neoclassical economics stands out clearly in this quotation, we often fail to realize that the world economic and moral order today is not very far from such logic. For example, after an airline crash, compensation paid to families of victims depends on their nationality and estimates of what their forgone lifetime earnings would have totaled. There is now a market for babies from "overpopulated" societies such as India or China, or from poorer segments of white populations in the former Soviet Union and East bloc, who are sold to childless couples in Western societies. There is a thriving market in the harvesting of organs such as livers and kidneys from third-world populations to prolong life expectancy of the affluent in first and third worlds alike. Recent decades have seen the unprecedented commodification of water (think of the ubiquity of bottled water for sale and privatization of water supply in many third-world cities), of air (the rich protect themselves from pollution through air conditioned homes, offices, and cars, and in gated communities that are densely treed and landscaped, while the rest breathe in subhuman conditions), space (through marketing of bandwidths for telecommunications), oceans, and so on. The idea that Africa is underpolluted (a remarkable and absurd word, when one stops and thinks about it) and therefore deserving of more toxic waste makes perfect sense in a thoroughly commodified world where nothing is sacred or outside the dictates of the market system.

What is common to these diverse practices is a set of attributes: the idea that society is comprised of atomistic individuals whose worth is dependent on what their skills can command in a competitive market; that nature is a repository that exists solely for the benefit of man and a place onto which he can dump his wastes, toxic or otherwise; that the relentless competition between humans and between different societies will redound to the collective benefit of humanity and of the planet as a whole. In other words, it presupposes a thoroughly commodified world. As one critic noted in response to Summers's memo, "Your reasoning is perfectly logical but totally insane. . . . Your thoughts (provide) a concrete example of the unbelievable alienation, reductionist thinking, social ruthlessness and the arrogant ignorance of many conventional 'economists' concerning the world we live in."[3]

One finds here the echoes of the important critique of a market society made by the Viennese economist and philosopher Karl Polanyi. This critique, which was in many ways anticipated what has throughout this book been described as a postcolonial perspective, represents an important philosophical and political resource for those opposed to the current market fundamentalism. Polanyi's landmark work *The Great Transformation* was first published in 1944, the same year as the Bretton Woods institutions were being established.[4] After a historical survey of ancient and medieval societies, he looked at the emergence of capitalist modernity in England and northwestern Europe and underlined an evident truth: The economy is embedded in a wider sociopolitical milieu, and efforts to naturalize the market economy as a timelessly rational way of ordering society is profoundly political, historically recent, and ethically immoral.

Polanyi pointed out that historical and anthropological research does not bear out Smith's idea that humans had a natural tendency to barter, truck, and trade. In fact, the weight of such research indicated that most societies were more concerned with reciprocity, redistribution, and prevention of an excessive concentration of wealth. Trade, exchange, and business were subordinate activities that did not preoccupy premodern societies and were seen as at best a means to an end, rather than ends in themselves. The ideas of the importance of the trading spirit of man, the commodification of everything, and the emergence of the self-centered, utility-maximizing homo economicus were not merely attributes of modern societies; they were self-fulfilling prophecies in that if we began to interact with others on these premises, our very actions would create the world that was ostensibly our referent.[5]

It was, however, based on this essentialization of the core characteristic of individuals in all times and at all places as a homo economicus that the idea of the self-regulating market as the ideal and rational social order gained its sway. Polanyi observed that there were some aspects that were simply not susceptible to commodification, notably nature (land) and labor (humans):

> [L]abor, [and] land are obviously *not* commodities; the postulate that anything that is bought and sold must have been produced for sale is emphati-

cally untrue in regard to them. In other words, according to the empirical definition of a commodity they are not commodities. Labor is only another name for a human activity which goes with life itself, which in its turn is not produced for sale but for entirely different reasons, nor can that activity be detached from the rest of life, be stored or mobilized; land is only another name for nature, which is not produced by man. . . . The commodity description of labor [and] land . . . is entirely fictitious. Nevertheless, it is with the help of this fiction that the actual markets for labor [and] land are organized; they are being actually bought and sold on the market; their demand and supply are real magnitudes; and any measures or policies that would inhibit the formation of such markets would ipso facto endanger the self-regulation of the system. . . . To allow the market mechanism to be the sole director of the fate of human beings and their natural environment . . . would result in the demolition of society. For the alleged commodity "labor power" cannot be shoved about, used indiscriminately, or even left unused, without affecting the human individual who happens to be the bearer of this particular commodity. In disposing of a man's labor power the system would, incidentally, dispose of the physical, psychological, and moral entity "man" attached to that tag. Robbed of the protective covering of cultural institutions, human beings would perish from the effects of social exposure; they would die as victims of acute social dislocation through vice, perversion, crime and starvation. Nature would be reduced to its elements, neighborhoods and landscapes defiled, rivers polluted, military safety jeopardized, the power to produce food and raw materials destroyed.[6]

Polanyi saw the politics of Britain and other Western societies from the nineteenth century onward as oscillating between a conservative market-mandated morality and a more ethical position that saw the economy (the production of material goods for the satisfaction of needs) as merely a small part of a larger set of concerns that should animate a society. He was objecting to the use of the market metaphor to ethically justify and promote a form of social Darwinism within countries as well as in the realm of interstate relations. To the enthusiasts of an unbridled free market, just as inefficient firms and producers fall by the wayside under competitive capitalism, so too must inefficient humans (races) and societies (poorer nations) pay the price for their lack of ability or competitiveness. Such an ethic, Polanyi argued, went against the grain of history and was unique to the modern epoch. He made a powerful case for the intervention of politics to ensure that capitalist growth based on private enterprise and the market did not destroy those who were weaker and less able. As was indicated in Chapter 1, the ascendancy of such commodification of human relations and the sanctity of the market were critical in what Mike Davis described as the holocausts of the Victorian era, resulting in between 30 and 60 million deaths in the third world.[7]

Polanyi's critique is philosophically crucial as it reminds us that far from being the reservoir of the ethical, a market society derives its ethics from an impoverished logic of the economy, which is then used to de-politicize society. Postcolonialism, in its narration of the history of capital-ist development as inextricably intertwined with colonialism, racism, and genocide, in its critique of modernization theory and the myth of laissez-faire, and in its contemporary engagement with neoliberal globalization has anchored itself precisely against this reduction of the ethicopolitical realm to that of the economy. And it has done this by consistently histori-cizing the claims of neoliberal globalization and showing them to be em-pirically untrue and historically false. In making this argument, postcolo-nial study, especially in its emphasis on capitalism as a worldwide process that simultaneously produces development and underdevelopment, growth and poverty, affluence and misery, has consistently refuted the ten-dency of neoliberal theories of modernization to confine our focus to the level of competitive nation-states. It is to this critique of the method of ne-oliberalism that we now turn.

THE POVERTY OF METHODOLOGICAL NATIONALISM

For all the talk about the importance of free trade and the need for the re-moval of barriers to the mobility of the factors of production, the economic profits and gains of neoliberal globalization rest to a significant degree on the relative immobility of unskilled and semiskilled labor. The energetic policing of immigration, the violence rampant across every border separat-ing affluent and poor nations, the presence of tens of thousands of illegal aliens in refugee camps all across such frontiers, and repeated news reports of horrendous deaths of those trying to enter the first world in containers or precarious dinghies, or as stowaways on international carriers, index into the tremendous effort involved in arresting the mobility of one of the most important factors of production, namely, labor. In essence, the supply of labor in the world's population does not determine global wage levels, as it would in a genuinely free and globalized free-market economy. This is prevented through the erection of national barriers restricting its mobility. The continued salience of such national boundaries and its role in cor-ralling labor are key elements in the ongoing accumulation of capital in dif-ferent parts of the world today.

Yet, it is also something from which proponents of neoliberal global-ization avert their eyes. Typifying their amnesia is the words of Thomas Friedman. After waxing eloquent about labor conditions in a lingerie fac-tory in Sri Lanka, which produced for Victoria's Secret and Marks and Spencers, Friedman notes in an almost off-handed way, "Wages were about $80 to $100 a month, including breakfast, and there was a waiting list for jobs. In terms of working conditions, this factory was world-class. *Wages aside, I would let my own daughters work there.*"[8] It is precisely that which is set aside, namely, wages, that constitutes the nub of the issue here. Were it not for these very low wages, there would be little reason for Victoria's Secret or Marks and Spencers to relocate production facilities to Sri Lanka. The difference in wages compared to the West, alongside the lowering of what are called transaction costs (due to transportation, tariffs, time re-quired for production in faraway sites) under globalization, allows for the making of profit. In effect, the working or laboring classes of different parts of the world are pitted against one another, and as various poorer countries compete with one another to make themselves more attractive to foreign investment, wages are driven down further, environmental and other reg-ulations weakened further, unions are busted and/or prevented from or-ganizing, and, ironically, tax breaks and incentives are used by the poor to entice the rich to invest in their countries.

One of the key moments in the consolidation of neoliberal hegemony arises from our inability to conceive of ourselves outside a national cartog-raphy of the world. As indicated in Chapter 1, Walt Rostow's notion of eco-nomic development as a race between distinct nation-states arrayed on dis-crete tracks does not capture its interrelated character on a global scale. Yet, the Rostowian metaphor continues to hold us in its thrall. A promis-ing aspect of some movements that have resisted neoliberal globalization in recent years has been their willingness to imagine a way of being that is nonnational and to counter the transnational power and linkages of a world capitalist class with similarly transnational alliances of workers, ac-tivists, and grassroots organizations. In his work on such movements, specifically in the context of the North American Free Trade Agreement (NAFTA) and opposition to the World Trade Organization (WTO), Mark Rupert argues that there is an incipient imagination of a global democracy that offers grounds for optimism. He notes in this regard:

> In an attempt to begin to reconstruct popular common sense, and to (re)politicize the linkage between domestic and global economies, these progressive critics envisioned the world as divided by fundamental

political-economic inequalities. Accordingly, they represented NAFTA as augmenting the power of multinational capital relative to workers, unions, women, and local communities. Beginning to frame an alternative vision of global political economy based on democratic self-determination and transnational linkages among working people and citizens—rather than allowing markets and the criterion of private profit to determine social outcomes—they counterposed the common sense value of "democracy" to liberalism's traditional valorization of private property. Progressive NAFTA opponents thus aimed at a central tension in liberal common sense in order to attempt to develop an alternative political agenda to that of multinational capital.[9]

Like Rupert, I do not wish to overstate the supranational imaginary that energizes the antiglobalization movements. Nevertheless, when labor activists in the United States argue that NAFTA should result in better working conditions, higher wages, the right to unionize, observance of strict environmental laws, and standardization of these regulations in Mexico, they are explicitly fighting against the tendency of globalization to become a nationalist race to the bottom and articulating an alternative vision that raises working conditions in all parts of an interrelated world economy.

Although the connections are by no means direct, postcolonialism has enabled our ability to think critically outside the nation-state. It does so in a variety of ways that have been outlined in previous chapters, but it might be worth recalling some specifics here. At a broad level, as the first two chapters outlined, it has consistently viewed capitalist development as occurring on a world scale and preferred to view the world as divided into imperial/colonial powers and colonies or peripheries, rather than as nation-states. In Robert Young's terms, postcolonialism emphasizes "Tricontinentalism" rather than the ideology of the nation-state. More recent examples of postcolonial theory are also explicit in their critique of methodological nationalism, even if their focus is less on economic development and more on matters of cultural representation. This was outlined in some detail previously (see Chapter 3), so only the salient points will be summarized here.

Edward Said's work urges us to regard culture or literature not as the aesthetic corpus of a settled, territorially demarcated, and already constituted entity called the nation. Rather, Said sees culture as something that emerges from the agonistic and antagonistic encounter between the unceasing movements of ideas, peoples, languages, and literatures in a world marked by imperial conquest and resistance. Historically and today, the idea that culture is the property or unique genius of a nation or a people has been a tremendous catalyst for narrow forms of patriotism and xenophobia. In "worlding" the emergence and history of culture, in other words, by politicizing it, Said is able to help us see ourselves not as eternally divided citizens of distinct entities called nations or civilizations, but rather as constituted together by conjoined histories. By refusing a politics of resistance anchored on a self-assured and ahistorical notion of cultural identity, Said commits himself to the more difficult and longer-term task of affiliation on humanist grounds. In this, his politics is aligned with and enables those who see the need for transnational linkages between resistance movements in different parts of the world.

Said's entire career as a scholar and public intellectual committed to the Palestinian cause demonstrates that such a critique of methodological nationalism is in no way antithetical or hostile to the notion that the different peoples of this planet do inhabit different territories and have rights to their traditional homelands, and that their expropriation through colonialism or imperialism is unjust and ought to be opposed. He is against the reification of such spatially bounded structures of feeling into forms of nationalist chauvinism or jingoism, and emphasizes the ways in which all cultures are constituted through interaction and intermingling.

In Chapter 5, another aspect of the powerful critique leveled by postcolonial studies on forms of methodological nationalism was examined. Following on Said's work on Orientalism, that chapter explained how U.S. hegemony throughout the twentieth century was underwritten by its imperialistic and militarist policies across the developing world. In its contemporary form, the critique of so-called Islamic terrorism mimics earlier notions of containment of communism. Where containment often misrecognized third-world economic nationalism to be communism, today terrorism is used as a blanket term to misrecognize any and all forms of resistance to Western hegemony as religiously inspired, barbaric, and unthinking. Postcolonial theory, with its continuous emphasis on the need to understand economic and sociopolitical-cultural developments as intertwined, draws our eyes to the ways in which the contemporary war on terror is used to further a narrow notion of patriotism and cement existing hierarchies in the world order.

In a related vein, Homi Bhabha problematizes the idea of the nation as a settled community with a mainstream or hegemonic culture or civilization. He instead locates the production of contemporary culture predominantly among the supposed margins of societies—migrants, exiles, minorities, the indigenous, and all those uncomfortable in their skin and place. In doing this, he helps deconstruct the idea of the nation as the embodiment of an essence and representative of the apogee of its values, an idea that has energized much of contemporary and historical interstate violence. Such ideas are regnant in the views of someone such as Samuel Huntington in his theses regarding the clash of civilizations, or the idea that the United States is once and forever a Euro-American society, with its core values emanating from something called a Judeo-Christian heritage. When Bhabha argues that contemporary culture is the work not of the sovereign, self-assured, and plenitudinous citizen but that of the unsure and atypical resident seeking through art to construct and inhabit a community of fellow being, he pluralizes and democratizes the idea of a nation. When he argues that the nation is not so much an essential entity as it is a performative and narrative category, Bhabha's politics converges with those who find that opposition to the WTO, for instance, requires labor unions in one country to fight for the rights of labor to organize in others, or those who argue that working conditions be standardized upward rather than driven to the rock bottom in a quest for profits. By questioning the sanctity and the density of the nation as a category, the project of postcolonial studies is convergent with new movements against neoliberal globalization that cannot escape the imperative of transnational alliances and linkages.

When Spivak, who works on the subaltern tribal woman in a backward state in India, points out that the latter's spiritual practices do not even qualify as "religion" in the eyes of the state, she draws attention to the limits of our ideas and imagination of rights, the nation, democracy, and our practices of inclusiveness and tolerance. Similarly, her work on landless laborers reminds us that in certain contexts membership in the class of workers is itself a privilege in comparison with those whose work is not even recognized as constituting labor. The fight for unionization and working conditions so prominent in struggles against NAFTA or against the WTO has to be enlarged to include the rights of those so destitute that they do not qualify to even enter the category of nation or class. By drawing attention to the subaltern who is outside these historical categories, Spivak's work enlarges the domain of democratic struggle against neoliberal globalization.

The critique of methodological nationalism that informs the work of Spivak can be best illustrated by the following episode. The Minnesota-based computer and telecommunications giant Control Data is often commended within the United States for its relatively progressive attitude toward women in the workplace and for the fact that it offers its employees paid leaves or sabbaticals during which they could enhance their professional and personal lives. In May 1982, the U.S.-based *Ms* magazine praised Control Data for such policies and encouraged other firms to emulate the firm in the way it recruited, promoted, and supported the careers of its women employees. Spivak juxtaposes this Western feminist accolade for Control Data with what the firm was doing at the same time in Seoul, South Korea, in a factory owned by it. In March 1982, 237 women South Korean workers at Control Data's factory went on strike for higher wages. Six of their union leaders (all women) were fired and imprisoned. The prolonged standoff between the women employees and Control Data ended a few months later, in July, with the male Korean employees of the factory assaulting the resisting women and ending the strike. Many of the women sustained severe injuries and two of them had miscarriages.

Spivak uses this episode to urge us to be vigilant about the multinational and gendered character of economic exploitation and the crucial role that a myopic methodological nationalism plays in our inability to critique neoliberal globalization. A nationally self-contained feminism, as reflected by *Ms* magazine in this instance, becomes an unwitting accomplice in global injustice against women in other contexts. Just as was asked earlier (in Chapter 5, for instance) why the trampling of human rights in Britain's colonies or why U.S. support for military dictatorships in third-world countries never seems to sully their status as the world's leading liberal democracies; in assessing the feminist and progressive credentials of a firm like Control Data, one should take into consideration its worldwide operations and not merely its treatment of its U.S. (women) employees. In a related vein, Spivak points out that methodological nationalism should not blind us to the fact that it was South Korean men, in this instance, who were the accomplices who broke the strike of the women and brought it to a violent end. None of the familiar categories mobilized in struggle—nation, gender, ethnicity, class—remains an unproblematic pole for progressive politics, and only a ceaseless vigilance can aid us in the struggle.[10]

In their different ways, postcolonial theorists remind us that politics is often a matter of imagining the beyond. Movements of resistance to neoliberal globalization have to conceive of a politics that is beyond the nation-state, beyond the idea that nature exists only as a corpus for human exploitation and self-aggrandizement, beyond the idea that we are atomized individuals locked in eternal competition with one another for finite resources, and that out of such abasing competition collective benefits will magically accrue to humanity as a whole. By refusing the safe pieties of guaranteed victory, because of the eventual coalescence of class as ideology, or women as gender, or the indigenous as a given and always already liberatory category, or the nation as a cultural essence, postcolonial theorists both complicate and enhance our vision of the political in many ways. Such work may well be critiqued by those who desire secure guarantees that we are on a trajectory of moral and political success. It is the refusal to provide any such guarantees, even as it strives for such an overcoming, that defines the postcolonial standpoint.[11]

ASHIS NANDY: POSTCOLONIALITY AS BEYOND GLOBALIZATION

Although there are a number of points through which one might enter the highly insightful and profound work of the Indian thinker Ashis Nandy, I would like to do so through one of his arguments that strikes me as emblematic. In his 1983 book, *The Intimate Enemy*, Nandy suggests that the enterprise of colonialism may have been, in the end, far more damaging to the psyche and society of the colonizer than the colonized.[12] Colonial rule demanded of the colonizer a degree of unambiguous belief in his racial superiority, masculinity, and the civilizing mission of science and rationality, which could be achieved only through a phenomenal effort of repressing alternative notions of ethics and being. Constantly afraid of not appearing as a superior being in the eyes of the colonized, and mindful of the tremendous violence that underwrote colonialism, the colonizer had to always exaggerate the degree of belief in the colonial project, and could never give the appearance of doubt or ambivalence toward it. In maintaining this facade, colonialism gravitated to one pole of a set of antinomies found in all societies—between masculinity and femininity, hetero- and homosexuality, science and religion, control and freedom, materialism and spirituality, to name a few—and became vituperative in its contempt for the opposite pole. Such contempt reduced the space for alternative ways of being in both the society of the colonizer and the colonized, but, Nandy argues, more so in the former.

To illustrate Nandy's point here about the greater damage inflicted by colonialism on the humanity of the colonizer rather than the colonized, it would be useful to recall George Orwell's essay on "Shooting an Elephant."[13] There Orwell recounts his experience as a young colonial police official posted in a small town in southern Burma tasked with maintaining "law and order" among a people he hardly knew. One day an elephant ran amok and the natives, in their hundreds, came running to Orwell for help. Though both the Burmese and Orwell were fully aware that such episodes were hardly uncommon in elephants, and that it would soon spend its rage and return peacefully to its "mahout," he found that he had no choice but to shoot the elephant. His recollection bears repeating:

> The people expected it of me and I had got to do it; I could feel their two thousand wills pressing me forward, irresistibly. And it was at this moment, as I stood there with the rifle in my hands, that I first grasped the hollow-ness, the futility of the white man's dominion in the East. Here was I, the white man with his gun, standing in front of the unarmed native crowd—seemingly the leading actor of the piece; but in reality I was only an absurd puppet pushed to and fro by the will of those yellow faces behind. I per-ceived in this moment that when the white man turns tyrant it is his own freedom that he destroys. He becomes a sort of hollow, posing dummy, the conventionalized figure of a sahib. For it is the condition of his rule that he shall spend his life in trying to impress the "natives," and so in every crisis he has got to do what the "natives" expect of him. He wears a mask, and his face grows to fit it. I had got to shoot the elephant. I had committed myself to doing it when I sent for the rifle. A sahib has got to act like a sahib; he has got to appear resolute, to know his own mind and do definite things. To come all that way, rifle in hand, with two thousand people marching at my heels, and then to trail feebly away, having done nothing—no, that was im-possible. The crowd would laugh at me. And my whole life, every white man's life in the East, was one long struggle not to be laughed at.[14]

Nandy argues that Orwell's predicament above is emblematic of the en-tire colonial project: it traduces the humanity of the colonizer, throws into relief some of the worst qualities of his society, represses his ethical and hu-manistic instincts, and divides him from his fellow beings. Nandy compli-cates the binary of colonizer and colonized by pointing out colonialism was not a one-sided imposition of the values of a militarily superior soci-ety on a passive recipient. Rather, colonialism was a pact entered into by certain sections of society in both colonizer and colonized, at the expense of others in either society. Especially the aspiring middle classes in the col-onized society ingested the values of the colonizer and used it in ways that created and cemented their supposed superiority over their own country-men. In both societies, colonialism produced an overemphasis on hyper-masculine, patriarchal, heteronormal, and acquisitive values at the expense of the feminine, spiritual, queer, and subaltern classes. Such emphasis was now moreover justified as a civilizing mission and essential for a transition to a desired modernity. The intimacy of the enmity of colonizer and colonized lay precisely in the fact the latter could not easily exorcize the thought-worlds and beliefs of the former. Even as colonial middle classes struggled for decolonization and independence, often their purpose in doing so seemed to be that they could then do to their own countrymen what colonialism had promised to do, civilize, develop, industrialize, scientize, rationalize, and democratize, in other words, modernize them. Nandy points out that the decades of "independent" economic development in places like India have been extraordinarily violent in their treatment of indigenous peoples, tribals, the poor, and the environment in a relentless pursuit of industrialization and national security along the modernist model.

Writing thus in the early 1980s at a time when binary critiques of colonialism reigned supreme, for Nandy to emphasize the co-construction of colonial domination by third-world elites and middle class in collusion with the colonizer was audacious. The nationalist and left-intellectual fashion at the time emphasized the one-way domination of the West and the colonizers and exaggerated the supposed innocence of the third world as supine victims. In talking of colonialism not as a "Western" malady but a social formation that was, in its own way, a pact among elites or the so-called educated classes in both societies, Nandy was not playing the patriot games of third-world nationalism or socialism. Indeed, his critiques of science, mega-development projects, modern medicine, the national security state, and other aspects of modernization indicated that he saw capitalism, state-led socialism, or third-world modernization as all parts of the same problem, the hegemony of a certain industrialized and hyperrational vision of humanity and the planet.[15]

Nandy's debt to the insights of Mohandas Gandhi, especially in his critique of industrial society and modernist civilization, is apparent. Although his writings have ranged across a fascinating series of subjects, for the purpose of this chapter, the focus here will be on his critique of the impossibility of a civilized and ethical life under the conditions of industrial modernity and its latter-day version of neoliberal globalization. Like Polanyi, Nandy argues the commodification of man, and nature sanctions unprecedented levels of inequality and violence besides rendering the poor expendable or redundant. In his critique of neoliberal globalization, Nandy makes an acute distinction between poverty and destitution. He argues that poverty has perhaps always been with us, and was not necessarily as degrading and inhuman in earlier times as it seems today. In traditional or premodern societies, for the most part, to be poor did not disqualify one from membership in the community, nor did it warrant one being treated as less than human. With the disappearance of the commons across the world (through the ascent of private property) and the erosion of the idea of a moral economy (the notion that no fellow humans should ever be so poor and bereft that they cannot feed, clothe, and house themselves to some minimal degree), poverty has been replaced by mass destitution. Nandy observes that destitution is perhaps iatrogenic to the very process of economic development that has reigned supreme over the past few decades. This model, which avers development to be the collectively optimal or beneficial result of the self-interested and utility-maximizing actions of individuals interacting in an overall milieu marked by the commodification of nature and human relationships, cannot address the needs of those deemed deficient in these qualities. In Western developed societies, such poor individuals (usually also racial and ethnic minorities who were once either enslaved or the indigenous) are seen as undeserving welfare parasites. In the non-Western world, they are seen as incapable of imbibing modern values and hence simply redundant on the way to national arrival as a developed society. As Nandy notes:

> Large parts of Africa, Latin America and Asia were poor by contemporary standards of income and consumption before colonial administrators and development planners began to identify them as poor. That does not mean that they had massive destitution or that the quality of life there was abysmally poor. Destitution, or at least large-scale destitution, is a more recent phenomenon. It has been increasing among many traditionally poor communities over the last hundred years, partly as a direct result of urbanization and development. The most glaring instances of destitution are not found in traditional, isolated tribal communities, but among the poor communities that are uprooted and fragmented and move into cities as individuals and nuclear families. It is also found among landless agricultural laborers who for some reason lose their jobs in a situation where agriculture is industrialized and becomes nonprofitable. They are the ones who find themselves unable to cope with the demands of an impersonal market or the culture of a modern political economy. . . . Poverty in societies unfortunately left outside the loving embrace of modernity did not mean starvation or the collapse of life-support systems. For lifestyles in such societies were not fully monetized and the global commons were relatively intact. Even with no income one could hope to survive at a low, but perhaps not entirely meaningless level of subsistence.[16]

In arguments that anticipate those of Mike Davis in *Late Victorian Holocausts*, as was mentioned in Chapter 1, Nandy argues that a certain ideology of modern economic thinking renders nature (in the form of land) into private property, which enables its access to some and the alienation of others from the possibility of life itself. The purpose of life itself becomes the endless accumulation of goods and the pursuit of consumption, irrespective of needs and governed by insatiable wants. Nandy suggests that destitution is incomparably more devastating than mere poverty and is intertwined with modernity to a degree that renders it impossible to address satisfactorily. He notes:

> Destitution usually means zero income in a fully modern, contractual political economy. In an impersonal situation where individualism reigns, in the absence of money income, one can no longer depend or fall back upon the global commons, either because it is exhausted or depleted, or because it has been taken over by the ubiquitous global market. Neither can you live off the forest and the land nor can you depend on the magnanimity of your relatives and neighbors. The neighbors are no longer neighbors; you discover that they have become individualized fellow citizens, who neither expect nor give any quarter to anyone, often not even to their own families.[17]

In effect, Nandy is suggesting here that destitution is not something that is aberrant in modern development but is rather intrinsic to its very logic. This is a fundamental indictment of the very strategies of economic development that are now hegemonic the world over and indicates the dystopia toward which a world energized by neoliberal globalization is headed. Nandy argues that it is the so-called defeated subcultures and civilizations of the world that will manage to retain the values and worldviews necessary for our survival as a planet or a species. Such supposedly defeated peoples and subcultures are not burdened with that Orwellian imposition of being successful, hypermasculine, rational, and in-control at all times. They have retained humility and a distance from hubris that may be more conducive to our survival as a planet and as a species rather than the instrumental rationality of modernization.[18] The latter has produced spectacular technological successes, but these are indissociable from the sort of industrialized violence that characterized the Nazi concentrations camps and the genocide of the Jews in Germany, or the nuclear apocalypse that has threatened the planet for over six decades now. To illustrate Nandy's point about how the supposedly defeated cultures and civilizations may yet be our source of redemption, consider the following: as agriculture is industrialized the world over and the planet's genetic biodiversity is narrowed to a precariously small pool, we may yet have to turn to those last few remaining tribes and cultures outside the modern industrial ambit in the event of a catastrophe. It is precisely their distance from the desired modern that allowed them to retain such biodiversity in the first place. Nandy remains hopeful of averting the dystopia of globalization through the actions of those often dismissed as unrealistic utopians or naive idealists, those who flooded the streets of Seattle in 1999 and who are at the forefront of movements articulating a different world. As he notes:

> Mine is an effort to capture the tacit faith of tens of thousands of social and political activists and environmentalists, who often include our own children. They constitute today a global underworld, a substratum of consciousness that defies at every step the mainstream culture of global economics. Frequently they go about their job foolishly, sometimes hypocritically, but occasionally with a degree of ideological commitment and moral passion, too. However woolly-headed they may look to us, we shall have to learn with that underworld in the new century.[19]

In line with the rest of postcolonial theory, Nandy offers no guarantees in the struggle against neoliberal globalization or the strategies of development that have emerged in its wake. What he has always done so effectively is allow us to imagine a beyond to the world of neoliberal globalization. The ethicopolitical importance of that imagination is best left to him to articulate:

> [N]o system becomes morally acceptable only on the grounds that human creativity or ingenuity has not yet found a better system. Nor does any system acquire an intrinsic moral stature or the right to snuff out alternative human possibilities by virtue of the fact that earlier systems were worse.[20]

CONCLUSION

In her critique of the relevance of postcolonial theory to our times, Ella Shohat notes the absence of the names and ideas of avowedly postcolonial theorists in the movement against the war in Iraq.[21] This book has argued that if one were to widen the ambit of analysis beyond such a narrow accounting of names and slogans, one finds that the ideas and insights of postcolonialism constitute an inseparable part of the movements against war and neoliberal globalization, and more generally, against the commodification of humans and nature that seems intrinsic to modernity. Throughout, the ways in which postcolonial theory does this have been indicated: by its relentless focus on understanding economic development and the production of wealth and inequality as worldwide, rather than nation-state specific, processes; through its continuous expansion of who gets to be counted within the provenance of "human"; through its exposure of the Orientalism that underlies the contemporary war on "terror"; in its critique of the very idea of nation-states as territorial enclosures of essences; and through its realization that colonialism is not just political imposition and economic exploitation but a form of violent planetary consciousness that afflicts us all collectively.

These ideas and beliefs of postcolonialism are consequential and important in the struggle against the impoverishing ideational and material effects of neoliberal globalization, and its epistemic progenitor in modernization. As with every intellectual movement in our time, postcolonialism too is enabled by the material conditions of the self-same neoliberal world it seeks to critique and change. Postcolonialism has argued that its ideas come neither with a guarantee of political success nor intellectual certitude. If the former promotes an unrelenting insistence on the need for informed participation in the politics of our times, the latter instills a sense of humility about the open-ended nature of the very future we seek to attain.

This seemingly contradictory combination of struggling for a better tomorrow without predetermining its content captures the essence of the postcolonial standpoint.[22] It is perhaps best illustrated by an episode involving the thinker who epitomizes postcolonial thought, Edward Said, and serves as an appropriate way to end this book. At a conference on the politics of the Middle East, Said was lavishly complimented by a commentator for his steadfast commitment to the cause of the Palestinian nation and for his patriotism. Said gently deflected the praise by noting that "he was working for the Palestinian state to establish itself so that he could then become its critic."[23] As the tethered shadow to globalization in its multiple forms over the past few centuries, the vocation of postcolonialism remains that of an endless and yet ethical critique operating with neither intellectual guarantee nor political piety.

NOTES

INTRODUCTION:
GLOBALIZATION AND POSTCOLONIALISM

1. See Denis Kux, *India and the United States: Estranged Democracies, 1941–1991* (Washington, DC: National Defense University Press, 1993), 337.

2. Although there are a number of works that have theorized about time–space compression, readers may wish to consult two books in particular that are useful in this regard. Marshall Berman's *All that Is Solid Melts into Air: The Experience of Modernity* (New York: Simon and Schuster, 1982) charts time–space compression as reflected in economic, literary, spatial, cultural, and other dimensions in the late nineteenth and early twentieth centuries through a persuasive Marxist lens, while David Harvey's *The Condition of Post-Modernity: An Enquiry into the Origins of Cultural Change* (Oxford: Blackwell, 1989) takes the story forward into the second half of the twentieth century.

3. For a similar distinction between globalization and globalism, see especially Manfred Steger, *Globalism: The New Market Ideology* (Lanham, MD: Rowman & Littlefield, 2001).

CHAPTER 1:
INTELLECTUAL AND HISTORICAL BACKGROUND

1. Such a division of the world into first, second, and third worlds emerged in the 1950s and has remained current in colloquial usage to this day. The second world referred to the communist nations—the former Soviet Union, the Eastern European nations under the Soviet umbrella, China, Vietnam, Cuba, Angola, and a few others. With the end of the communist experiment in the Soviet Union and most of its erstwhile satellites, and with China's unique form of capitalism under

the leadership of Communist Party elite, there is no second world anymore in the sense of an ideological communist alternative to capitalism. The term third world, referring to the countries of Asia, Africa, and Latin America, many of which had experienced some form of direct or indirect colonialism or Western domination, remains very current, even as it recognizes that a handful of countries in that zone have experienced rates of economic growth in recent decades that have elevated them to an intermediate position between third and first worlds. These countries, often referred to as the newly industrialized countries (NICs), are South Korea, Taiwan, Hong Kong, and Singapore.

2. See Anup Shah, "Causes of Poverty: Facts and Stats," 2006. <http://www .globalissues.org/TradeRelated/Facts.asp> (accessed 22 May 2008).

3. As we will see at later points, the idea that we live in a grossly unequal and diverging world is not necessarily shared by everyone. A significant number of economists and development theorists argue that the second half of the twentieth century, especially the period from about 1945 to 1970, witnessed unprecedented growth rates across the world. For the first time in human history, despite populations increasing at unheard of rates, the global food supply outpaced it, and per capita GDP growth rates were at a historical high across the third world. During these same decades, such economists argue, it is a fact that the Western, developed countries grew even faster than the third world—and hence the gap between them widened. However, such rising inequality should not allow one to dismiss the fact the substantial and sustained growth was achieved by many third-world countries in the postwar period. Ultimately, whether a glass is half-full or half-empty is a matter of interpretation—and there is no "higher authority" who can resolve such a difference of views with finality.

4. See L. S. Stavrianos, *Global Rift: The Third World Comes of Age* (New York: William Morrow, 1981), 38.

5. A list of works comprising the modernization school would be inordinately long. For a comprehensive summary and analysis of the school, see Alvin Y. So, *Social Change and Development: Modernization, Dependency and World-Systems Analysis* (London: Sage Publications, 1990).

6. Although the term "the invisible hand of the market" was used three times by Smith in his writings, whether this made him an uncritical proponent of laissez-faire (a word he never once used) or free trade remains a matter of controversy. Certainly as someone who was a philosopher, a pioneer in the field of political economy, and who had written a prior work on the theory of moral sentiments, Smith was an unlikely champion of the distinctness of the economic realm and its insulation from that of the political. His works are both immersed in history and continuously working through the interconnections between the economic and political realms. It is important to note that his comments about the invisible hand of the market and the superiority of freer trade come in the specific context of debates with the mercantilists. These latter were economists who believed that it was in the self-interest of each nation to maximize the amount of gold within its borders, and one way of

doing so was to export as much as possible while keeping imports from other nations minimal. This would maximize the amount of wealth retained within national borders. To the mercantilists, international trade was a zero-sum game; that is, like in a poker game the winnings of some had to come at the cost of the losses of others. In order to minimize imports and maximize exports a country would have to, in essence, give up on the principle of specialization because the only way to minimize imports is to produce within one's own country all of the goods that are needed. Moreover, if every country tried to operate on mercantilist principles, international trade would soon collapse, as it is logically impossible for everyone to be an exporter while unwilling to be an importer. Smith, like many in his time, was vehemently critical of the flawed economic theory of the mercantilists. The latter were, in any case, for the glory of the nation and its sovereign; unlike Smith who was among the first moral philosophers to argue that economic growth should result in the betterment of the people at large. It is in the context of debates with mercantilists that Smith's theory of the invisible hand of the market and the desirability of relatively free trade is made. To elevate this preference to a nostrum that is true for all times, places, and countries is something that emerged later, and not necessarily something that Smith would have agreed with. For a recent engagement with these issues, see James Buchan, *The Authentic Adam Smith: His Life and Ideas* (New York: W. W. Norton, 2006). For an interesting "politicization" of Smith in this regard and on the implications of conservative readings of his texts for international political economy, see Naeem Inayatullah and David L. Blaney, *International Relations and the Problem of Difference* (New York: Routledge, 2004).

7. As Smith notes, "What is prudence in the conduct of every private family can scarce be folly in that of a great kingdom. If a foreign country can supply us with a commodity cheaper than we can ourselves make it, better buy it of them with some part of the produce of our own industry employed in a way in which we have some advantage." Adam Smith, *Wealth of Nations*, ed. K. Sutherland (Oxford: Oxford University Press, 1993), 292–93. The kernel of the theory of comparative advantage is clearly present here, although David Ricardo would provide formal proof of the veracity of this notion a few decades after Smith. These ideas constitute the core of liberal theories of globalization to the present day and especially its emphasis on free trade as an engine for the development of all parts of the world. It is important to understand that they are not necessarily wrong, but rather, to elevate the formal proof of these dicta to a truth that holds irrespective of time and space is folly. As we see later in this chapter, the economic histories of countries like the United States, Germany, Japan, the NICs of the late twentieth century (South Korea and Taiwan, for example) and now China show, periods in which societies protect certain key industries or sectors of the economy from foreign competition are neither unusual nor economically counterproductive. On the contrary, such periods of consolidation and maturing are critical to both the retention of economic and political sovereignty, as well as the ability to compete effectively in the global economy at a later time.

8. Walt W. Rostow, *The Stages of Economic Growth: A Non-Communist Manifesto* (New York: Cambridge University Press, 1960).

9. See So, *Social Change and Development* for a comprehensive list and comparison of various works within the underdevelopment approach. So, following many others, sees the underdevelopment approach as Marxian in its inspiration and comprising mainly of the dependency and world-systems approaches to the study of world economic development.

10. See the reissue of Alexander Hamilton's influential *Report on the Subject of Manufactures* (original 1791; New York: Cosimo Classics, 2007).

11. See Friedrich List, *The National System of Political Economy* (original 1841; New York: A. M. Kelley, 1966).

12. The literature examining various aspects of colonial underdevelopment in India is vast. Those interested in exploring it further would do well to begin with the following texts: Bipan Chandra, *The Rise and Growth of Economic Nationalism in India* (New Delhi: Peoples Publishing House, 1966); Sumit Sarkar, *Modern India: 1885–1947* (New Delhi: Macmillan, 1983); and Dharma Kumar, ed., *The Cambridge Economic History of India: 1757–1970*, Vol. II, (Cambridge,UK: Cambridge University Press, 1982).

13. See Mike Davis, *Late Victorian Holocausts: El Niño Famines and the Making of the Third World* (London: Verso, 2002).

14. Davis, *Late Victorian Holocausts*, 9–11.

15. This broad-brush summarization obviously does not allow one to nuance the picture greatly. During the twentieth century, some colonies like India did experience a certain degree of growth in domestically owned manufacturing industries, notably textiles, steel, chemicals, locomotives, paper, and others. These industries were often established by native industrialists in the teeth of opposition by the colonial regime, despite its imposed free-trade policies. Insistence on such free trade, and the colonial state's refusal to erect tariffs to protect the infant industries of the natives, made nationalists out of many industrialists and fed the growing movement for independence in such countries. At the same time, international wars and colonial subcontracting to other parts of empire made such native industrialists often dependent on the colonial state for their prosperity. For more on this, see Amiya Kumar Bagchi, *Private Investment in India: 1900–1939* (Cambridge, UK: Cambridge University Press, 1972).

16. A casual visitor to cities such as London, Amsterdam, or Madrid cannot help but be staggered by the sheer architectural magnificence and beauty of these urban spaces. Even a superficial investigation would lead one to realize the overwhelming role played by colonial conquest, plunder, loot, and pillage in the construction of such wonderful monuments, palaces, churches and cathedrals, abbeys, museums, parks, plazas, mansions, and estates. When one considers the fact that international tourism is the top contributor of foreign exchange to the national exchequers of these countries, it becomes obvious that the colonial legacy is a gift that keeps on giving right up to the present time. The irony of Indian tourists pay-

ing through their noses to see the Crown jewels (a goodly chunk of which were looted from colonial India) housed in the Tower of London is unfortunately probably lost on the average visitor.

17. Karl Marx, *Capital*, Vol. I, (1867). Quoted from Andre Gunder Frank, *World Accumulation: 1492–1789* (New York: Monthly Review Press, 1978), 214. Emphases mine.

18. Adam Smith, *An Inquiry into the Nature and Causes of the Wealth of Nations* (1776), quoted in Andre Gunder Frank, *World Accumulation: 1492–1789* (New York: Monthly Review Press, 1978), 213–14. Emphases mine.

19. Smith, *Wealth of Nations* (1993), 21.

20. See Karl Marx and Friedrich Engels, "Manifesto of the Communist Party" (1848) www.anu.edu.au/polsci/marx/classics/manifesto.html (accessed 22 May 2008). The causal forces for the transition from feudalism to capitalism in late medieval Europe, the role of long-distance trade, the emerging class of burghers in the cities and towns and the yeoman farmers in the countryside, the rise of urban centers, and class struggles within European society in this transition are matters of intense debate among historians. For an excellent summarization of this debate see Rodney Hilton, ed., *The Transition from Feudalism to Capitalism in Europe* (London: Verso, 1976). Although the details of the debate are not germane to us, it hinged on differences between those who emphasized the importance of long-distance trade and the rising power of merchants in the urban centers in the rise of capitalism versus those who emphasized the changing class structure of rural society in England, France, Holland, and the northwest tier of Europe generally as the prime mover in the emergence of capitalism. One might term this a debate between trade-centric explanations and class-centric explanations, or Smithian versus Marxian explanations. The salience of this debate for contemporary discussions of globalization and economic development in poorer countries is immense and outlined at length below.

21. The best illustration of the crucial role that political sovereignty, capitalism, and colonialism played in development or underdevelopment can be found in the contrasting histories of India and Japan. The latter's geographical remoteness and lack of mineral resources during the early modern period kept it off the radar of colonizing Western nations. Japan retained her political and economic sovereignty through the Meiji Restoration of the late 1860s, while India's conquest by Britain was being completed after the Revolt of 1857. This enabled Japan to join the ranks of the developed nations in the twentieth century, and even the devastation of World War II could not stop her from doing so. In contrast, India's political fragmentation in the 1700s, alongside her riches, resulted in the loss of her economic and political sovereignty, namely, colonialism and underdevelopment.

22. Immanuel Wallerstein, the scholar who pioneered the world-systems approach to understanding history, thus describes the Soviet and Chinese revolutions of 1917 and 1949 not so much as communism but as instances of a mercantilist semiwithdrawal from the world capitalist economy to reorganize production under

strong states. Realizing that they were economically in no position to compete under liberal trading regimes with the West, these societies withdrew (temporarily, as Wallerstein presciently argued) until they established the self-sufficient infrastructure to later compete on an equal footing in the world capitalist system. See Immanuel Wallerstein, *Geopolitics and Geoculture: Essays on the Changing World System* (New York: Cambridge University Press, 1991).

23. Although there are a number of works that demonstrate the emergence of the "social sciences"—economics, sociology, anthropology, political science—in the course of the nineteenth century, the connections between the emergence of these "disciplines" and issues of modernity are made most clearly in Timothy Mitchell, "Fixing the Economy," *Cultural Studies* 12, no. 1 (Jan. 1998): 82–101; Mitchell, "The Limits of the State," *American Political Science Review* 85, no.1 (March 1991): 77–96; and Immanuel Wallerstein, *Unthinking Social Science: The Limits of Nineteenth Century Paradigms* (Cambridge, UK: Polity Press, 1991). Nearly 150 years after its publication, the best work on the separation of the political and the civil and of how under liberal electoral democracy issues divisive issues such as property, wealth, assets, and so forth are deemed no longer politically relevant because of equality under the law and equality of the vote remains Karl Marx's brilliant essay "On the Jewish Question," in *Karl Marx: Early Writings*, trans. Rodney Livingstone and Gregor Benton (New York: Vintage, 1975), 211–42.

24. Inter alia, such a belief in the core, unchanging, and ahistorical attributes of social entities might be described as essentialism. It attributes essential or unchanging characteristics to nationalities, races, genders, or other groupings of people and tries to derive the content of their actions from such characteristics. Thus, believing that all Muslims are inherently violent (because they are enjoined to do so by the Qur'an), or that all women are instinctively more caring about the environment (because they have capacity to bear children), would be examples of essentialist thinking.

25. Writing out of a German philosophical tradition of dialectics, Marx argued that this contradiction—of a mode of production that was simultaneously the most dynamic in every way, and yet harbored the seeds of its own undoing—made capitalism the penultimate stage in the evolution of mankind on this planet. Here, Marx, the utopian heir of the Enlightenment, comes shining through. He argued that the in-built contradictions of capitalism would both advance mankind to an unprecedented apogee in terms of productivity, technology, the democratic impulse, individual liberties, and freedoms, but would also sharpen class contradictions by the creation of an ever-shrinking number of capitalist producers alongside a global proletariat. The awakening to class consciousness and to the realities of their own exploitation by this global class would herald the new, and final, social revolution, namely communism.

CHAPTER 2: INDEPENDENCE OR NEOCOLONIALISM?

1. Although there are a number of works in the field of international political economy that have charted the decline of Britain as the world's leading economic power at the turn of the twentieth century and the consequences of that decline in terms of interimperial rivalries and world wars, one of the clearest expositions may be found in John Agnew and Stuart Corbridge, *Mastering Space: Hegemony, Territory and International Political Economy* (New York: Routledge, 1995), 13–45.

2. See Mark Rupert, *Producing Hegemony* (Cambridge: Cambridge University Press, 1995); David Harvey, *The Condition of Post-Modernity* (London: Blackwell, 1989); and John Agnew and Stuart Corbridge, *Mastering Space* (New York: Routledge, 1995).

3. On the strength of communist and socialist parties across Europe immediately after World War II, see John Nagle, *System and Succession: The Social Bases of Political Elite Recruitment* (Austin: University of Texas Press, 1977).

4. See Walden Bello et al., "Notes on the Ascendancy and Regulation of Speculative Capital," in *Global Finance: New Thinking On Regulating Speculative Capital Markets*, eds. Walden Bello et al. (London: Zed Books, 2000), 2.

5. In the years 1945 to 1973, a conservative list of countries that the United States intervened in would be the following: Cambodia, Chile, Cuba, Dominican Republic, El Salvador, Ghana, Greece, Guatemala, Iran, Iraq, Korea, Laos, Lebanon, Mali, Panama, Philippines, Turkey, Vietnam, and Zaire. In a number of other societies, the United States provided money and assistance to individuals and political parties that were hostile to communist ideology and in favor of free enterprise. Among many works that detail the history of such American interventions, see Stephen Kinzer, *Overthrow: America's Century of Regime Change from Hawaii to Iraq* (New York: Times Books, 2006). Another work that insightfully teases out the connections between capitalist economic development and the national security "imperatives" of the developed countries is Mark R. Duffield, *Development, Security and Unending War: Governing the World of Peoples* (Cambridge, UK: Polity Press, 2007).

6. Unsurprisingly, there was a convergence between a U.S. foreign policy of "containment" of global communism and a domestic policy that alternately attacked communists (as in the McCarthyist Red Scare of the early 1950s) and pacified labor through its inclusion in the social structure of accumulation that emerged after the war. The quid pro quo between American capital and labor union leaders at this time essentially amounted to labor giving up its socialist and revolutionary impulse in exchange for security of jobs, wages linked to rising productivity, and a partnership with capital, instead of an adversarial relationship. This pact, which lasted from the end of the war until the early 1970s, brought industrial peace as well as rising real wages, security, and social inclusion for the U.S. working

class. However, its longer-term costs were at least as severe: it calcified a conservative union leadership and diminished any shop-floor activism or intellectual autonomy; labor became largely hostile to emerging issues such as gender and racial equality; it lagged behind on progressive issues such as the rights of gays and migrants; and it equated patriotism with uncritical support for U.S. foreign policy. When American capital turned its back on labor from the late 1970s onward, the latter was unable to articulate a political, moral, intellectual, and historical critique, and was bereft of any allies worth the name.

7. Although the literature on the economics of developing societies is vast, one of the best texts on the overall patterns, debates, statistics, and various strategies attempted is Michael Todaro, *Economic Development in the Third World*, 4th ed. (New York: Longman, 1989).

8. For example, India's efforts at self-reliant development were marked by a large state sector, detailed economic planning, import substitution, and export pessimism, all within high protectionist walls. Although this elicited critiques from a neoclassical perspective, both within the nation and internationally, it also commanded an impressive degree of support. For a work that illustrates the ecumenical and tolerant milieu in which such self-reliant third-world strategies of development were attempted, in contrast to the market fundamentalism of today, see Dharma Kumar and Dilip Mookherjee, eds., *D. School: Reflections on the Delhi School of Economics* (New Delhi: Oxford University Press, 1995). Also see Sankaran Krishna, "Transition in the Era of US Hegemony: Indian Economic Development and World-Systems Analysis," in *Pacific-Asia and the Future of the World-System*, ed. Ravi Arvind Palat (Westport, CT: Greenwood, 1992), 119–31.

9. See Lloyd G. Reynolds, "Spread of Economic Growth to the Third World," *Journal of Economic Literature* 21 (Sept. 1983): 961.

10. On the other hand, the fact that growth in food output and increases in per capita GDP growth rates have occurred, despite the phenomenal increase in third-world population, is seen as a cause for celebration. Exemplifying this, Richard Cooper, professor of economics at Harvard, observes that "the world economy [has] performed outstandingly well during the second half of the 20th century. Worldwide growth in per capita income exceeded two percent a year (historically unprecedented), many poor countries became rich, infant mortality declined, diets improved, longevity increased, diseases were contained if not vanquished. Poverty on the World Bank definition of $1 a day (in 1985$) declined dramatically, and the number of persons in poverty was halved despite a more than doubling of the world population . . . on average sub-Saharan Africa fared much less well than other regions. Declines in national per capita income were rare, and concentrated in Africa. . . . On the whole, it was a good half century for mankind. The substantial poverty and misery that still exists should not lead to neglect or even denial of these achievements." See Richard N. Cooper, "A Half Century of Development," Paper No. 04-03, Weatherhead Center for International Affairs, Harvard University, Cambridge, MA, May 2004. <http://www.cid.harvard.edu/cidwp/pdf/118.pdf> (accessed 22 May 2008).

11. The GDP per capita growth rates mentioned here are taken from Todaro, *Economic Development in the Third World*, 48–49. His book has no data for Taiwan; the information for the latter is found in Thomas B. Gold, *State and Society in the Taiwan Miracle* (Armonk, NY: M. E. Sharpe, 1986), 6.

12. The debate over market versus state-led explanations for the success of South Korea and other NIC economies such as Hong Kong, Singapore, and Taiwan has been energetic over the years. Useful works include Robert Wade, *Governing the Market: Economic Theory and the Role of Government in East Asian Industrialization* (Princeton, NJ: Princeton University Press, 2003); Alice Amsden, *Asia's Next Giant: South Korea and Late Industrialization* (New York: Oxford University Press, 1989); Meredith Woo-Cumings, *Race to the Swift: State and Finance in Korean Industrialization* (New York: Columbia University Press, 1991); Frederic Deyo, *The Political Economy of the New Asian Industrialism* (Ithaca, NY: Cornell University Press, 1987); Stephen Haggard, *Pathways from the Periphery: The Politics of Growth in the Newly Industrializing Countries* (Ithaca, NY: Cornell University Press, 1990); and Leroy Jones and Il Sakong, *Government, Business, and Entrepreneurship in Economic Development: The Korean Case* (Cambridge, MA: Harvard University Press, 1980). Although some neoclassical economists took the view that NIC success was proof of the wisdom of the World Bank's emphasis on export promotion, liberalization of trade and investment, and a retreat of the state (see for example Bela Balassa, *The Newly Industrializing Countries in the World Economy* [New York: Pergamon, 1981]; and Colin I. Bradford Jr. and William H. Branson, eds., *Trade and Structural Change in Pacific Asia* [Chicago: University of Chicago Press, 1987]), the consensus drew back to underlining the extraordinarily important role of "political factors," such as the state, bureaucracy, the nature of state-dominant class relationships, the repression of trade unions, and the significant role of international geopolitical factors in the rise of the East Asian NICs in the 1960s to 1980s.

13. "Land reform, done properly, peacefully, and legally, ensuring that workers get not only land but access to credit, and the extension services that teach them about new seeds and planting techniques, could provide an enormous boost to output. But land reform represents a fundamental change in the structure of society, one that those in the elite that populates the finance ministries, those with whom the international financial institutions interact, do not necessarily like. If these institutions were really concerned about growth and poverty alleviation, they would have paid considerable attention to the issue: land reform preceded several of the most successful instances of development, such as those in Korea and Taiwan." This quote summarizing the critical role of land reforms in Korean and Taiwanese success comes from Joseph Stiglitz, a Nobel laureate in economics who served on President Bill Clinton's Council of Economic Advisers, and was chief economist and senior vice president of the World Bank from 1997 to 2000. He is far removed from a believer in a peasant revolution and yet underlines the critical importance of land reform as a precursor to equitable growth. See Joseph Stiglitz, *Globalization and Its Discontents* (New York: W. W. Norton, 2002), 81.

14. The crucial work on the role played by Japanese ministries and bureaucrats in collaboration with private capital in the rise of the postwar economy there remains Chalmers Johnson, *MITI and the Japanese Miracle* (Stanford, CA: Stanford University Press, 1981).

15. See Sankaran Krishna, "India: Globalization and Information Technology," *South Asian Journal* (April–June 2005): 146–58.

16. It is important to point out that Cooper's data are divided regionally rather than in terms of first, second, and third worlds. This means that his growth rates for Asia include Japan, which tends to present a more favorable picture than would be the case without it. For instance, for the period 1940–80, Indian per capita growth rates were on the order of about 1.3 percent per annum, which weighs down all of Asia quite considerably. Similarly, the impact of the late 1990s' East Asian economic crisis, which led to negative growth in Korea, Malaysia, Indonesia, and Thailand for some years, is swamped by the double-digit growth averaged by China during that same time and therefore does not register in Cooper's data. Since his table is used here to primarily indicate the sharp downturn in the global economy since the early 1970s and to mark the reversals in the case of Africa, Latin America, and the former communist bloc after 1980, this aspect of his data is less of a problem than it might have been otherwise.

17. Susan George, "A Short History of Neoliberalism: Twenty Years of Elite Economics and Emerging Opportunities for Structural Change," in *Global Finance*, eds. Bello et al., 33. For data on the phenomenal increase in the concentration of wealth in the United States since Reagan, see especially Kevin Phillips, *The Politics of Rich and Poor: Wealth and the American Electorate in the Reagan Aftermath* (New York: Random House, 1990), and his more recent *Wealth and Democracy: A Political History of the American Rich* (New York: Broadway Books, 2002). David Harvey's *A Brief History of Neoliberalism* (New York: Oxford University Press, 2005) offers a comprehensive statistical picture of the concentration of wealth all across the Western developed countries in the wake of neoliberalism.

18. "Development economics" can be defined as a branch within the discipline of economics that focuses mainly on third-world or developing societies. As its very name suggests, the field holds that there is something special or distinctive about the history and contemporary attributes of such societies that is inadequately addressed by the more general discipline and warrants special attention. The extraordinary prominence of this field in the years 1945–80 contrasts with its virtual disappearance in the decades that follow. Its demise is another sign of the hegemonic sway of the neoliberal globalizing worldview: there is only way to develop and that is through the liberalization and fuller participation in world trade and capital movements.

19. The changing nature of capital inflows to Latin America in the post–World War II period is a good illustration of the growing power of finance capital in the contemporary world. Although loans from institutions like the IMF and World

Bank, and Official Development Assistance constituted close to 60 percent of average annual foreign resource inflows into Latin America in the period 1961–65, this had dropped to merely 12 percent by the late 1970s. Moving in precisely the opposite direction, foreign bank loans, private investment capital, and bonds rose from about 7 percent of the average annual resource inflow in the early 1960s to as much as 65 percent by the late 1970s. For the world as a whole, private financial flows to the developing nations went from $44 billion in 1990 to $244 billion in 1996, about half of this colossal amount was in forms of speculative capital that was likely to desert the countries instantaneously at the whim of finance managers located in the first world. See Robin Broad and John Cavanagh, "The Death of the Washington Consensus?" in *Global Finance*, eds. Bello et al., 88.

20. See Cheryl Payer, *Lent and Lost: Foreign Credit and Third World Development* (London: Zed, 1991).

21. The nature of such speculative financial investments and the ways in which they make their profits are often not well explained in the literature. In one of the more lucid passages, the following is offered: "Diminishing, if not vanishing, returns to key industries have led to capital being shifted from the real economy to squeezing 'value' out of the financial sector. The result is essentially a game of global arbitrage, where capital moves from one financial market to another seeking to turn a profit from the exploitation of the imperfections of globalized markets. This is done via arbitrage between interest-rate differentials, targeting gaps between nominal currency values and 'real' currency values, or short-selling in stocks, that is, borrowing shares to artificially inflate share values and then selling. Not surprisingly, volatility, being central to global finance, has become the driving force of the global capitalist system as a whole." See Bello et al., "The Ascendancy and Regulation of Speculative Capital," 6.

22. In the early 1990s, the supply-driven capital of Western banks and investment funds turned to East Asia as the new emerging market darlings of the world. For example, net portfolio investments reached $24 billion in the years 1994–97 in Thailand, and an additional $50 billion entered the country as loans to Thai businesses and banks. This surge of investment into Thailand led governments in Malaysia, Indonesia, Korea, and the Philippines to follow suit in terms of liberalizing their capital markets, and private investment in these countries collectively went from $37.9 billion in 1994 to close to $100 billion by 1996. See Bello et al., "The Ascendancy and Regulation of Speculative Capital," 13–14. It is worth pondering how a group of countries that collectively attracted investments of this magnitude in the years 1994–97 could become, a few months later, societies that were always crony capitalist, lacking in stable institutions and in need of serious restructuring through the advice of the IMF.

23. To take just one example of the extent to which such debt crises and financial bubbles are driven by an excess of capital in Western countries seeking super profits and their lack of any relation to economic fundamentals, consider the

following: in the early 1990s, in just four years, Mexico was the recipient of $91 billion in foreign capital inflows, constituting as much as one-fifth of all capital flows to the third world. Yet, during these same four years, the Mexican GDP was actually contracting, half the people were mired in poverty, and unemployment levels were as high as 40 percent. For all the talk of the rational signals sent out by the market, these figures indicate that capitalism in the era of global financial flows may be better explained or understood by mob psychology than by rational choice economics.

24. Thomas L. Friedman, *The Lexus and the Olive Tree: Understanding Globalization* (New York, Anchor Books, 2000).

25. Jeffrey Winters, "The Financial Crisis in Southeast Asia," paper delivered at the Conference on the Asian Crisis, Murdoch University, Fremantle, Western Australia, August 1998: quoted in Bello et al., "The Ascendancy and Regulation of Speculative Capital," 16.

26. Anna Lowenhaupt Tsing, *Friction: An Ethnography of Global Connection* (Princeton, NJ: 2005), 44–45.

27. Share of people living on less than $1 (PPP US$) a day (percent) (original data from World Bank, reproduced in the Human Development Report 2005, "International Cooperation at a Crossroads: Aid, Trade and Security in an Unequal World," <http://hdr.undp.org/en/media/hdr05_complete.pdf>, 34 (accessed 22 May 2008).

28. Robert Wade has consistently made the argument that in a number of countries, especially China and India, the rise in growth rates preceded the liberalization of their economies to international trade and investment, and hence the argument that globalization reduces poverty is difficult to establish. Wade argues that we live in what he calls a 1:3:2 world today: there are 1 billion people living in affluent developed nations which have low-to-moderate economic growth rates; 3 billion in developing nations (comprised mainly of China and India) with growth rates that exceed that of the developed nations; and another 2 billion in slow or negative growth regions (mainly Africa). The key issue for Wade is how and when the slow-growth nations and their 2 billion will make common cause with the faster-growing 3 billion to remake the world economic order in their collective self interest. See Robert Wade, "Questions of Fairness," *Foreign Affairs* (September–October 2006).

29. Margaret Thatcher, quoted in the Human Development Report 2005, 51.

30. Margaret Thatcher, quoted in Susan George, "A Short History of Neoliberalism," 30.

31. Nelson Mandela, quoted in Patrick Bond, *Against Global Apartheid: South Africa Meets the World Bank, the IMF and International Finance* (London: Macmillan, 2003), 119.

32. Perry Anderson, quoted in Manfred Steger, *Globalism: The New Market Ideology* (Lanham, MD: Rowman & Littlefield, 2002), 139.

CHAPTER 3: GENEALOGIES OF THE POSTCOLONIAL

1. Michel Foucault, "Nietzsche, Genealogy, History," in *Language, Counter-Memory, Practice: Selected Essays and Interviews by Michel Foucault*, ed. Donald Bouchard (Ithaca, NY: Cornell University Press, 1977), 148, 151–52.

2. Hamza Alavi, "The State in Post-Colonial Societies: Pakistan and Bangladesh," *New Left Review* 74 (July–Aug. 1972): 59–81.

3. Alavi's discussion of state autonomy as a result of the standoff between the three dominant propertied classes echoes Marx's famous formulation of the Bonapartist state in postrevolutionary France in his *Eighteenth Brumaire of Louis Napoleon*, see Karl Marx and Frederick Engels, *Selected Works* (New York: International Publishers, 1986), 97–180. His essay entered an ongoing and energetic debate among Marxists, most notably Ralph Miliband and Nicos Poulantzas, at the time about the degree to which modern capitalist states were autonomous from or acting at the behest of the dominant class(es) of their societies. For more on the latter debate that took place largely in the pages of the *New Left Review*, see Clyde W. Barrow, "The Miliband-Poulantzas Debate: An Intellectual History," in *Paradigm Lost: State Theory Reconsidered*, eds. Stanley Aronowitz and Peter Bratsis (Minneapolis: University of Minnesota Press, 2002), 3–52.

4. Alavi's thesis on the "overdeveloped" character of the postcolonial state and its "relative autonomy" from dominant propertied classes in such nations has been taken up by a wide range of authors and is one of the most influential formulations made in the context of any analyses of third-world societies, or peripheral societies, as he termed them. To mention only a few, it became the basis of works that analyzed the collapse of African democracies into military rule after decolonization, such as that of John Saul (*The State and Revolution in Eastern Africa: Essays* [New York: Monthly Review Press, 1979]) and Issa Shivji (*Class Struggles in Tanzania* [New York: Monthly Review Press, 1976]); it forms the core argument of one of the most influential books on India's postindependence period, namely, Pranab Bardhan's *The Political Economy of Development in India* (New York: Blackwell, 1984) as well as that of Pakistan as seen in Ayesha Jalal's *The State of Martial Rule: The Origins of Pakistan's Political Economy of Defense* (New York: Cambridge University Press, 1990).

5. Robert Young, *Postcolonialism: An Historical Introduction* (Oxford, UK: Blackwell, 2001).

6. Young's truly global view of the inspirational sources of postcolonial thought even extends to conservative critics of British imperialism such as Edmund Burke or Jeremy Bentham in the eighteenth and early nineteenth centuries. Such thinkers were less interested in the welfare of South Asians or Africans or Malays and more concerned about the possibly of impoverishing effects of British colonialism on its own economy and its threat to the emerging bourgeois liberties and freedoms therein. And yet, especially in someone such as Burke, one can clearly discern a

critique of the ethnocentric assumptions that underlie colonial and imperial conquest, the idea that what is good for one's own society must necessarily be good for others. Burke's critique of English imperialism contained within it the idea that one can never really know another society, and respecting its alterity (or otherness) is an important human value. For an elaboration of Burke's thought in this regard, and for the complex links between conservative thinking in this era and the enterprise of empire, see Uday Singh Mehta, *Liberalism and Empire* (Chicago: University of Chicago Press, 1999).

7. See, for example, Sudipta Kaviraj, "Marxism and the Darkness of History," in *Emancipations: Modern and Postmodern*, ed. Jan Nederveen Pieterse (London: Sage, 1992), 54–83.

8. Bill Ashcroft, Gareth Griffiths, and Helen Tiffin, *The Empire Writes Back: Theory and Practice in Post-Colonial Literature* (New York: Routledge, 1989).

9. As the authors note, "People in the discipline of 'English' in 1989 were barely aware of the existence of colonialism as a major force in shaping two-thirds of the modern world directly, and, indirectly, affecting the entire world. Specifically, they were unaware of the significance of writing by peoples outside the UK or US. [Edward] Said's work had received only scant attention and had had little impact on reshaping syllabuses and altering critical methodologies. The literary world was still profoundly Eurocentric, as anyone teaching in the period will attest." Ashcroft et al., *The Empire Writes Back*, 2nd ed. (2002), 244.

10. Ashcroft et al., *The Empire Strikes Back* (1989), 2. Emphasis mine.

11. Ashcroft et al., *The Empire Strikes Back* (2002), 200.

12. Edward Said, *Orientalism* (New York: Vintage, 1978).

13. The crucial work in this regard is Said's *The Question of Palestine* (New York: Vintage, 1979).

14. See Edward Said, *Out of Place: A Memoir* (London: Granta, 1999), 20.

15. *Beginnings: Intention and Method* (New York: Columbia University Press) had been published in 1975, and a year later it was awarded the first annual Lionel Trilling Award instituted by Columbia University.

16. In an interview conducted in 1997, in New Delhi, India, Said disavowed affiliation with postcolonial studies when he noted that "I would rather not talk about it [the field of postcolonial studies] because I do not think I belong to that. First of all, I don't think colonialism is over, really. I don't know what they are really talking about. I mean colonialism in the formal sense is over, but I am very interested in neocolonialism, I am very interested in the workings of the International Monetary Fund and the World Bank and I have written about them. I care very much about the structures of dependency and impoverishment that exist, well certainly in this part of the world and my part of the world and in all parts in what is now referred to as the global South. So I think to use the word postcolonialism is really a misnomer and I think I referred to the problems of that term in the Afterword to *Orientalism*." See Edward Said, "In Conversation with Neeladri Bhattacharya, Suvir Kaul, and Ania Loomba," in *Relocating Postcolonialism*, eds. David

Theo Goldberg and Ato Quayson (London: Blackwell, 2002), 2, my bracketed addition.

17. The word Orient can mean different things in different places. In England and much of Europe, the term Orient referred to Turkey and lands farther east, beginning with Istanbul or Constantinople. It referred primarily to what we would today call the Middle East. In the United States, however, the Orient has usually referred to what is often called the Far East, that is, mainly China and Japan. The changing geographic content of the Orient is itself an indicator that it is an imagined or discursive construct rather than a specific locale or area.

18. Said, *Orientalism*, 200–204, emphasis in original.

19. Said, *Orientalism*, 6–7.

20. Said, *Orientalism*, 326, emphasis mine.

21. For more on ethnophilosophy and the tensions between such views and those of universalism, see the essays in Kwame Anthony Appiah's book *In My Father's House: Africa in the Philosophy of Culture* (New York: Oxford, 1992).

22. Said, *Orientalism*, 322, emphasis mine.

23. Edward Said, *Culture and Imperialism* (New York: Vintage, 1994).

24. For two useful works that meditate on the tension between nationalism and the urge toward an inclusionary universalist humanism, see Terry Eagleton, Fredric Jameson, and Edward W. Said, *Nationalism, Colonialism, and Literature*, introduction by Seamus Deane (Minneapolis: University of Minnesota Press, 1990); and Ashis Nandy, *Illegitimacy of Nationalism: Rabindranath Tagore and the Politics of Self* (New Delhi: Oxford University Press, 1994).

25. Here is Said on Foucault, whose political passivity post-1968 he contrasts with that of a committed revolutionary like Fanon: "Foucault seems actually to represent an irresistible colonizing movement that paradoxically fortifies the prestige of both the lonely individual scholar and the system that contains him. Both Fanon and Foucault have Hegel, Marx, Freud, Nietzsche, Canguilhelm, and Sartre in their heritage, yet only Fanon presses that formidable arsenal into anti-authoritarian service. Foucault, perhaps in his disenchantment with both the insurrections of the 1960s and the Iranian Revolution, swerves away from politics entirely . . . European theory and Western Marxism . . . haven't in the main proved themselves to be reliable allies in the resistance to imperialism—on the contrary, one may suspect that they are part of the same invidious 'universalism' that connected culture with imperialism for centuries." Said, *Culture and Imperialism*, 278.

26. Said, *Culture and Imperialism*, 278.

27. Said, *Culture and Imperialism*, 319.

28. By the time Said was writing this in the preface to the silver jubilee edition of *Orientalism*, he had been diagnosed with cancer and was undergoing chemotherapy and other debilitating treatments for the disease. His autobiography *Out of Place* describes the circumstances in which the writings of his last years took place.

29. See Said, Preface to twenty-fifth anniversary edition of *Orientalism* (New York: Vintage, 2003), xxiii–xxix.

30. Anwar Abdel Malek, "Orientalism in Crisis," *Diogenes* 44 (Winter 1963): 107–8, quoted in Said, *Orientalism*, 97.

31. For more on what its author has insightfully called the "epidemiology" of Said's work within the history of ideas, see Patrick Wolfe's review essay, "History and Imperialism: A Century of Theory, from Marx to Postcolonialism," *American Historical Review* 102, 2 (April 1997): 408. Wolfe's essay mentions other works that significantly anticipated the content of Said's argument in *Orientalism*.

32. The SSC has changed composition over time, and at the outset it consisted of Ranajit Guha, Gyanendra Pandey, Shahid Amin, Dipesh Chakrabarty, Partha Chatterjee, David Arnold, David Hardiman, and Gautam Bhadra.

33. In actuality, in the British Indian army, subaltern often referred to the lowest class of officer, not soldier. Gramsci's use of the term is connected to the circumstances of his scholarship—in a fascist prison and with heavy scrutiny and censorship. He may have used the word subaltern as a synonym for proletarian just as he used the term the philosophy of Praxis when he meant Marxism.

34. Guha, Preface, in *Selected Subaltern Studies*, eds. Ranajit Guha and Gayatri Chakavorty Spivak (New York: Oxford University Press, 1988), 35.

35. Guha, "On Some Aspects of the Historiography of Colonial India," in *Selected Subaltern Studies*, eds. Guha and Spivak, 44, emphasis original.

36. See, for instance, John Gallagher, Gordon Johnson, and Anil Seal, eds., *Locality, Province, and Nation: Essays on Indian Politics 1870 to 1940* (Cambridge: Cambridge University Press, 1973); David Washbrook, *The Emergence of Provincial Politics* (Cambridge: Cambridge University Press, 1976); Anil Seal, *The Emergence of Indian Nationalism* (Cambridge: Cambridge University Press, 1968); Christopher Baker, *The Politics of South India, 1920–1937* (Cambridge: Cambridge University Press, 1976).

37. Guha, "On Some Aspects of the Historiography of Colonial India," 38.

38. Guha, "On Some Aspects of the Historiography of Colonial India," 39, emphasis original.

39. Guha, "On Some Aspects of the Historiography of Colonial India," 40, emphasis original.

40. Guha, "On Some Aspects of the Historiography of Colonial India," 41–42, emphasis original.

41. One of many works that makes such an argument is that of Partha Chatterjee's *Nationalist Thought and the Colonial World: A Derivative Discourse* (Minneapolis: University of Minnesota Press, 1993). This was a study dedicated to Ranajit Guha. In a book that has achieved the status of a canonical work in postcolonial studies, Chatterjee argued that Indian nationalism, while it opposed British colonialism, was trapped within a contradiction: even as it embarked on a project of national independence, it remained unable to think beyond a "post-Enlightenment" framework of modern science, industrialization, rationality, and a Eurocentrism masquerading as universalism. In other words, the project of third-world nationalism harbored a deep contradiction because it seemed as if the point of

independence was to autonomously imitate and replicate the pasts of the erstwhile colonial powers. Chatterjee argues that at various points, Gandhi seemed to veer from this hegemonic narrative and conceive of an India that was genuinely different and outside the imperium of Western thought. With his completely different take on industrial civilization, his ascetic emphasis on needs rather than wants, his critique of the alienating character of modern science, and his overall philosophy that was so orthogonal to the modern scientific, rational, and consumerist temper, Gandhi might have constituted a genuine rupture within the discourse of mimetic third-world nationalism. Yet, ultimately, this radical revisioning of the nation was recuperated within the discursive fold, even during Gandhi's time, by elevating him to a suprapolitical moral saint ("the Mahatma"), thereby precluding a serious engagement with his political and economic thought, more so certainly after his death. Gandhi's truly alternative conception of India was possibly the real source of his charisma and mass following among subaltern classes who intuited in his actions and symbolism something closer to what they were seeking. Tragically, Chatterjee argues, the moment came and went: Gandhi was expediently used by the rest of the nationalist elite to gain independence (he was, after all, the only one among them who could really bring the masses out into the streets), but the radical nature of his thinking was jettisoned at the earliest opportunity, even before but certainly after 1947. Along the way, Chatterjee shows how the subaltern energy of the masses, especially the peasantry, invariably exceeded the nationalism of the elite but was always tamed by the latter's emphasis on nonviolence, orderly politics, and maintaining a united national front against alien rule. Once again, the peasantry could not represent itself but had to be represented.

42. Guha, "On Some Aspects of the Historiography of Colonial India," 43, emphasis original.

43. Specifically, Guha uses Gramsci's notion of the "passive revolution" to indicate that Indian independence meant no more than a narrow political decolonization that did little to disrupt the enduring hierarchies—both material and symbolic, class and caste—that characterized India. Gramsci had used the term "passive revolution" to describe how in the nineteenth century, the national unification of Italy was led by diplomatic and military elites. The middle classes, led by Mazzini and Garibaldi, forewent an historical opportunity to ally with the peasantry and impart to Italian unification and nationalism a genuinely democratic and popular character and instead chose to cast their lot with the conservative and feudal elites. The Italian nation that emerged was therefore socially fractured and dominated by a conservative leadership with no hegemony (that is, moral and consensual leadership) over the masses. Gramsci traced the early twentieth-century descent of this state into fascism in this incomplete or "passive revolution" that formed the Italian nation-state in the first place. For more on the significance of Gramsci for Guha and the subaltern studies project in general, see David Arnold, "Gramsci and Peasant Subalternity in India," *Journal of Peasant Studies* 11, 4 (1984): 155–77.

44. Marx himself was disparaging of the peasantry, describing them, in the context of mid-nineteenth-century France, as a "sack of potatoes" for their inability to transcend a narrow self-centered economism and unite as a class. In fact, Marx does so in the same paragraph of the essay from which Said drew his epigraph for *Orientalism* ("They cannot represent themselves, they must be represented"), namely, the *Eighteenth Brumaire of Louis Napoleon*, Marx and Engels, in *Selected Works*, 172.

45. I should emphasize that, as is often the case with intellectual movements of this sort, many of the authors and works that came to be coalesced under Subaltern Studies had arrived at similar (although by no means identical) views as Guha on their own and were not writing merely out of allegiance to his manifesto. There was a convergence of ideas here, especially about the violence of abstractions such as nation, class, and politics, and how they occluded our understandings of what was really happening among nonelite social groups and classes. These ideas were perhaps usefully adumbrated by Guha, and it is important to realize that these authors were, in that sense, his fellow travelers rather than followers. Among the early works notable for a distinctive use of sources and a consequently rich reading of the often autonomous and radical nature of subaltern involvement in political movements at this time, see especially the essays by Shahid Amin, "Gandhi as Mahatma," Dipesh Chakrabarty on "Conditions for Knowledge of Working-Class Conditions," Gyanendra Pandey, "Peasant Revolt and Indian Nationalism 1919–1922," and David Arnold, "Touching the Body: Perspectives on the Indian Plague," in *Selected Subaltern Studies*, eds. Guha and Spivak.

46. Spivak, "Editor's Note," in *Selected Subaltern Studies*, eds. Guha and Spivak, xii.

47. Gyanendra Pandey, "Peasant Revolt and Indian Nationalism 1919–1922," in *Selected Subaltern Studies*, eds. Guha and Spivak, 233–87.

48. Shahid Amin, "Gandhi as Mahatma," *Selected Subaltern Studies*, eds. Guha and Spivak, 288–348.

49. Partha Chatterjee, *The Nation and Its Fragments: Colonial and Postcolonial Histories* (Princeton, NJ: Princeton University Press, 1993), 167.

50. Chatterjee, *The Nation and Its Fragments*, 168.

51. See Dipesh Chakrabarty, *Provincializing Europe: Postcolonial Thought and Historical Difference* (Princeton, NJ: Princeton University Press, 2000).

52. See, for examples of such early critiques, Sangeeta Singh, Minakshi Menon, Pradeep Kumar Dutta, Biswamoy Pati, Radhakanta Barik, Radhika Chopra, Partha Dutta, and Sanjay Prasad, "Subaltern Studies II: A Review Article," *Social Scientist* 12, 8 (1984): 3–41; Rosalind O'Hanlon, "Recovering the Subject: Subaltern Studies and Histories of Resistance in Colonial South Asia," *Modern Asian Studies* 22, 1 (1988): 189–224; Chris Bayly, "Rallying around the Subaltern," *Journal of Peasant Studies* 11, 1 (1988): 110–20; B. B. Chaudhuri, "Subaltern Autonomy and the National Movement," *Indian Historical Review* (New Delhi) 12, 1–2 (July 1985–Jan. 1986): 391–99; Mridula Mukherjee, "Peasant Resistance and Peasant Conscious-

ness in Colonial India: 'Subalterns' and Beyond," *Economic and Political Weekly* 23, 41 (8 October 1988): 2109–20; 23, 42 (15 October 1988): 2174–85; Yang, Anand, Review of Subaltern Studies II, *Journal of Asian Studies* 45, 1 (Nov. 1985): 178; Alam, Javeed, "Peasantry, Politics and Historiography: Critique of New Trend in Relation to Marxism," *Social Scientist* 117, 11:2 (Feb. 1983): 43–54; Gayatri Chakravorty Spivak, "Subaltern Studies: Deconstructing Historiography," in *Selected Subaltern Studies*, 2–32; and Spivak, "Can the Subaltern Speak?" in *Marxism and the Interpretation of Cultures*, eds. Cathy Nelson and Lawrence Grossberg (Urbana, IL: University of Illinois Press, 1988), 271–315.

53. Over a dozen volumes of Subaltern Studies essays have been published, beginning with the first in 1982. However, these were all printed and sold by Oxford University Press (India), which caters mainly to South Asia, and are not for sale in metropolitan markets. *Selected Subaltern Studies* (1988) was, however, printed in and marketed from Oxford's English and American outlets, making its purchase and its use for courses in Western universities much easier in comparison to these earlier (and later) volumes. By 1988, Edward Said was a well-recognized name in a number of disciplines, including English, history, cultural studies, and ethnic studies. Spivak was only slightly less famous by this time in Western academic circles. Her translation (and "Translator's Preface") to Jacques Derrida's *Of Grammatology* (Baltimore: Johns Hopkins University Press) in 1974, followed by a series of brilliant essays on a variety of topics in the fields of comparative literature, feminist studies, Marxist theory, and cultural studies, had already secured her reputation. Emerging into the Western academy with the imprimatur of Said and Spivak undoubtedly helped launch Selected Subaltern Studies into an academic space already energized by multiculturalism and the culture wars of the 1980s.

54. See Latin America Subaltern Studies Group, "Founding Statement," *boundary 2* 20 (Fall 1993): 110–21; and Florencia E. Mallon, "The Promise and Dilemma of Subaltern Studies: Perspectives from Latin American History," *American Historical Review* 99, 5 (Dec. 1994): 1491–515.

55. It would take us too far afield to discuss this at any length, but many critics routinely charge postcolonial studies and Subaltern Studies with essentially doing no more than applying Western postmodern and poststructural insights onto materials from the third world. As Arif Dirlik puts it, "indeed, their most original contribution would seem to lie in their rephrasing of older problems in the study of the Third World in the language of poststructuralism," see Dirlik, "The Postcolonial Aura: Third World Criticism in the Age of Global Capitalism," in *Dangerous Liaisons: Gender, Nation and Postcolonial Perspectives*, ed. Anne McClintock, Aamir Mufti, and Ella Shohat (Minneapolis: University of Minnesota Press, 1997), 520. In contrast, when one reads the early volumes of the Subaltern Studies Collective, or an intellectual history of the Subaltern Studies Collective as written by Dipesh Chakrabarty, for example, it is clear that there was simultaneity of ideas, interests, and insights that make such a charge seem both unfair and empirically inaccurate. See Chakrabarty, "A Small History of Subaltern Studies" in his *Habitations of*

Modernity: Essays in the Wake of Subaltern Studies (Chicago: University of Chicago Press, 2002), 3–19. The work of Antonio Gramsci, and its profound implications for the history of societies such as India, was part of the intellectual debates in Calcutta and Delhi long before anything comparable was happening within Marxist circles in the United States. See, for example, Asok Sen, *Iswar Chandra Vidyasagar and His Elusive Milestones* (Calcatta: Riddlu-India, 1977). Similarly, the implications of modern institutions like the Census for what Foucault would come to term "governmentality," and the power/knowledge nexus underlying the production of Orientalist notions, such as caste and unchanging "village" of Indian anthropological discourse, are both abundantly evident in the work of Bernard Cohn on colonial India published in the 1950s and 1960s. See, for instance, Ranajit Guha's introduction to Bernard S. Cohn, *An Anthropologist Among Historians and Other Essays* (Delhi: Oxford University Press, 1987), and Nicholas Dirks's foreword to Bernard S. Cohn, *Colonialism and Its Forms of Knowledge: The British In India* (Princeton, NJ: Princeton University Press, 1996).

56. Gyan Prakash, *Another Reason: Science and the Imagination of Modern India* (Princeton, NJ: Princeton University Press, 1999).

57. Homi Bhabha, *The Location of Culture* (New York: Routledge, 1994), 100.

58. Bhabha, *Location of Culture*, 44. Emphasis original.

59. Bhabha, *Location of Culture*, 45. Emphasis mine.

60. Jean Baudrillard, *For a Critique of the Political Economy of the Sign*, trans. Charles Levin (St. Louis, MO: Telos Press), 1981.

61. Baudrillard, *For a Critique of the Political Economy of the Sign*, 205.

62. Homi Bhabha and John Comaroff, "Speaking of Postcoloniality in the Continuous Present: A Conversation," in *Relocating Postcolonialism*, eds. David Theo Goldberg and Ato Quayson (Malden, MA: Blackwell Publishers, 2002), 21, 24.

63. It is entirely apposite that Bhabha's early work was on V. S. Naipaul, for I can think of no other writer who has mined his own alienation from any sovereign sense of selfhood more creatively and brilliantly than him. Naipaul is perhaps the best living proof of Bhabha's view, drawing from Lacan, that interdiction of desire produces value, especially literary value and insight. Another way of understanding Bhabha's emphasis on interdiction, thwarted desire, or a sense of alienation that comes from being colonized and of never quite being at home anywhere in the world, and its immense role in creativity, is to ponder the meaning of Rushdie's statement in an interview regarding the sources of his own creativity: "I wanted to write about a thing I find difficult to admit even to myself, which is the fact that I left home." Salman Rushdie, "Interview with Sean French," in *The Rushdie File*, eds. Lisa Appignanesi and Sara Maitland (London: Fourth Estate, 1989), 9.

64. Kalpana Seshadri-Crooks, "Surviving Theory: A Conversation with Homi K. Bhabha," in *The Pre-Occupation of Postcolonial Studies*, eds. Fawzia Afzal-Khan and Kalpana Seshadri-Crooks (Durham, NC: Duke University Press, 2000), 379, emphasis mine.

65. Bhabha, *The Location of Culture*, 33–34. Emphasis mine.

66. The project is self-contradictory: if the native could be successfully colonized and made into an authentic replica of the original, what then is the need for colonialism, in what sense is he an "other" who is different from the Western or colonizing self, and where does this leave the idea of the selfhood of the colonizer?

67. Bhabha, *Location of Culture*, 112.

68. Bhabha, *Location of Culture*, 121. Emphasis in original.

69. Benita Parry, "The Institutionalization of Postcolonial Studies," in *The Cambridge Companion to Postcolonial Literary Studies*, ed. Neil Lazarus (New York: Cambridge University Press, 2004), 76.

70. For instance, here is Bhabha in *The Location of Culture*, 20: "I am convinced that, in the language of political economy, it is legitimate to represent the relations of exploitation and domination in the discursive division between the First and Third World, the North and the South. Despite the claims to a spurious rhetoric of 'internationalism' on the part of the established multinationals and the networks of the new communications technology industries, such circulations of signs and commodities as there are, are caught in the vicious circuits of surplus value that link First World capital to Third World labour markets through the chains of the international division of labour, and national comprador classes . . . there is a sharp growth in a new Anglo-American nationalism which increasingly articulates its economic and military power in political acts that express a neo-imperialist disregard for the independence and autonomy of peoples and places in the Third World. Think of America's 'backyard' policy towards the Caribbean and Latin America, the patriotic gore and patrician lore of Britain's Falklands Campaign or, more recently, the triumphalism of the American and British forces during the Gulf War." Elsewhere in this same work (4–6), Bhabha is quite clear that the "post" in postcolonial does not mean that colonialism is in the past or is done with in any way. Rather, he argues, that these histories of colonial domination and conquest are points of departure for our investigations into the present and are responsible for the world of diasporas, migrants, exiles, and dispossessed that we find ourselves in.

71. See Gayatri Chakravorty Spivak, *In Other Worlds: Essays in Cultural Politics* (New York: Routledge, 1997), 159.

72. In his preface to the *Phenomenology of Spirit*, Hegel notes: "Lacking strength, Beauty hates the Understanding for asking of her what it cannot do. But the life of Spirit is not the life that shrinks from death and keeps itself untouched by devastation, but rather the life that endures it and maintains itself in it. It wins its truth only when, in utter dismemberment, it finds itself. This *tarrying with the negative* is the magical power that converts it into being." Hegel quoted in Slavoj Žižek, *Tarrying with the Negative* (Durham, NC: Duke University Press, 1993), vii, emphasis original. Žižek is following Hegel here in understanding Being as something emergent from antagonistic encounter rather than threatened by it. In a similar vein, I argue that for Spivak, politics is something that emerges from the fractured and

irretrievably nonsovereign selves of the contemporary world. Like Bhabha, she too argues that fissures and fractures are constitutive of our identity and politics, not their negation or diminution. Meaning, action, and politics are all emergent from inhabiting structures that one *cannot not want* to inhabit.

73. Gayatri Charkavorty Spivak, *Outside in the Teaching Machine* (New York: Routledge, 1993), 60.

74. Spivak, *Outside in the Teaching Machine*, 281. Emphasis original.

75. Spivak, *Outside in the Teaching Machine*, 237. Emphasis mine.

76. Spivak, *Outside in the Teaching Machine*, 236. Emphasis mine.

77. Spivak, "The Postcolonial Critic," in *The Postcolonial Critic*, ed. Sarah Harasym (New York: Routledge, 1990), 72.

78. Derrida, *Writing and Difference* [1967], trans. Alan Bass (London: Routledge, 1978), 111, quoted in Young, *Postcolonialism*, 418.

79. Spivak, *Outside in the Teaching Machine*, 5. Emphasis original.

80. Spivak, *Outside in the Teaching Machine*, 80.

81. Spivak, *Outside in the Teaching Machine*, 122.

82. This is Spivak's description of *A Critique of Postcolonial Reason: Toward a History of the Vanishing Present* (Cambridge: Harvard University Press, 1999), 421.

83. It is this kind of overdone self-effacement that draws the ire of someone such as Dirlik who notes with heavy sarcasm that "Postcolonial intellectuals, in their First World institutional locations, are ensconced in positions of power not only vis-à-vis the 'native' intellectuals back at home but also vis-à-vis their First World neighbors here. My neighbors in Farmville, Virginia, are no match in power for the highly paid, highly prestigious postcolonial intellectuals at Columbia, Duke, Princeton, or the University of California at Santa Cruz; some of them might even be willing to swap positions with the latter and take the anguish that comes with hybridity so long as it brings with it the power and prestige it seems to command." Dirlik, "The Postcolonial Aura," in *Dangerous Liaisons*, 513.

84. Spivak interview in *The Postcolonial Critic,* 71. Emphasis mine.

85. Spivak, *Critique of Postcolonial Reason*, 358.

CHAPTER 4: CRITIQUES OF POSTCOLONIAL THEORY

1. Ella Shohat, "Notes on the Postcolonial," in *The Pre-Occupation of Postcolonial Studies*, eds. Fawzia Afzal-Khan and Kalpana Seshadri-Crooks (Durham, NC: Duke University Press, 2000), 126–27. Emphasis original.

2. Bill Ashcroft, Gareth Griffiths, and Helen Tiffin, *Key Concepts in Post-Colonial Studies* (New York: Routledge, 1998).

3. A good illustration of the distinction between base and superstructure can be found in a discussion of political correctness. Marxists would argue that proscribing words that demean blacks or women only superficially addresses the problem of racism or male dominance. Such bowdlerization of the English language has to

be accompanied by structural economic and political changes that result in genuine equality for blacks and women, otherwise the change in terminology would be merely cosmetic.

4. Arif Dirlik, "The Postcolonial Aura: Third World Criticism in the Age of Global Capitalism," in *Dangerous Liaisons: Gender, Nation and Postcolonial Perspectives*, eds. Anne McClintock, Aamir Mufti, and Ella Shohat (Minneapolis: University of Minnesota Press, 1997), 502–3. Emphasis mine.

5. Benita Parry, "The Institutionalization of Postcolonial Studies," in *The Cambridge Companion to Postcolonial Literary Studies*, ed. Neil Lazarus (Cambridge: Cambridge University Press, 2004), 66–67. It has to be mentioned that despite her claim that many postcolonial theorists regard issues such as the ongoing economic exploitation of the third world by Western countries as past and done with, Parry does not cite a single exemplary author or quote in support. Her style of argument, in the context of such critique at least, is of a form wherein the "absence of evidence" is equated with the "evidence of absence." That is, because an author like Homi Bhabha is attentive to ambivalence and ambiguity in colonial discourses, or the sly parody of colonial power effected by exaggerated mimicry on the part of the colonized, and does not explicitly reference North-South inequalities, this implies he is deliberately neglectful or chooses to ignore the latter set of issues.

6. One of the clearest statements on how the distaste for binarisms, the critique of essentialism, and the suspicion of teleological reasoning combine to depoliticize postcolonial theory and disable its analysis of neoliberal globalization can be found in the work of Simon During. See his "Postcolonialism and Globalization: A Dialectical Relation After All?" *Postcolonial Studies* 1, 1 (1998): 31–47.

7. Dirlik, "The Postcolonial Aura," 525.

8. Parry, "The Institutionalization of Postcolonial Studies," 76.

9. Keya Ganguly, "Adorno, Authenticity, Critique," in *Marxism, Modernity, and Postcolonial Studies*, eds. Crystal Bartolovich and Neil Lazarus (Cambridge, UK: Cambridge University Press, 2002), 241.

10. Parry, "The Institutionalization of Postcolonial Studies," 74–75.

11. Neil Larsen, "DetermiNation: Postcolonialism, Poststructuralism, and the Problem of Ideology," in *The Pre-Occupation of Postcolonial Studies*, 147–48.

12. Aijaz Ahmad, *In Theory: Classes, Nations, Literatures* (New York: Verso, 1992), 86. See also Ania Loomba and Suvir Kaul, "Location, Culture, Post-Coloniality," *Oxford Literary Review* 16 (1994): 3–30, for more on the conflation of distinctive and often painful histories connoted by words such as diaspora and exile with the more anodyne experiences of middle-class economic migration engaged in by many postcolonial intellectuals in Western academies.

13. Sumit Sarkar, "The Decline of the Subaltern in Subaltern Studies," in *Mapping Subaltern Studies and the Postcolonial*, ed. Vinayak Chaturvedi (New York: Verso, 2000), 317–18.

14. This point about the irrelevance of postcolonial theory in home societies is made by Seshadri-Crooks in her introduction to *The Pre-Occupation of Postcolonial*

Studies, as well as Ania Loomba, Suvir Kaul, Matti Bunzel, Antoinette Burton, and Jed Esty in their introduction to Fredrick Cooper, Laura Chrisman, Timothy Brennan, Nivedita Menon, Neil Lazarus, Vilashini Cooppan, Kelwyn Sole, Ania Loomba, and Jed Esty's *Postcolonial Studies and Beyond* (Durham, NC: Duke University Press, 2005).

15. Lazarus's use of the word "idealist" here explicitly indicates the base-superstructure model that underlies his analysis of the limits of the critique of Eurocentrism made by postcolonial theorists like Dipesh Chakrabarty or Partha Chatterjee.

16. Neil Lazarus, "The Fetish of 'the West' in Postcolonial Theory," in *Marxism, Modernity, and Postcolonial Studies*, 43–44.

17. The same points regarding Eurocentrism are made by others, notably Arif Dirlik, "The Postcolonial Aura," and Timothy Brennan, *At Home in the World: Cosmopolitanism Now* (Cambridge: Harvard University Press, 1997).

18. See especially Aijaz Ahmad's chapter "Orientalism and After: Ambivalence and Metropolitan Location in the Work of Edward Said," in his *In Theory*, 159–220, for a critique of such reverse racism on the part of postcolonial studies.

19. Dirlik, "The Postcolonial Aura," 517, 520.

20. Prakash, "Writing Post-Orientalist Histories of the Third World: Perspectives from Indian Historiography," in *Mapping Subaltern Studies and the Postcolonial*, 176–77.

21. Dirlik, "The Postcolonial Aura," 521.

22. Dirlik, "The Postcolonial Aura," 515–16.

23. The phrase is from Ranajit Guha, "On the Historiography of Colonial India," in *Selected Subaltern Studies*, eds. Ranajit Guha and Gayatri Chakravorty Spivak (New York: Oxford, 1988), 43. Emphasis original.

24. Shohat, "Notes on the Post-Colonial," 126. Emphasis original.

25. David Scott, "The Social Construction of Postcolonial Studies," in *Postcolonial Studies and Beyond*, 385–400.

26. Scott, "The Social Construction of Postcolonial Studies," 399. One of the best aspects of Scott's essay is its rebuttal of the charge of binarism that is often leveled at many depictions of colonialism. Scott points out that many who use binary descriptions, such as core/periphery, black/white, first/third world, colonizer/colonized (including such clearly insightful and complex thinkers like Fanon or Albert Memmi), were not unaware of the multiple nuances that informed relations between colonizer and colonized. They were intervening on the debate over colonialism in a specific political context: they fought, in the case of Fanon and Memmi, to see countries like France (in Algeria, Vietnam, and elsewhere) shed their colonial ambitions and rid themselves of notions of civilizational superiority. It was in this *political* context that these authors self-consciously used binarist modes of reasoning. To critique them of a narrow and unnuanced reading of the complexities of the colonial encounter is, literally, to miss the point. Such an abstract critique of binarism is precisely what Scott refers to as an instance of political criticism gradually degenerating into abstract method.

27. Loomba et al., *Postcolonial Studies and Beyond*, 4.

28. Loomba et al., *Postcolonial Studies and Beyond*, 9–13.

29. Shohat, "Notes on the Postcolonial," 136.

30. Linda Tuhiwai Smith, "Imperialism, History, Writing, and Theory," in *Post-colonialisms: An Anthology of Cultural Theory and Criticism*, eds. Gaurav Desai and Supriya Nair (New Brunswick, NJ: Rutgers University Press, 2005), 99.

31. Cynthia Franklin and Laura Lyons, "Remixing Hybridity: Globalization, Native Resistance, and Cultural Production in Hawai'i," *American Studies* 45, 3 (Fall 2004): 51.

32. Franklin and Lyons, "Remixing Hybridity," 52. Emphasis mine. In making such an argument, they deny quite explicitly the claim of someone such as Gyan Prakash that postcolonial thought has been "arousing, inciting, and affiliating with the subordinated others in the First World . . . to connect with minority voices." Gyan Prakash, "Writing Post-Orientalist Third World Histories," *Comparative Studies in Society and History* 32, 2 (April 1990): 403.

33. Franklin and Lyons, "Remixing Hybridity," 52.

34. Franklin and Lyons, "Remixing Hybridity," 53–54. Another work that similarly critiques postcolonial studies from the standpoint of indigenous politics, and specifically on the grounds that essentialisms may be necessary at specific stages of political struggles, is Eric Cheyfitz, "The (Post)Colonial Predicament of Native American Studies," *Interventions* 4, 3 (2002): 405–27. bell hooks had similarly critiqued the antiessentialism of postcolonial studies from the perspective of black studies in her *Yearning: Race, Gender, and Cultural Politics* (Boston: South End, 1990).

35. See Edward Said, *Culture and Imperialism* (New York: Knopf, 1993).

36. The idea that one could use essentialism in a strategic or calculated way to advance certain contextual political aims, without actually fully believing in its truth, was first articulated by Gayatri Chakravorty Spivak. She emphasized both the provisional nature of such use in certain political contexts and the scrupulous attention that ought to be paid to its dangers. She has since distanced herself from the concept, arguing that too many have become enamored of the license to essentialism it provides and careless about the injunctions regarding scrupulousness, care, and contingency that she had hoped to emphasize. For one gloss on the strategic use of essentialism and its enablements and dangers, see Spivak, "Subaltern Studies: Deconstructing Historiography," in *Selected Subaltern Studies*, 3–32. For her own later skepticism regarding how the concept had become misused, see her interview with Sara Danius and Stefan Jonsson in *boundary 2* 20, 2 (1993): 24–50.

37. Homi Bhabha, *The Location of Culture* (New York: Routledge, 1994), 5–6. Emphasis original.

38. Gauri Viswanathan, *Masks of Conquest: Literary Study and British Rule in India* (New York: Columbia University Press, 1989).

39. Lata Mani, *Contentious Traditions: The Debate on Sati in Colonial India* (Berkeley: University of California Press, 1998).

40. Quote from "Introduction," in *Sovereign Bodies: Citizens, Migrants, and States in the Postcolonial World*, eds. Thomas Blom Hansen and Finn Stepputat (Princeton, NJ: Princeton University Press, 2005), 19.

41. Franklin and Lyons, "Remixing Hybridity," 50.

CHAPTER 5: POSTCOLONIAL ENCOUNTERS

1. I did find another letter from the same person on August 20, 2006 in the *New York Times Magazine* which is, I suppose, an even better (or should I say worse?) example of what one might call everyday Orientalism. In that letter, Haskill noted that the Middle East was "a strange, timeless place where nothing has changed for thousands of years, where fierce hatreds are as ancient as the deserts and cannot be tamed or reasoned with in Western terms. We will never understand it."

2. Emphases in original. For the full list of fifteen rules, the reader may consult Friedman's column in the *New York Times* dated December 20, 2006.

3. Friedman's belief that the United States is unquestionably the bastion of democracy, equality, trust, freedom, rationality, and pragmatism, and that it is justified in proselytizing such values to the rest of the world, is an article of faith that is widely shared by the media and the U.S. public at large. One would have to read the likes of Noam Chomsky, Howard Zinn, Gabriel Kolko, and alternative media sources to get a discourse other than this hegemonic self-representation. For example, the fact that a small handful of megacorporations own the vast majority of media outlets in the United States, and that this might color the ways in which they cover issues such as economic inequality, legislation affecting business interests, corporate tax rates, free trade agreements with neighboring countries, or the unionization of labor, never seems to occur to Friedman. On the other hand, that a media outlet like Al Jazeera or any other such entity in the Middle East must be incorrigibly biased and lack any credibility is simply assumed in the United States.

4. Bernard Lewis, "The Roots of Muslim Rage," *The Atlantic*, September 1990. <http://www.theatlantic.com/doc/199009/muslim-rage> (29 March 2008). Emphasis mine.

5. In the context of the interview, it is evident that the societies the Federal Bureau of Investigation director was referring to here were "Arab societies." Barak's quotation reproduced from Mahmood Mamdani, *Good Muslim, Bad Muslim: America, The Cold War, and the Roots of Terror* (New York: Doubleday, 2004), 215.

6. For instance, in February 2003, a month before the war, as many as 72 percent of the U.S. public believed that Saddam Hussein must have been personally involved in the attacks of 9/11. Seymour Hersh, "Selective Intelligence," *The New Yorker*, May 12, 2003. <http://www.newyorker.com/archive/2003/05/12/030512fa_fact> (accessed 29 May 2008).

7. Jeff Stein, "Can You Tell a Sunni from a Shiite?" *New York Times*, Oct. 17, 2006. Emphasis mine.

8. For the text of the report see <http://www.israeleconomy.org/strat1.htm> (accessed 28 May 2008). This section owes a great deal to the concise and persuasive argument of Rashid Khalidi, *Resurrecting Empire: Western Footprints and America's Perilous Path in the Middle East* (Boston: Beacon Press, 2004), 49–55.

9. As Richard Clarke, the national coordinator for counterterrorism in the Bush administration until March 2003, observed in his book written after the war began, it was obvious that the neoconservative cabal was determined to use 9/11 as an alibi to oust Saddam Hussein, never mind the absence of any evidence regarding the various allegations trotted out by the administration. He noted that "Having been attacked by Al Qaeda, for us now to go bombing Iraq would be like our invading Mexico after the Japanese attacked us at Pearl Harbor." Richard Clarke, *Against All Enemies: Inside America's War on Terror* (New York: Free Press, 2004), 30–31, quoted in Tarak Barkawi, *Globalization and War* (Lanham, MD: Rowman & Littlefield, 2006), 157.

10. Khalidi, *Resurrecting Empire*, 51–52.

11. Thomas L. Friedman, "Anti-Terror Fight Has to be a Marathon Run on Wilsonian Principle, Not Cheap Oil." Text of a speech delivered at the Yale Center for the Study of Globalization, January 30, 2003. <http://yaleglobal.yale.edu/article.print?id=913> (accessed 29 May 2008). If the style of one's prose as much as its content offers an insight into what one really thinks about people, statements like "buying off the judge with a goat" indicates the deep-seated contempt that runs through Friedman's depictions of Muslims in the Middle East and elsewhere. In any event, besides atmospherics, Friedman's argument is palpably wrong even on empirical grounds. Aziz Premji is not so much symptomatic of India's Muslim minority as he is the exception that proves the rule regarding their second-class status in that country. A "Prime Minister's High Level Committee" set up by the Hindu majoritarian Bharatiya Janata Party (BJP) announced its findings regarding the status of India's Muslim minority on November 30, 2006. The Justice Rajinder Sachar Committee Report found that while Muslims were 14 percent of India's population, their share of government employment is 4.9 percent, they constitute only 3.9 percent of India's various security agencies (police, border security force, and so forth), and only 2.7 percent of the district judges. On almost every positive yardstick—literacy, access to subsidized loans or rural poverty alleviation programs, per capita incomes—Muslims, the committee found, were represented at levels far below their share of the overall population. The areas in which they were overrepresented include their share of the incarcerated and the severity of judicial sentences meted out to them. The committee concluded that in many instances this was a direct result of discrimination by the government and the majority community. For a summary and detailed analysis of the Sachar Committee Report, see the newsmagazine *Frontline's* report: http://pay.hindu.com/ebook%20%20ebfl20061215part1.pdf (accessed 28 May 2008).

12. Just as Britain was regarded as the home of democracy even when it was the architect of the world's largest modern empire built on the denial of basic freedoms to the hundreds of millions in its colonies, Americans never question the notion that they are a democracy even if the United States has supported one dictator after another in every part of the world when it has suited their economic and strategic interests. The denial of basic civil liberties and the right to free and fair elections in these countries are always seen as signs of *their* inadequacy and not as at least partially the outcomes of U.S. intervention. It is through such instances that one realizes the immense power of a methodological nationalism that informs our understanding of the world. What the United States does outside its borders is somehow deemed irrelevant to our assessment of its democratic credentials. Such methodological nationalism also informs debates such as the "democratic peace" debate that has so exercised the discipline of international relations in recent years. All too many IR scholars in this exchange seem to have an anemic understanding of democracy, one that ahistorically and uncritically categorizes Western nations as democratic irrespective of their historical and ongoing complicity in colonialism and neocolonialism. For an excellent work that critiques the limits of this debate, see Tarak Barkawi and Mark Laffey, eds., *Democracy, Liberalism and War: Rethinking the Democratic Peace Debate* (Boulder, CO: Lynne Rienner, 2001). For a critique of the discipline of International Relations, specifically on its willful forgetting of racism and colonization, see Sankaran Krishna, "Race, Amnesia and the Education of International Relations," *Alternatives* 26, 4 (2001): 401–24.

13. Woodrow Wilson's support for the right of self-determination of incipient nations was intended primarily for the emerging states in the Balkans and Eastern Europe generally. However, movements all across the colonial world saw this as support for their own independence from colonial powers generally.

14. Khalidi, *Resurrecting Empire*, 165.

15. To argue in this fashion begins from the presupposition that words like "terrorist" foreclose explanation rather than further it. It is necessary to remember that from the perspective of the English royalty in the late eighteenth century, the founding fathers of the United States were terrorists. Ronald Reagan described the anti-Soviet Afghan mujahideen and the Nicaraguan Contras in the mid-1980s as the moral equivalents of America's founding fathers.

16. U.S. media coverage would give one the impression that the Iraqi invasion of Kuwait was the violation of a long-established and recognized international sovereign entity and border. Iraqi perspectives differ. The boundaries of the Iraqi nation were created during the breakup of the Ottoman Empire, under the auspices of British colonial authorities who had no legal mandate over the territory. The creation of Kuwait as an independent sovereign entity had long been a bone of contention among many Iraqis, and Saddam's invasion of that country in 1991 was seen as a redress of a historical error. I am not justifying the invasion of Kuwait by Iraq in 1991, but I am suggesting that media coverage that includes historical per-

spectives from within the region might lessen the focus on demonizing an individual (Saddam) and widen it to include the complicity of Western nations in the creation of geopolitical conflicts that are legacies of colonial and neocolonial interference in these regions.

17. For details on the first Gulf War of 1991, see Sankaran Krishna, "The Importance of Being Ironic: A Postcolonial View on Critical International Relations Theory," *Alternatives* 18 (1993): 385–417. One has to ask what is particularly valorous about the aerial bombing of a country from thousands of feet above ground, when its air defense systems are weakened, its air force much smaller, and whose technology and armaments were at least a generation behind that of the United States. Yet, the bravery of U.S. soldiers and treacherous and cowardly nature of the adversary are reiterated within mainstream Western media depictions. Just a glance at the kill ratios, hundreds of thousands of Iraqis killed to about 400 Allied soldiers dead, should indicate the incredibly one-sided nature of the conflict. Yet that does not stop a military historian like Sir John Keegan from observing that "Westerners fight face to face, in stand-up battle . . . [observing] rules of honour. Orientals . . . shrink from pitched battle . . . preferring ambush, surprise, treachery and deceit," quoted in Tarak Barkawi, *Globalization and War*, 134 n. 9. The reliance on Orientalist stereotyping in such a sentence is transparent, and such contrasts are ubiquitous within the Western, especially American, media. As Barkawi points out, when one is up against overwhelming odds because of the superiority of one's adversary in weaponry and resources, resort to tactics such as ambush or surprise or guerrilla insurgency is routine in the history of war.

18. Mamdani, *Good Muslim, Bad Muslim*, 185.

19. Mamdani, *Good Muslim, Bad Muslim*, 189.

20. Quoted in Mamdani, *Good Muslim, Bad Muslim*, 192. It is worth remembering that so many of these atrocities on the civilians of Iraq happened during the eight years of the Clinton administration. For those who still believe that the two-party system in the United States offers a genuine choice in terms of foreign policy, or domestic policy for that matter, this ought to be a sober reminder of the incredibly narrow range of options that that "choice" represents in reality.

21. See the BBC website <http://news.bbc.co.uk/2/hi/middle_east/4525412 .stm> 2006 (accessed 28 May 2008), for the full report.

22. See the Canadian Broadcasting Corporation (CBC) report, "Casualties in the Iraq War": <http://www.cbc.ca/news/background/iraq/casualties.html> (accessed 29 May 2008), for the report on Bush's estimate.

23. For the latest figures on the Iraqi war dead, and for details on the methodology used in estimating the casualties, see Iraq Body Count's website: <http://www .iraqbodycount.org/ (accessed 28 May 2008).

24. For a work that carefully demonstrates how U.S. aid and support to the Pakistani military during the 1950s and 1960s thwarted the consolidation of democratic regimes in that country and wound up consolidating the military in its

rivalry with the political parties and bureaucracy for state power, see Ayesha Jalal, *The State of Martial Rule: The Origins of Pakistan's Political Economy of Defence* (Cambridge, UK: Cambridge University Press, 1990).

25. Faisal Devji, *Landscapes of the Jihad: Militancy, Morality, Modernity* (Ithaca, NY: Cornell University Press, 2005), xiv.

26. For a recent work that empirically analyzes suicide bombers and concludes that their motivations are far from religious and arise more from a sense of occupation, see Robert Pape, *Dying to Win: The Strategic Logic of Suicide Terrorism* (New York: Random House, 2005).

27. Ramzi Yousef's courtroom deposition, as reproduced in Friedman, *The Lexus and the Olive Tree: Understanding Globalization* (New York: Anchor Books, 2000), 404.

28. Osama Bin Laden, in his interview with Al Jazeera, October 2001, as quoted in Devji, *Landscapes of the Jihad*, 140–41.

29. See Noam Chomsky, *Failed States: The Abuse of Power and the Assault on Democracy* (New York: Holt, 2007), 18–22.

30. See Michael Scheuer, *Imperial Hubris: Why the West Is Losing the War on Terror* (Dulles, VA: Brassey's, 2004), quoted in Chomsky, *Failed States*, 23.

31. Thus, Under Secretary of State Douglas Dillon observed in March 1960, that "the Cuban people are responsible for the regime," and President Eisenhower justified the embargo by saying that "if [the Cuban people] are hungry they will throw Castro out," and Kennedy agreed by noting that the "rising discomfort among hungry Cubans" would hasten the demise of the Castro regime. The Deputy Secretary of State Lester Mallory noted in April 1960 that "through disenchantment and disaffection based on economic dissatisfaction and hardship every possible means should be undertaken promptly to weaken the economic life of Cuba [in order to] bring about hunger, desperation and overthrow of the government." All quotes from Chomsky, *Failed States*, 113.

32. Ayman al-Zawahiri, quoted in Faisal Devji, *Landscapes of the Jihad*, 99–100 n. 25. See also the quotations from Osama Bin Ladin's interview in 1998 regarding the responsibilities of civilians for the regimes they elect in a democracy at <http://www.pbs.org/wgbh/pages/frontline/shows/binladen/who/interview.html> 2007 (accessed 28 May 2008), cited in Devji, *Landscapes of the Jihad*, 173.

33. Devji, *Landscapes of the Jihad*, 100.

34. Devji, *Landscaptes of the Jihad*, 98–99.

CONCLUSION: POSTCOLONIALISM AND GLOBALIZATION

1. See, in particular, Mark Rupert, *Ideologies of Globalization: Contending Visions of a New World Order* (New York: Routledge, 2000); Manfred Steger, *Globalism: The New Market Ideology* (Lanham, MD: Rowman & Littlefield, 2002); Richard P. Ap-

pelbaum and William I. Robinson, eds., *Critical Globalization Studies* (New York: Routledge, 2005).

2. Emphasis mine. Summers's memo was leaked to the public in February 1992. It was later stated that it was written in an ironic tone by one of his junior staff members (a graduate student in economics at the time, who went on to join the Harvard Economics department as faculty), and that Summers signed the memo without reading it in its entirety. Summers was praised by some for not hanging his junior colleague out to dry and instead taking the blame himself. For the quote and an analysis placing it at the heart of the World Bank and the International Monetary Fund's structural adjustment policies in Africa, see Asad Ismi, "Impoverishing a Continent: The World Bank and the IMF in Africa," report commissioned by the Halifax Initiative Commission, July, 2004. <http://www.halifax-initiative.org/updir/ImpoverishingAContinent.pdf> (28 May 2008).

3. This was the comment by Jose Lutzenberger, the secretary of the environment of Brazil. He was fired from his position soon thereafter. See Asad Ismi, "Impoverishing a Continent," 27.

4. Karl Polanyi, *The Great Transformation: The Political and Economic Origins of Our Time* (Boston: Beacon Press, 1944).

5. As he noted in his summarization of the existing anthropological and ethnographic research on many premodern societies, "Broadly, the proposition holds that all economic systems known to us up to the end of feudalism in Western Europe were organized either on the principles of reciprocity or redistribution, or householding, or some combination of the three. These principles were institutionalized with the help of a social organization which, inter alia, made use of patterns of symmetry, centricity, and autarchy. In this framework, the orderly production and distribution of goods was secured through a great variety of individual motives disciplined by general principles of behavior. Among these motives gain was not prominent. Custom and law, magic and religion co-operated in inducing the individual to comply with rules of behavior, which, eventually, ensured his functioning in the economic system." Polanyi, *The Great Transformation*, 55.

6. Polanyi, *The Great Transformation*, 72–73. Emphasis original.

7. Mike Davis, *Late Victorian Holocausts: El Niño Famines and the Making of the Third World* (London: Verso, 2002).

8. Thomas Friedman, *The Lexus and the Olive Tree: Understanding Globalization* (New York: Anchor Books, 2000), 177. Emphasis mine.

9. Rupert, *Ideologies of Globalization*, 67.

10. For details on this episode and a typically insightful reading of the limits of categories such as the nation, ethnicity, gender, capital, and labor in understanding and critiquing capitalist exploitation, see "Feminism and Critical Theory," in Gayatri Chakravorty Spivak, *In Other Worlds: Essays in Cultural Politics* (New York: Routledge, 1998), 102–23.

11. I have elaborated at length on the ethics of such a postcolonial standpoint in my *Postcolonial Insecurities: India, Sri Lanka and the Question of Nationhood* (Minneapolis: University of Minnesota Press, 1999), and in "Boundaries in Question," in *A Companion to Political Geography*, eds. John Agnew et al. (Malden, MA: Blackwell, 2003), 302–14.

12. Ashis Nandy, *The Intimate Enemy: Loss and Recovery of Self Under Colonialism* (Delhi: Oxford University Press, 1983). Other crucial texts by Nandy would include *At the Edge of Psychology: Essays in Politics and Culture* (Delhi: Oxford University Press, 1980); *The Illegitimacy of Nationalism: Rabindranath Tagore and the Politics of Self* (Delhi: Oxford University Press, 1994); *The Savage Freud and Other Essays on Possible and Retrievable Selves* (Princeton, NJ: Princeton University Press, 1995); *Time Warps: Silent and Evasive Pasts in Indian Politics and Religion* (New Brunswick, NJ: Rutgers University Press, 2002); *The Romance of the State and the Fate of Dissent in the Tropics* (Delhi: Oxford University Press, 2003). These are only some of Nandy's impressive oeuvre. One of the best ways of entering Nandy's unique take on modernity is to read his extended conversation with Vinay Lal in a special issue of the journal *Emergences* titled "Plural Worlds, Multiple Selves: Ashis Nandy and the Post-Columbian Future," 7–8 (1995–96).

13. The original essay was published as part of a collection titled "Burmese Days." An online version is available at <http://www.online-literature.com/orwell/887> (accessed 29 May 2008).

14. Orwell, "Shooting an Elephant."

15. See especially his edited volume, *Science, Hegemony and Violence: A Requiem for Modernity* (Delhi: Oxford University Press, 1988).

16. Ashis Nandy, "The Beautiful Expanding Future of Poverty: Popular Economics as a Psychological Defense," *International Studies Review* 4, no. 2 (Summer 2002): 115–16.

17. Nandy, "The Beautiful Expanding Future of Poverty," 117–18.

18. Although Nandy has variations on this argument in many of his essays, one of the most compelling can be found in his "Shamans, Savages and the Wilderness: On the Audibility of Dissent and the Future of Civilizations," *Alternatives* 14 (1989): 263–77.

19. Nandy, "The Beautiful, Expanding Future of Poverty," 121.

20. Nandy, "The Beautiful Expanding Future of Poverty," 119.

21. Ella Shohat, "Notes on the 'Post-Colonial'," in *The Pre-Occupation of Postcolonial Studies*, eds. Fawzia Afzal-Khan and Kalpana Seshadri Crooks (Durham, NC: Duke University Press, 2000), 126–39.

22. I have elaborated at length on this in my *Postcolonial Insecurities: India, Sri Lanka and the Question of Nationhood*, Minneapolis: University of Minnesota Press, 1999.

23. See Spivak, *In Other Worlds*, 171, for a recounting of this episode and its import.

BIBIOGRAPHY

Agnew, John, and Stuart Corbridge. *Mastering Space: Hegemony, Territory and International Political Economy*. New York: Routledge, 1995.

Ahmad, Aijaz. *In Theory: Classes, Nations, Literatures*. New York: Verso, 1992.

Alavi, Hamza. "The State in Post-Colonial Societies: Pakistan and Bangladesh." *New Left Review* 74 (July–August, 1972): 59–81.

Amin, Shaid. "Gandhi as Mahatma." Pp. 288–348 in *Selected Subaltern Studies*, edited by Ranajit Guha and Gayatri Chakravorty Spivak. New York: Oxford University Press, 1988.

Amsden, Alice. *Asia's Next Giant: South Korea and Late Industrialization*. New York: Oxford University Press, 1989.

Appelbaum, Richard P., and William I. Robinson, eds. *Critical Globalization Studies*. New York: Routledge, 2005.

Appiah, Kwame Anthony. *In My Father's House: Africa in the Philosophy of Culture*. New York: Oxford University Press, 1992.

Appignanesi, Lisa, and Sara Maitland, eds. *The Rushdie File*. London: Fourth Estate, 1989.

Ashcroft, Bill, Gareth Griffiths, and Helen Tiffin. *The Empire Writes Back: Theory and Practice in Post-Colonial Literature*. New York: Routledge, 1989 (2nd ed. 2002).

———. *Key Concepts in Post-Colonial Studies*. New York: Routledge, 1998.

Bagchi, Amiya Kumar. *Private Investment in India: 1900–1939*. Cambridge: Cambridge University Press, 1972.

Baker, Christopher. *The Politics of South India, 1920–1937*. Cambridge: Cambridge University Press, 1976.

Balassa, Bela. *The Newly Industrializing Countries in the World Economy*. New York: Pergamon, 1981.

Bardhan, Pranab. *The Political Economy of Development in India*. New York: Black-well, 1984.

Barkawi, Tarak. *Globalization and War*. Lanham, MD: Rowman & Littlefield, 2006.

Barkawi, Tarak, and Mark Laffey, eds. *Democracy, Liberalism and War: Rethinking the Democratic Peace Debate*. Boulder, CO: Lynne Rienner, 2001.

Barrow, Clyde W. "The Miliband-Poulantzas Debate: An Intellectual History." Pp. 3–52 in *Paradigm Lost: State Theory Reconsidered*, edited by Stanley Aronowitz and Peter Bratsis. Minneapolis: University of Minnesota Press, 2002.

Baudrillard, Jean. *For a Critique of the Political Economy of the Sign*. Trans. Charles Levin. St. Louis, MO: Telos Press, 1981.

BBC [British Broadcasting Company] News. "Iraq Body Count: War Dead Figures." 2006. <http://news.bbc.co.uk/2/hi/middle_east/4525412.stm> (28 May 2008).

Bello, Walden, Kamal Malhotra, Nicola Bullard, and Marco Mezzera. "Notes on the Ascendancy and Regulation of Speculative Capital." Pp. 1–26 in *Global Finance: New Thinking on Regulating Speculative Capital Markets*, edited by Walden Bello, Nicola Bullard, and Kamal Malhtora. London: Zed Books, 2000.

Berman, Marshall. *All that Is Solid Melts Into Air: The Experience of Modernity*. New York: Simon and Schuster, 1982.

Bhabha, Homi. *The Location of Culture*. New York: Routledge, 1994.

Bhabha, Homi, and John Comaroff, "Speaking of Postcoloniality in the Continuous Present: A Conversation." Pp. 15–46 in *Relocating Postcolonialism*, edited by David Theo Goldberg and Ato Quayson. Malden, MA: Blackwell Publishers, 2002.

Bond, Patrick. *Against Global Apartheid: South Africa Meets the World Bank, the IMF and International Finance*. London: Macmillan, 2003.

Bradford, Colin I., Jr., and William H. Branson, eds. *Trade and Structural Change in Pacific Asia*. Chicago: University of Chicago Press, 1987.

Brennan, Timothy. *At Home in the World: Cosmopolitanism Now*. Cambridge: Harvard University Press, 1997.

Broad, Robin, and John Cavanagh. "The Death of the Washington Consensus?" Pp. 83–95 in *Global Finance: New Thinking on Regulating Speculative Capital Markets*, edited by Walden Bello, Nicola Bullard, and Kamal Malhotra. New York: Zed Books, 2000.

Buchan, James. *The Authentic Adam Smith: His Life and Ideas*. New York: W. W. Norton, 2006.

CBC [Canadian Broadcasting Corporation]. "Casualties in the Iraq War." 2007. <http://www.cbc.ca/news/background/iraq/casualties.html> (29 May 2008).

Chakrabarty, Dipesh. *Provincializing Europe: Postcolonial Thought and Historical Difference*. Princeton, NJ: Princeton University Press, 2000.

———. *Habitations of Modernity: Essays in the Wake of Subaltern Studies*. Chicago: University of Chicago Press, 2002.

Chandra, Bipan. *The Rise and Growth of Economic Nationalism in India*. New Delhi: Peoples Publishing House, 1966.

Chatterjee, Partha. *The Nation and Its Fragments: Colonial and Postcolonial Histories.* Princeton, NJ: Princeton University Press, 1993.

Cheyfitz, Eric. "The (Post)Colonial Predicament of Native American Studies." *Interventions* 4, no. 3 (2002): 40527.

Chomsky, Noam. *Failed States: The Abuse of Power and the Assault on Democracy.* New York: Holt, 2007.

Clarke, Richard. *Against All Enemies: Inside America's War on Terror.* New York: Free Press, 2004.

Cohn, Bernard S. *An Anthropologist Among Historians and Other Essays.* Delhi: Oxford University Press, 1987.

———. *Colonialism and Its Forms of Knowledge: The British in India.* Princeton, NJ: Princeton University Press, 1996.

Cooper, Richard N. "A Half Century of Development." Paper No. 04-03. Weatherhead Center For International Affairs, Harvard University, Cambridge, MA, May 2004. <http://www.cid.havard.edu/cidwp/118.pdf> (22 May 2008).

Davis, Mike. *Late Victorian Holocausts: El Nino Famines and the Making of the Third World.* London: Verso, 2002.

Derrida, Jacques. *Of Grammatology.* Trans. Gayatri Chakravorty Spivak. Baltimore: Johns Hopkins University Press, 1974.

———. *Writing and Difference.* Trans. Alan Bass. London: Routledge, 1978.

Devji, Faisal. *Landscapes of the Jihad: Militancy, Morality, Modernity.* Ithaca, NY: Cornell University Press, 2005.

Deyo, Frederic. *The Political Economy of the New Asian Industrialism.* Ithaca, NY: Cornell University Press, 1987.

Dirlik, Arif. "The Postcolonial Aura: Third World Criticism in the Age of Global Capitalism." Pp. 501–28 in *Dangerous Liaisons: Gender, Nation and Postcolonial Perspectives,* edited by Anne McClintock, Aamir Mufti, and Ella Shohat. Minneapolis: University of Minnesota Press, 1997.

Duffield, Mark R. *Development, Security and Unending War: Governing the World of Peoples.* Cambridge, UK: Polity Press, 2007.

During, Simon. "Postcolonialism and Globalization: A Dialectical Relation After All?" *Postcolonial Studies* 1, no. 1 (1998): 31–47.

Eagleton, Terry, Fredric Jameson, and Edward W. Said. *Nationalism, Colonialism, and Literature.* Minneapolis: University of Minnesota Press, 1990.

Foucault, Michel. "Nietzsche, Genealogy, History." Pp. 139–64 in *Language, Counter-Memory, Practice: Selected Essays and Interviews by Michel Foucault,* edited by Donald Bouchard. Ithaca, NY: Cornell University Press, 1977.

Frank, Andre Gunder. *World Accumulation: 1492–1789.* New York: Monthly Review Press, 1978.

Franklin, Cynthia, and Laura Lyons. "Remixing Hybridity: Globalization, Native Resistance, and Cultural Production in Hawai'i." *American Studies* 45, no. 3 (Fall 2004): 49–80.

Friedman, Thomas. *The Lexus and the Olive Tree: Understanding Globalization.* New York: Anchor Books, 2000.

———. "Anti-Terror Fight Has to Be a Marathon Run on Wilsonian Principle, Not Cheap Oil." Text of speech delivered at the Yale Center for the Study of Globalization, January 30, 2003. <http://yaleglobal.yale.edu/article.print?id=913> (29 May 2008).

Frontline (India). "Community on the Margins." 2006. <http://pay.hindu.com/ebook%20-%20ebfl20061215part1.pdf> (28 May 2008).

Gallagher, John, Gordon Johnson, and Anil Seal, eds. *Locality, Province and Nation.* Cambridge: Cambridge University Press, 1973.

Ganguly, Keya. "Adorno, Authenticity, Critique." Pp. 240–56 in *Marxism, Modernity, and Postcolonial Studies,* edited by Crystal Bartolovich and Neil Lazarus. Cambridge: Cambridge University Press, 2002.

George, Susan. "A Short History of Neoliberalism: Twenty years of Elite Economics and Emerging Opportunities for Structural Change." Pp. 27–35 in *Global Finance: New Thinking on Regulating Speculative Capital Markets,* edited by Walden Bello. London: Zed Books, 2000.

Gold, Thomas B. *State and Society in the Taiwan Miracle.* Armonk, NY: M. E. Sharpe, 1986.

Guha, Ranajit. "On Some Aspects of the Historiography of Colonial India." Pp. 37–44 in *Selected Subaltern Studies,* edited by Ranajit Guha and Gayatri Chakravorty Spivak. New York: Oxford University Press, 1988.

Haggard, Stepehen. *Pathways from the Periphery: The Politics of Growth in the Newly Industrializing Countries.* Ithaca, NY: Cornell University Press, 1990.

Hamilton, Alexander. *Report on the Subject of Manufactures.* New York: Cosimo Classics, 2007.

Hansen, Thomas Blom, and Finn Stepputat, eds. *Sovereign Bodies: Citizens, Migrants, and States in the Postcolonial World.* Princeton, NJ: Princeton University Press, 2005.

Harvey, David. *The Condition of Post-Modernity: An Enquiry into the Origins of Cultural Change.* Oxford: Blackwell, 1989.

———. *A Brief History of Neoliberalism.* New York: Oxford University Press, 2005.

Hersh, Seymour. "Selective Intelligence." *The New Yorker,* 12 May 2003. <http://www.newyorker.com/archive/2003/05/12/030512fa_fact> (29 May 2008).

Hilton, Rodney, ed. *The Transition from Feudalism to Capitalism in Europe.* London: Verso, 1976.

hooks, bell. *Yearning: Race, Gender, and Cultural Politics.* Boston: South End, 1990.

Inayatullah, Naeem, and David L. Blaney. *International Relations and the Problem of Difference.* New York: Routledge, 2004.

Institute for Advanced Strategic and Political Studies. "A Clean Break: A New Strategy for Securing the Realm." <http://www.israeleconomy.org/strat1.htm> (28 May 2008).

Iraq Body Count. 2008. <http://www.iraqbodycount.org/> (28 May 2008).

Ismi, Asad. "Impoverishing a Continent: The World Bank and the IMF in Africa." Report commissioned by the Halifax Initiative Commission, July 2004. <http://www.halifaxinitiative.org/updir/ImpoverishingAContinent.pdf> (28 May 2008).

Jalal, Ayesha. *The State of Martial Rule: The Origins of Pakistan's Political Economy of Defence.* New York: Cambridge University Press, 1990.

Johnson, Chalmers. *MITI and the Japanese Miracle.* Stanford, CA: Stanford University Press, 1981.

Jones, Leroy, and Il Sakong. *Government, Business, and Entrepreneurship in Economic Development: The Korean Case.* Cambridge, MA: Harvard University Press, 1980.

Kaviraj, Sudipta. "Marxism and the Darkness of History." Pp. 54–83 in *Emancipations: Modern and Postmodern,* edited by Jan Nederveen Pieterse. London: Sage, 1992.

Khalidi, Rashid. *Resurrecting Empire: Western Footprints and America's Perilous Path in the Middle East.* Boston: Beacon Press, 2004.

Kinzer, Stephen. *Overthrow: America's Century of Regime Change from Hawaii to Iraq.* New York: Times Books, 2006.

Krishna, Sankaran. "Transition in the Era of US Hegemony: Indian Economic Development and World-Systems Analysis." Pp. 119–31 in *Pacific-Asia and the Future of the World-System,* ed. Ravi Arvind Palat. Westport, CT: Greenwood, 1992.

———. "The Importance of Being Ironic: A Postcolonial View on Critical International Relations Theory." *Alternatives* 18 (1993): 385417.

———. *Postcolonial Insecurities: India, Sri Lanka and the Question of Nationhood.* Minneapolis: University of Minnesota Press, 1999.

———. "Race, Amnesia and the Education of International Relations. *Alternatives* 26, no. 4 (2001): 401–24.

———. "Boundaries in Question." Pp. 302–14 in *A Companion to Political Geography,* edited by John Agnew, Katharyne Mitchell, and Gerard Toal. Malden, MA: Blackwell, 2003.

———. "India: Globalization and Information Technology." *South Asian Journal* (April–June 2005): 146–58.

Kumar, Dharma, ed. *The Cambridge Economic History of India: 1757–1970,* Vol. II. Cambridge: Cambridge University Press, 1982.

Kumar, Dharma, and Dilip Mookherjee, eds. *D. School: Reflections on the Delhi School of Economics.* New Delhi: Oxford University Press, 1995.

Kux, Denis. *India and the United States: Estranged Democracies, 1941–1991.* Washington, DC: National Defense University Press, 1993.

Lal, Vinay, ed. "Plural Worlds, Multiple Selves: Ashis Nandy and the Post-Columbian Future." *Emergences* nos. 7–8 (1995–96).

Larsen, Neil. "DetermiNation: Postcolonialism, Poststructuralism, and the Problem of Ideology." Pp. 140–56 in *The Pre-Occupation of Postcolonial Studies,* edited by Fawzia Afzal-Khan and Kalpana Seshadri-Crooks. Durham, NC: Duke University Press, 2000.

Latin American Subaltern Studies Group. "Founding Statement." *boundary 2* 20, no. 2 (Fall 1993): 110–21.

Lazarus, Neil. "The Fetish of 'the West' in Postcolonial Theory." Pp. 43–64 in *Marxism, Modernity, and Postcolonial Studies*, edited by Crystal Bartolovich and Neil Lazarus. Cambridge: Cambridge University Press, 2002.

Lewis, Bernard. "The Roots of Muslim Rage." *The Atlantic* (September 1990). <http://www.theatlantic.com/doc/199009/muslimrage> (29 March 2008).

List, Friedrich. *The National System of Political Economy.* New York: A. M. Kelley, 1966.

Loomba, Ania, and Suvir Kaul. "Location, Culture, Post-Coloniality." *Oxford Literary Review* 16 (1994): 3–30.

Malek, Anwar Abdel. "Orientalism in Crisis." *Diogenes* 44 (Winter 1963): 107–8.

Mallon, Florenica E. "The Promise and Dilemma of Subaltern Studies: Perspectives from Latin American History." *American Historical Review* 99, no. 5 (December 1994): 1491–515.

Mamdani, Mahmood. *Good Muslim, Bad Muslim: America, the Cold War, and the Roots of Terror.* New York: Doubleday, 2004.

Mani, Lata. *Contentious Traditions: The Debate on Sati in Colonial India.* Berkeley: University of California Press, 1998.

Marx, Karl. "On the Jewish Question." Pp. 211–42 in *Karl Marx: Early Writings.* Trans. Rodney Livingstone and Gregor Benton. New York: Vintage, 1975.

Marx, Karl, and Frederick Engels. "Manifesto of the Communist Party." 1848. <http://www.anu.edu.au/polsci/marx/classics/manifesto.html> (22 May 2008).

———. "Eighteenth Brumaire of Louis Napoleon." Pp. 97–180 in *Karl Marx and Friedrich Engels: Selected Works in One Volume.* New York: International Publishers, 1986.

Mehta, Uday Singh. *Liberalism and Empire.* Chicago: University of Chicago Press, 1999.

Mitchell, Timothy. "The Limits of the State." *American Political Science Review* 85, no.1 (March 1991): 77–96.

———. "Fixing the Economy." *Cultural Studies* 12, no. 1 (January 1998): 82–101.

Nagle, John. *System and Succession: The Social Bases of Political Elite Recruitment.* Austin: University of Texas Press, 1977.

Nandy, Ashis. *At the Edge of Psychology: Essays in Politics and Culture.* Delhi: Oxford University Press, 1980.

———. *The Intimate Enemy: Loss and Recovery of Self Under Colonialism.* Delhi: Oxford University Press, 1983.

———. *Science, Hegemony and Violence: A Requiem for Modernity.* Delhi: Oxford University Press, 1988.

———. "Shamans, Savages and the Wilderness: On the Audibility of Dissent and the Future of Civilizations." *Alternatives* 14 (1989): 263–77.

———. *Illegitimacy of Nationalism: Rabindranath Tagore and the Politics of Self.* New Delhi: Oxford University Press, 1994.

——. *The Savage Freud and Other Essays on Possible and Retrievable Selves*. Princeton, NJ: Princeton University Press, 1995.

——. "The Beautiful Expanding Future of Poverty: Popular Economics as a Psychological Defense." *International Studies Review* 4, no. 2 (Summer 2002): 107–21.

——. *Time Warps: Silent and Evasive Pasts in Indian Politics and Religion*. New Brunswick, NJ: Rutgers University Press, 2002.

——. *The Romance of the State and the Fate of Dissent in the Tropics*. Delhi: Oxford University Press, 2003.

Orwell, George. "Shooting an Elephant." 1936. <http://www.online-literature.com/orwell/887>. (29 May 2008).

Pandey, Gyanendra. "Peasant Revolt and Indian Nationalism 1919-1922." Pp. 233–87 in *Selected Subaltern Studies*, edited by Ranajit Guha and Gayatri Chakravorty Spivak. New York: Oxford University Press, 1988.

Pape, Robert. *Dying to Win: The Strategic Logic of Suicide Terrorism*. New York: Random House, 2005.

Parry, Benita. "The Institutionalization of Postcolonial Studies." Pp. 66–80 in *The Cambridge Companion to Postcolonial Literary Studies*, edited by Neil Lazarus. Cambridge: Cambridge University Press, 2004.

Payer, Cheryl. *Lent and Lost: Foreign Credit and Third World Development*. London: Zed Books, 1991.

PBS [Public Broadcasting Service]. "Interview: Osama bin Laden." 1998. <http://www.pbs.org/wgbh/pages/frontline/shows/binladen/who/interview.html> (28 May 2008).

Phillips, Kevin. *The Politics of Rich and Poor: Wealth and the American Electorate in the Reagan Aftermath*. New York: Random House, 1990.

——. *Wealth and Democracy: A Political History of the American Rich*. New York: Broadway Books, 2002.

Polanyi, Karl. *The Great Transformation: The Political and Economic Origins of Our Time*. Boston: Beacon Press, 1944.

Prakash, Gyan. "Post-Orientalist Third World Histories." *Comparative Studies in Society and History* 32, no. 2 (April 1990): 382–408.

——. *Another Reason: Science and the Imagination of Modern India*. Princeton, NJ: Princeton University Press, 1999.

——. "Writing Post-Orientalist Histories of the Third World: Perspectives from Indian Historiography." Pp. 163–90 in *Mapping Subaltern Studies and the Postcolonial*, edited by Vinayak Chaturvedi. New York: Verso, 2000.

Reynolds, Lloyd G. "Spread of Economic Growth to the Third World." *Journal of Economic Literature* 21, no. 3 (September 1983): 961–80.

Rostow, Walt W. *The Stages of Economic Growth: A Non-Communist Manifesto*. New York: Cambridge University Press, 1960.

Rupert, Mark. *Producing Hegemony*. Cambridge: Cambridge University Press, 1995.

————. *Ideologies of Globalization: Contending Visions of a New World Order.* New York: Routledge, 2000.

Said, Edward. *Beginnings: Intention and Method.* New York: Columbia University Press, 1975.

————. *Orientalism.* New York: Vintage, 1978 (25th anniversary ed., 2003).

————. *The Question of Palestine.* New York: Vintage, 1979.

————. *Culture and Imperialism.* New York: Knopf, 1993.

————. *Out of Place: A Memoir.* London: Granta, 1999.

————. "In Conversation with Neeladri Bhattacharya, Suvir Kaul, and Ania Loomba." Pp. 1–14 in *Relocating Postcolonialism*, edited by David Theo Goldberg and Ato Quayson. London: Blackwell, 2002.

Sarkar, Sumit. *Modern India: 1885–1947.* New Delhi: Macmillan, 1983.

————. "The Decline of the Subaltern in Subaltern Studies." Pp. 300–323 in *Mapping Subaltern Studies and the Postcolonial*, edited by Vinayak Chaturvedi. New York: Verso, 2000.

Saul, John. *The State and Revolution in Eastern Africa: Essays.* New York: Monthly Review Press, 1979.

Scheuer, Michael. *Imperial Hubris: Why the West Is Losing the War on Terror.* Dulles, VA: Brassey's, 2004.

Scott, David. "The Social Construction of Postcolonial Studies." Pp. 385–400 in *Postcolonial Studies and Beyond*, Ania Loomba, Suvir Kaul, Matti Bunzi, Antoinette Burton, and Jed Esty, eds. Durham, NC: Duke University Press, 2005.

Seal, Anil. *The Emergence of Indian Nationalism.* Cambridge: Cambridge University Press, 1968.

Sen, Asok. *Iswar Chandra Vidyasagar and His Elusive Milestones.* Calcutta: Riddhi, 1977.

Shah, Anup. "Causes of Poverty: Facts and Stats." 2006. <http://www.globalissues.org/TradeRelated/Facts.asp> (22 May 2008).

Shivji, Issa. *Class Struggles in Tanzania.* New York: Monthly Review Press, 1976.

Shohat, Ella. "Notes on the Postcolonial." Pp. 126–39 in *The Pre-Occupation of Postcolonial Studies*, edited by Fawzia Afzal-Khan and Kalpana Seshadri-Crooks. Durham, NC: Duke University Press, 2000.

Smith, Adam. *Wealth of Nations.* Ed. K. Sutherland. Oxford: Oxford University Press, 1993.

Smith, Linda Tuhiwai. "Imperialism, History, Writing, and Theory." Pp. 94–115 in *Postcolonialisms: An Anthology of Cultural Theory and Criticism*, edited by Gaurav Desai and Supriya Nair. New Brunswick, NJ: Rutgers University Press, 2005.

So, Alvin Y. *Social Change and Development: Modernization, Dependency and World Systems Analysis.* London: Sage Publications, 1990.

Spivak, Gayatri Chakravorty. "Can the Subaltern Speak?" Pp. 271–315 in *Marxism and the Interpretation of Cultures*, edited by Cathy Nelson and Lawrence Grossberg. Urbana: University of Illinois Press, 1988.

———. "Subaltern Studies: Deconstructing Historiography." Pp. 3–32 in *Selected Subaltern Studies*, edited by Ranajit Guha and Gayatri Chakravorty Spivak. New York: Oxford University Press, 1988.

———. "The Postcolonial Critic." Pp. 67–74 in *The Postcolonial Critic*, edited by Sarah Harasym. New York: Routledge, 1990.

———. "Interview with Sara Danius and Stefan Jonsson." *boundary 2* 20, no. 2 (Fall 1993): 24–50.

———. *Outside in the Teaching Machine*. New York: Routledge, 1993.

———. *In Other Worlds: Essays in Cultural Politics*. New York: Routledge, 1998.

———. *A Critique of Postcolonial Reason: Toward a History of the Vanishing Present*. Cambridge, MA: Harvard University Press, 1999.

Stavrianos, L. S. *Global Rift: The Third World Comes of Age*. New York: William Morrow, 1981.

Steger, Manfred. *Globalism: The New Market Ideology*. Lanham, MD: Rowman & Littlefield, 2001.

Stiglitz, Joseph. *Globalization and its Discontents*. New York: W. W. Norton, 2002.

Todaro, Michael. *Economic Development in the Third World*, 4th ed. New York: Longman, 1989.

Tsing, Anna Lowenhaupt. *Friction: An Ethnography of Global Connection*. Princeton, NJ: Princeton University Press, 2005.

United Nations. "Human Development Report 2005: "International Cooperation at a Crossroads: Aid, Trade and Security in an Unequal World." 2005. <http://hdr.undp/org/en/media/hdr05_complete.pdf> (22 May 2008).

———. "Growth and Development Trends, 1960–2005." World Economic and Social Survey, 2006: Diverging Growth and Development. 2006. <http://www.un .org/esa/policy/wess/wess2006files/toc.pdf> (22 May 2008).

Viswanathan, Gauri. *Masks of Conquest: Literary Study and British Rule in India*. New York: Columbia University Press, 1989.

Wade, Robert. *Governing the Market: Economic Theory and the Role of Government in East Asian Industrialization*. Princeton, NJ: Princeton University Press, 2003.

———. "Questions of Fairness." *Foreign Affairs* (September–October 2006).

Wallerstein, Immanuel. *Geopolitics and Geoculture: Essays on the Changing World System*. New York: Cambridge University Press, 1991.

———. *Unthinking Social Science: The Limits of Nineteenth Century Paradigms*. Cambridge, UK: Polity Press, 1991.

Washbrook, David. *The Emergence of Provincial Politics*. Cambridge: Cambridge University Press, 1976.

Winters, Jeffrey. "The Financial Crisis in Southeast Asia." Paper delivered at the Conference on the Asian Crisis, Murdoch University, Fremantle, Western Australia, August 1998.

Wolfe, Patrick. "History and Imperialism: A Century of Theory, from Marx to Postcolonialism." *American Historical Review* 102, no. 2 (April 1997): 388–420.

Woo-Cumings, Meredith. *Race to the Swift: State and Finance in Korean Industrialization*. New York: Columbia University Press, 1991.

Young, Robert. *Postcolonialism: An Historical Introduction*. Oxford, UK: Blackwell, 2001.

Žižek, Slavoj. *Tarrying with the Negative*. Durham, NC: Duke University Press, 1993.

INDEX

ABOUT THE AUTHOR

Sankaran Krishna is professor of political science at the University of Hawai'i at Mānoa.